D1263137

DEVELOPING LANGUAGE SKILLS

DEVELOPING LANGUAGE SKILLS SERIES
General Editor, Cecil E. Potts

Grade 3 CECIL E. POTTS
PHYLLIS A. MOORE

Grade 4 CECIL E. POTTS

Grade 5 CECIL E. POTTS
HUGH C. MacCORKINDALE

Grade 6 CECIL E. POTTS
ELLEN M. BUTLER
MARGARET M. KNECHTEL
MARGARET C. STEWART

Grade 7 CECIL E. POTTS
JACK G. NICHOLS

Grade 8 CECIL E. POTTS
JACK G. NICHOLS

EIGHT

Developing

LANGUAGE

Skills

Cecil E. Potts, B.A., B.Paed.,

Late Inspector of Public Schools,
Etobicoke, Ontario

Jack G. Nichols, B.A., B.Paed.,

Superintendent of Instruction, Peterborough County
Board of Education, Ontario

RYERSON EDUCATIONAL DIVISION
McGRAW-HILL COMPANY OF CANADA LIMITED

TORONTO · MONTREAL · NEW YORK · LONDON · SYDNEY
JOHANNESBURG · MEXICO · PANAMA · DÜSSELDORF · SINGAPORE
RIO DE JANEIRO · KUALA LUMPUR · NEW DELHI

COPYRIGHT, CANADA, 1958, BY
THE RYERSON PRESS, TORONTO

All rights reserved. No part of this book may be reproduced in any form (except by reviewers for the public
press), without permission in writing from the publishers.

ISBN 0-7700-3044-0

ACKNOWLEDGMENTS

The authors wish to express these words of appreciation to the host of teachers in both urban and rural schools who have used many of the ideas that are presented in this text. It is from their classrooms that the many examples of pupils' writing and the illustrative material found herein have come. The authors are grateful, too, to Mr. Campbell Hughes of The Ryerson Press for his stimulating enthusiasm for this project, for his valuable suggestions, and for his constructive criticisms of the draft manuscript.

Grateful acknowledgment is also made to the following for permission to use copyrighted material: AP Newsfeatures for two Associated Press items; the Audubon Society for an item from its magazine; Canadian Industries Limited for exercise material from the *C.I.L. Oval;* The Canadian Press for several news releases; the publishers of *Canada Unlimited* for material from that book; Dodd Mead & Company for selections reprinted from *Autumn across America* by Edwin Way Teale (Copyright *c.* 1950, 1951, by Edwin Way Teale. *c.* 1956 by Edwin Way Teale); Doubleday & Company, Inc., for selections from *Frozen Fire* by Armstrong Sperry (Copyright *c.* 1956 by Armstrong Sperry); General Motors Products of Canada for the use of a message; *The Globe and Mail*, Toronto, for an editorial and a news item; King Features Syndicate for a "Henry" cartoon by Carl T. Anderson; the estate of the late Hugh Lofting for a selection from *Dr. Dolittle in the Moon;* The Macmillan Company for selections adapted from *The Rain Forest* by Armstrong Sperry; Messrs. Oliver and Boyd for permission to use the schedule for marking written composition as used in *Backwardness in the Basic Subjects* by Fred J. Schonell; The Ryerson Press for "Indian Summer" by Wilfred Campbell; Trans Canada Airlines for the photograph on page 1; and A. P. Watt & Son, Alfred Noyes and Messrs. Wm. Blackwood & Sons Ltd. for a portion of "The Highwayman" from *Collected Poems of Alfred Noyes.*

Every reasonable care has been taken to trace the ownership of copyright material. Information will be welcomed which will enable the publishers to rectify any reference or credit in subsequent editions.

Illustrations were arranged or designed by the authors, with art work by Ken Zeally, Toronto, and photographs by The Kates Studio, Peterborough, and Albert Titley, St. Catharines.

23

PRINTED AND BOUND IN CANADA

FOREWORD TO THE TEACHER

This text is designed to follow DEVELOPING LANGUAGE SKILLS, GRADE VII. Its contents have been tested in all types of school situations and should provide an adequate basis for language study in Grade VIII.

In Part I of this text the authors have attempted to provide material that will be useful in a creative writing programme. They believe that the textbook must be *adapted* to the needs of the classroom language programme and that it should not be *adopted* as the programme. No textbook can suggest, or provide for, the infinite number of opportunities for the use of oral and written language that will arise in every classroom.

This book represents a shift away from the composition programme which provided a series of unrelated exercises designed to *teach* punctuation, paragraphing, correct usage, and other aspects of the structure and mechanics of language, and which provided only infrequently opportunities for pupils to write continuous prose. It first provides a planned series of writing activities in which pupils use language in expressing their own ideas, and then it provides specific related exercises to improve the effectiveness of the structure, or to overcome the weaknesses in mechanics, in accordance with pupils' needs.

If the authors have a basic principle, it lies in the words: "To learn to write, one must write. To learn to speak, one must speak." Gurrey[1] says, "But how very often the greater part of the time in a language period is taken up by the teacher explaining, instructing, admonishing—in fact by what he looks upon as teaching."

In a pamphlet of the United Kingdom Ministry of Education[2] the following is found, "In the last resort there can be only one answer: practice—frequent, careful, suitably chosen, suitably graded, well supervised, and done in such fashion as to give it some reality and, if possible, some interest. Such practice in continuous composition ought to take precedence over any other kind of linguistic exercise."

There are a greater number of writing opportunities in this text than any one pupil or class could possibly use in one year. Thus it will be possible to make a selection in accordance with needs and interests of the individual pupil.

This text provides a variety of devices to help pupils *to have something to say* before they begin to write. Models, selected from standard writers and from pupils' writing, will provide suitable patterns to follow. They will also help to stimulate the growth of ideas for original expression. Models of pupils' writing have not been revised to meet adult standards of achievement.

When they write for some purpose, pupils usually produce better results and have greater interest in what they write. Teachers are requested to examine carefully the content of Chapter V where several opportunities for writing with some sense of reality are presented. They have been designed to provide pupils with a purpose *for* writing. Teachers are also requested to read page 19 entitled Target for Today which suggests how purpose *in* writing may be established.

[1] *The Teaching of Written English*, Gurrey, Longmans, Green, 1954.
[2] *Language, Some Suggestions for the Teachers of English and Others*, Pamphlet No. 26, U.K. Ministry of Education.

Authorities generally agree on the procedure which should be followed when writing creatively. Pupils should not be expected to produce an errorless composition at the first sitting. Even adults do not write that way. Chapter II outlines a procedure which, it is suggested, pupils should learn to follow for much of their writing.

The "Marking" of composition has given way to the "appraisal" of composition, with the accent on the second syllable of the latter word. The teacher-pupil conference is recommended by most authorities as the most effective evaluation procedure. The marking scheme described on page 321 is considered to have merit by teachers who seek marks objectively for report card purposes, and who attempt to determine specific strengths and weaknesses in the writing of individual pupils.

After evaluation each teacher must formulate his own policy. "The sequel to evaluation whether by the teacher-pupil conference or otherwise is scrupulous revision by the pupil afterwards. When all is said and done about 'killing interest' it is difficult to see how practice can do much, or correction be worth much, if bad or inadequate work is not done again and done better."[2]

From the evaluation and appraisal procedures the teacher may determine the topics for language lessons that must be taught to meet group or class needs. Perhaps the class needs practice in overcoming the use of the run-on sentence. Perhaps commas are being used indiscriminately. Perhaps the pupils need practice in writing a greater variety of sentences. Practice activities related to these and other pupil needs can be found easily in this text by using the table of contents and the index.

It is suggested that, for the first few weeks of the term, language activities be selected from Chapter I, and that during this time the pupils become thoroughly acquainted with the content of Chapter II. A review of the various types of paragraphs, using material in Chapter III, might follow. After this introductory period, it is recommended that the teacher select from Part I and the Appendix, which includes the Almanac, the material that can be adapted best to the needs of the classroom language programme.

The material in Part II of the text, which presents the grammar for this grade, should be used in the order in which it appears. If three periods per week are devoted to the work in Part I of DEVELOPING LANGUAGE SKILLS, two periods per week might be spent with the material in Part II. So that pupils may attain mastery of the basic concepts of English grammar which are presented there, the attention of the teacher is drawn to the following:

1. Grammar must be taught in sequential steps.

2. It must be purposeful in that it must be related to the pupils' daily use of language.

3. It requires effective teaching.

4. A greater number of examples than can be provided in such a text as this are usually needed for the teaching lessons which develop each new topic.

5. The teacher must decide whether further drill on a particular topic is needed, or whether the pupils are prepared to proceed to the next one.

6. Frequent review and drill lessons are essential in the development of any skill.

7. Review exercises are provided here for the convenience of the teacher. Before they are assigned, review lessons are very necessary.

"In its right place, at the right time, and in right measure instruction in grammar is not only desirable but an essential part of the English course." (Ballard)

Any course in language must place the greater emphasis on developing in the pupil the ability to express his thoughts clearly, effectively, and accurately. There must be constant opportunity for pupils to write. This is the yardstick by which any course in ENGLISH should be measured. The study of grammar is a means of improving the expression of thought and provides standards for determining its correctness.

This text does not minimize the need for real effort on the part of both teachers and pupils. It has been designed in a sincere attempt to adjust subject matter so that the pupils of Grade VIII can use their mental ability, and to adjust method so that they will want to use it.

C. E. POTTS

J. G. NICHOLS

To
W.M.P. and M.I.N.
whose constant encouragement and co-operation
have been of invaluable assistance in the
preparation of this text for Canadian
boys and girls

CONTENTS

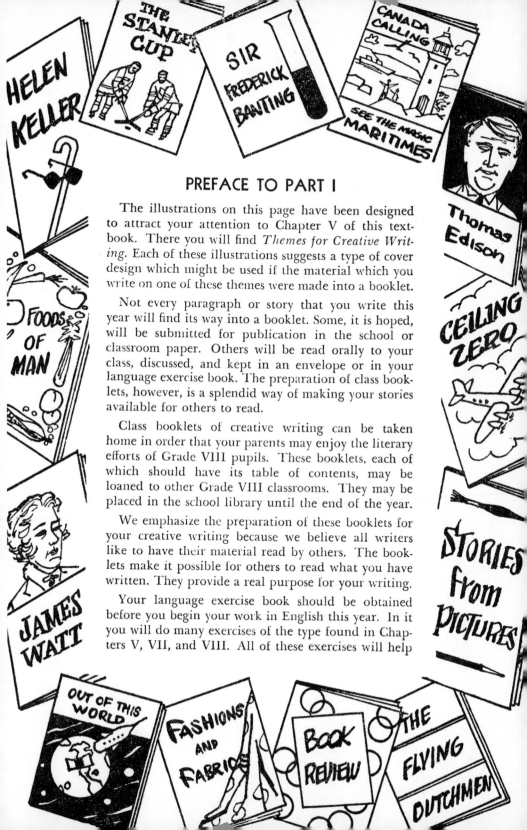

PREFACE TO PART I

The illustrations on this page have been designed to attract your attention to Chapter V of this textbook. There you will find *Themes for Creative Writing*. Each of these illustrations suggests a type of cover design which might be used if the material which you write on one of these themes were made into a booklet.

Not every paragraph or story that you write this year will find its way into a booklet. Some, it is hoped, will be submitted for publication in the school or classroom paper. Others will be read orally to your class, discussed, and kept in an envelope or in your language exercise book. The preparation of class booklets, however, is a splendid way of making your stories available for others to read.

Class booklets of creative writing can be taken home in order that your parents may enjoy the literary efforts of Grade VIII pupils. These booklets, each of which should have its table of contents, may be loaned to other Grade VIII classrooms. They may be placed in the school library until the end of the year.

We emphasize the preparation of these booklets for your creative writing because we believe all writers like to have their material read by others. The booklets make it possible for others to read what you have written. They provide a real purpose for your writing.

Your language exercise book should be obtained before you begin your work in English this year. In it you will do many exercises of the type found in Chapters V, VII, and VIII. All of these exercises will help to improve your ability to use language for its real purposes, that of writing well and of speaking well, in order that others may read or listen with both understanding and pleasure.

The development of language skills is somewhat similar to the development of skills for any sport or for the playing of a musical instrument. Practice, for example, is required on specific plays or on definite scales. In playing a game, or a selection, you use these skills and you use them to the best of your ability. In writing stories, letters, book reports, and articles for your school paper you use your skills in language in the same way. After you have done so, your teacher, who is your classroom coach, may decide that you need special practice on some particular skill to overcome a weakness which your writing or speaking has revealed.

Chapter I has been prepared for use at the opening of the new term. The exercises in it should be done in the order in which they appear. The content of Chapter II should be read carefully soon after school opens and referred to frequently during the year. Themes for creative writing will be found in Chapters IV and V. As the need arises, the exercises in the other chapters may be used.

It is our hope that you will find in *Developing Language Skills—Grade VIII* exercises and activities that will be both interesting and helpful.

—THE AUTHORS

Miller Services Ltd.

I ▲ CHECK-UPS

Perhaps you have seen a plane about to take off. You may have noticed that the pilot, before starting down the runway runs the engines at great speed although the aircraft does not move. This is the final check-up during which he carefully observes the many indicators on the instrument panel, and tests with his hands and feet to determine that all the controls are functioning properly. This procedure is always followed in order that the pilot may be satisfied that the plane is in condition for a smooth, safe flight.

For pupils starting on the language activities of a new grade the situation is similar. You, too, should first determine whether you are ready to proceed although for the time being you may feel that you are learning nothing new. Your mastery of the many language skills which you have practised in previous years can be tested by completing the exercises in this first chapter.

Check-Ups:

EXERCISE 1: A TEST OF SENTENCE SENSE, PUNCTUATION, AND CAPITALS.

This undivided paragraph has been printed without the use of capitals or punctuation. Copy the paragraph, using capital letters, periods, commas, and apostrophes where they are needed. Read the paragraph softly several times before beginning to write. This will help you to determine where the punctuation marks will be needed.

labour day which is celebrated annually throughout canada and the united states signifies the end of the vacation for school children regarding the origin of this holiday there is a difference of opinion some claim that peter j mcguire president of the carpenters brotherhood of new york first proposed in 1882 that a special day be proclaimed in honour of the nations workmen others maintain that george hewitt of the toronto coopers union suggested the idea in 1872 it is agreed however that the parades speeches games and picnics which made up the first labour day celebrations were well attended as a result the first monday in september became a legal holiday throughout most of north america

1. Read your written paragraph aloud and pay particular attention to the punctuation you have used. If it sounds well when you interpret the punctuation properly, the paragraph is probably punctuated correctly. By developing the habit of reading your written work aloud before considering it finished, you will detect and correct many errors. This reading to check for accuracy may be called *proofreading*.

2. Have you used the apostrophe three times? Did you use it on two occasions after the final "s"?

3. By dictionary research or by making inquiries of older people find answers to the following questions. Prepare to answer orally in complete sentences.

(a) What word in the paragraph indicates that governments have made laws to make Labour Day a holiday?

(b) From what countries did the people come whose surnames start with "Mc"?

(c) Read the sentences in which each of these words appear, but replace the given word with a synonym:

(i) proposed; (ii) origin; (iii) annually; (iv) proclaimed

4

Check-Ups:

EXERCISE 2: WRITING PARAGRAPHS.

(a) Read the following two paragraphs silently. Then read each aloud. Answer these questions orally: (i) In which paragraph has repetition been used effectively? (ii) In which paragraph is the structure of each of the sentences quite similar? Note how the writer used repetition and one sentence pattern to lead up to his closing sentence. (iii) Select phrases from each paragraph to illustrate that the writer obtained ideas by using each of these senses: (a) sight; (b) smell; (c) hearing; (d) feeling; (e) taste. (iv) Select and read the last sentence which is a real *summary sentence*. Read the last sentence which should be called a *closing sentence*.

1. Sitting there, I shared for a time the autumn excitement of those beautiful birds of passage. Perhaps it was a plaintive recurring note in the killdeer's call. Perhaps it was the smell of the dusty weeds, associated in my mind with a return to the city and to school, and with the end of the summer freedom at Lone Lake. Perhaps it was the faraway, lonely sound of the train whistle. Perhaps it was the singing of the September insects, the dry orchestral music that carries, like an overtone, the thought of swiftly passing life. Perhaps it was compounded of all of them—this wave of autumn sadness that enveloped me.

—AUTUMN ACROSS AMERICA by E. W. Teale

2. After I banked the fire, I climbed into my hammock. Outside the mosquito net, thwarted millions of insects hummed and buzzed and chirped. The natives, wrapped in their blankets around the fire, muttered sleepily for a few minutes, then fell silent. The dark river shimmered in a faint light from the stars. A wind was rising, and from far overhead on the roof of the forest there came a gentle patter, as of rain. Deep within the jungle the hoarse cough of a hunting jaguar could be heard, followed by the choked-off death cry of some smaller creature.

—FROZEN FIRE by Armstrong Sperry

(b) Write a paragraph on one of the following topics, or on any topic of your choice. Compose an effective closing or summary sentence. Create your own title.

1. That Last Day in June
2. It Was Fun While It Lasted
3. Food in Camp after Lights Out
4. Motoring with the Family
5. Holidays Can Be Too Long
6. As I Looked Forward to Opening Day
7. School Has Its Pleasant Side
8. My New School-Year's Resolutions

Check-Ups:

EXERCISE 3: LETTER WRITING.

This is an example of a real letter that might be written as a classroom exercise by any Grade VIII pupil. It is an invitation to his parents to attend a school function. It is not presented, however, in the form in which the parts of a letter should be arranged.

Read the letter carefully. Prepare to divide the body of the letter into three paragraphs. Write the letter in the proper form, using capital letters and punctuation marks where they are needed.

1992 inglewood road west vancouver b c october 12 195– dear parents on tuesday october 15 prince of wales school is holding its annual open house from 7.45 until 10.30 p.m. this is an invitation for you both to attend and i do hope that you will be able to come during the first hour there will be a meeting in the auditorium mr d bradley of the university of british columbia will speak on the subject is television interfering with school work the senior choir which won first prize at the kiwanis music festival and which is under the direction of miss park will provide the entertainment after the meeting the parents are invited to the classrooms to see a display of pupils work and to meet their childrens teachers if parents have problems to discuss they are asked to make an appointment with the principal or teacher on this occasion time will not be available during this evening for interviews refreshments will be served in the auditorium beginning at nine thirty these will be free here there will be an opportunity for you to obtain your home and school association (*or* parent teacher association) membership card for the usual fee your son norman

Proofread very carefully the letter which you have written. Reading the body of the letter softly will help you to determine where most of the punctuation marks are needed. Check the punctuation. Have you used only two apostrophes?

EXERCISE 4: LETTER WRITING.

Compose an original letter to any pupil in the class. If there is at least one pupil who has just arrived in your school make this letter part of a *Get Acquainted Day* programme. Address it to one of the new arrivals and give it to him, or her, when it is completed.

If your letter is of the *Get Acquainted* variety, describe your family, your activities outside of school, your pets, and the subjects you like best in school. Use a separate paragraph to tell about each topic. As your new friend may have many letters to read, do not make yours too long.

If your letter is to a person you already know tell him, or her, about your experiences during the summer vacation. Select the most interesting incidents and use a paragraph to describe each.

6

Check-Ups:

Start your letter with the heading you would use when writing from your home address. It will be well to write a draft first. Then make the revisions that are needed. Copy the revised letter on paper of good quality. Write on one side of the paper only.

(See Chapter X—LETTER WRITING, page 155.)

EXERCISE 5: AVOIDING EXTRAVAGANCE.

The choice of words determines the quality of our writing. The quantity of words is also an important characteristic. Sometimes more words than necessary are used. Needless repetition should be avoided.

Examine each of the following sentences to decide the word or words which should be omitted. Read the sentences ORALLY with the changes made. Be ready to explain the reason for each change.

1. While downtown we looked at the old antiques in that interesting shop.
2. The newspaper heading read "Young Winnipeg Youth Wins Shooting Prize."
3. At the graduation party she wore a new pair of shoes on her feet.
4. The team arrived on Saturday morning at ten a.m.
5. Each of the girls had an apple apiece.
6. The boys who had broken the window approached silently without saying a word.
7. Why are these automobiles being shown on display at this time of year.
8. In Algonquin Park we fed the deer some bread to eat.
9. Were the pair of twins on the same team? (This question refers to two people.)
10. That fellow has not never been able to have pets at home.

EXERCISE 6: SELECTING TITLES.

The boys and girls in a Grade VIII class wrote two-paragraph accounts to tell about their reactions, and those of their parents, to the first report card of the year. Read these two examples of pupils' writing.

When the moment came I was shaking with excitement. Then it happened. A big card was put on the top of my desk. It was my report. I took off the cover and opened it. Although it was not too bad, it was not too good either. Even to me it could have been better.

As I reached home I was still shaking a little. I kept wondering what mother and father were going to say. As there was only one way to find out, I gave them the report. Mother thought that it was good but that it might

Check-Ups:

have been much better. Father agreed and said that he was particularly pleased that all the entries in the citizenship column indicated satisfactory progress. I thanked them for their comments and promised that I would do my best to receive higher grades next time.   —Diane G.

It was Thursday morning just before the noon bell when I received my report card. A frown crept over my face as I read it. I had four A grades, four B's, five C's, one D and one F. I thought that, for me, it was not too bad. I soon discovered, however, as mother looked at me rather angrily, that she considered it terrible. She warned that if I did not work harder I would suffer the consequences.

Quickly I decided that from then on I would work harder than ever before, and that I would not dilly-dally although I would be careful not to work too fast. I made up my mind that the teacher would no longer find me daydreaming in school. Just think! Would it not be wonderful to see my next report with no grades below B on it?   —Tom B.

The titles which the pupils composed are arranged in three groups. (a) Select the most interesting title from each group and explain why it was chosen; (b) Select the group which contains the greatest number of interesting titles and explain why that group was chosen; (c) From these three groups select a title for each of the pupils' accounts that are printed above.

1. In this group note the repetition of the word "report." A Bad Report Card, An Embarrassing Report Card, Remarks On My Report, Receiving My Report, My Report—My Parents and I.

2. In this group what is the word that is common?
   R Day, The Exciting Day, A Special Day, What A Day!

3. What is the characteristic of this group?
   My Luck, Two Disappointed Looks, An Agreement, That Dreadful Moment.

EXERCISE 7: KINDS OF SENTENCES.

Rewrite each sentence and terminate it with the proper punctuation mark. In parenthesis (round brackets) after each, write the name of the kind of sentence. Among these sentences will be found at least one of the following kinds: assertive, interrogative, exclamatory, imperative.

1. Did you ever go boating to fly
2. For water fans that is not impossible these days
3. Buy a gyro-boat
4. What kind of craft is that
5. Add a ten-foot rotosail, or air paddles, to a small boat weighing less than two hundred pounds and you have one

➡

Check-Ups:

6. Explain that contraption in greater detail

7. The air paddles, which look like helicopter rotors, are mounted on a short mast attached near the stern of the boat

8. How does this wingless duck fly

9. When a fast motor boat tows the gyro-boat at a speed in excess of twenty miles an hour the spinning rotosail pulls the craft out of the water

10. What a dangerous way to imitate water birds

11. Its inventor claims a skilful pilot can manipulate the control stick to fly at sixty miles per hour at tree top height and that he will also be able to make banks and turns

12. Not for me

EXERCISE 8: SENTENCE BIOGRAPHIES.   The first part of this exercise tests your knowledge of famous people.   The second part gives you an opportunity to practise using reference books and to compose a well constructed sentence to make an informative statement about each person.   Begin by writing the names, surname first, in alphabetical order in a column in your language note book.   Leave two spaces between each name.

Horatio Nelson	Sir Winston Churchill	John James Audubon
St. Francis of Assisi	Edith Cavell	Florence Nightingale
Sir Isaac Brock	Orville Wright	Charles Lindbergh
Marie Curie	Louis Pasteur	Helen Keller
Robert Louis Stevenson	General James Wolfe	Samuel de Champlain
Louisa May Alcott	Louis Braille	David Livingstone
Samuel L. Clemens	Sir Frederick Banting	Maurice Richard

(a) Without consulting any book or asking any questions try to write beside each name one sentence which tells something about that person.

Example: Keller, Helen: Although deaf and blind from babyhood, Helen Keller has learned to speak and to read and has devoted her life to the helping of people with similar handicaps.

When called upon, read one or more of your sentences aloud to the class.

(b) Consult a reference book to obtain the information required. Compose a sentence for each of the names beside which you were unable to write any information while doing part (a) above.

9

Check-Ups:

EXERCISE 9: A SPELLING TEST. The following list presents the twenty words that were misspelled most frequently on the *Critic Sheets* used by several Grade VIII classes in connection with their opening exercises. (See page 299.)

(a) Arrange the words in a numbered list in alphabetical order. Write sentences using these words. More than one word from the list may be used in the same sentence. Master the spelling of these words.

fidgeting	refrain	mispronounced	convener
Bible	article	solemn	beginning
except	posture	preparation	practised
importance	straight	everyone	distinctly
everybody	comedy	too fast	all right

(b) As a test have someone dictate the words for you to write.

EXERCISE 10: PUNCTUATING A STORY WITH CONVERSATION.

Copy this story, using capital letters where needed and inserting the correct punctuation where required. Note that some capital letters have been provided and that the story has been divided into paragraphs. Compose a title.

Tim and Bob tiptoed quietly up to the classroom window and cautiously peeked out. Eagerly they looked at the ledge where just this morning some members of their class had erected a bird feeding station

Oh whispered Bob here comes our first visitor do you recognize him Tim

Yes it is Mr. Blackcap I think he is going to try the suet we put out for him and his friends

Why do you call him Mr. Blackcap when his real name is chickadee queried Bob

That is because of his shiny black-capped head see how it glistens as he bobs back and forth in the sunlight

I wish he wouldn't be so selfish he should call some other birds to help him could you bring your bird book to school Tim then we shall be able to find out the names of all our hungry guests

That is a good idea Bob We wouldn't be very good hosts if we didn't know the names of our callers

Well laughed Bob maybe it's a good thing Mr. Blackcap didn't bring any strangers here today

Just then the school bell rang with one backward glance the two boys made their way to their desks both were happy that all their science knowledge was not written neatly in their notebooks

Check-Ups:

EXERCISE 11: PARAGRAPHING A STORY WITH CONVERSATION.

Read the preceding exercise again. Note that the first paragraph, which contains no conversation, describes the setting of the story and that the last paragraph, which is also without conversation, tells what happened after the talking was over. Note also that each time the words of a different speaker are written a new paragraph must be started.

Copy the following story and make the divisions for proper paragraphing. Supply capital letters and punctuation as required.

While walking home from school one afternoon Bill and John were discussing a film which they had seen during the science period was that ever an interesting film exclaimed John why do you say that John didn't I tell you that the local representative of the department of agriculture has been helping my father to try out some of those ideas on our own farm replied John do you mean contour plowing and strip cropping Bill asked yes and many other ideas which some people have found to be of great help with many of the fences removed our farm seems much bigger now explained John tell your folks that you plan to come over to my place tomorrow afternoon I'll let you walk over some land that looks just like the pictures we saw today I would like to do that Bill replied a new fellow in the community certainly has a lot to learn the two boys parted at the crossroads after chatting for a few minutes about the new teacher they had agreed that there was plenty of evidence that it would be best for them to do all the homework assigned for that night and to do it well

EXERCISE 12: AVOIDING MONOTONY. When the same word is used too frequently, written or spoken language becomes monotonous. To avoid this monotony a person must refrain from repeating a word unnecessarily.

(a) Read the following selection silently and then read it aloud. Notice the effect that results from the repeated use of the word "good."

Although it was old it was a *good* car, and even though the roads were not as *good* as they might have been we had a *good* ride to the camp without one delay.

After a *good* night's sleep we wakened early. The fresh air had given us *good* appetites, and without saying much we ate a *good* breakfast of porridge, bacon and eggs, toast and milk. Before we left the table our counsellor made a *good* speech to welcome us. Still laughing we ran noisily to the dock which was a *good* distance away. There we received a *good* lecture on the advisability of not exercising too strenuously immediately after a meal.

We had so many *good* experiences during those two weeks that I cannot write about them all. Everyone was *good* to us, and all of us tried to be as *good* as possible in helping to keep the camp running smoothly. All of us shall look back on that holiday and think of what is really the *good* old summer time.

➡ 11

Check-Ups:

(b) Rewrite the selection in (a) replacing the word "good" in almost every case with one of the words selected from the list printed below. Use the word that best suits the context.

comfortable	emphatic	interesting	pleasant
considerable	healthy	kind	refreshing
cooperative	helpful	memorable	smooth
dependable	humorous	nourishing	stern

(c) Read the original selection aloud. Then read the revised selection aloud. Which is more pleasing to the ear? Which do you consider to be the better narrative? Give reasons for your answer.

To express ideas effectively words must be carefully chosen. Exercises to provide help in developing this skill will be found in Chapter VII.

EXERCISE 13: WRITING ABOUT FAMILY LIFE.

Write at least one paragraph to tell about some interesting incident that has happened to some member of your family. Perhaps, like a car on a very cold winter's morning, you too may need help to get started even when you are planning to write about what happens to those people you know best. If you do, these sentences may suggest a topic on which you may write. If you prefer to write an imaginative story, select one of the following sentences and use it as the opening sentence. Compose a reader-catching title. (See page 134.)

1. The look on my brother's (or sister's) face indicated very plainly that he (or she) had disobeyed.

2. When told that he would burst if he ate another bite, Johnny quietly asked everyone to please pass the cake and then to stand aside.

3. The other day my little brother showed us that he could really stick up for himself.

4. When my sister agreed to look after the children of three of our neighbours on the same afternoon she really had her hands full.

5. My big brother thought he could fix the drain in the kitchen sink.

(NOTE: For more activities in writing on the theme "Family Fun" see page 61.)

A motto worth adopting:
"If I cease becoming better, I shall soon cease to be good."
Oliver Cromwell

Check-Ups:

EXERCISE 14: PAYING MY WAY.

Everyone has had some experience with spending money. How that money is obtained, or how it might be earned, is another story. This exercise gives you the opportunity to tell something about your activities in "Paying Your Way."

Select one of the sentences from Part (a) below and use it as the opening sentence of your account on this theme "Paying My Way." If you prefer, select one of the titles given in Part (b) below, and develop a story based on it. Note that numbers 5 and 8 are particularly well-worded to catch the reader's eye. As a third choice you may select a topic closer to your own experiences and write on it.

(a)
1. The first collection day is one that will never let me forget my paper route.
2. Last summer I had my first job.
3. There is a rule around our house that anyone wanting to spend money must also earn some.
4. My friend and I decided to go into business.
5. The caddy cart is a machine that has displaced boy labour on the golf course.
6. Money seems to come my way whether I work or not.
7. Helping on a fruit farm makes me a temporary financial success.
8. Perhaps there are more pleasant ways of earning money than by doing housework.
9. Why am I banking the money I earn?
10. A delivery boy's job can be dangerous.
11. If I had my choice of jobs I would be an usher in a theatre.
12. Baby sitting before the children's bedtime can be a hazardous occupation.

(b)

1. My Saturday Job
2. My Diminishing Bank Account
3. Earning My Allowance
4. Hobbies Can Sometimes Be Profitable
5. Weeding My Way to the Ball Game

6. Needed—a Few Dollars More
7. The Magic Purse
8. Power Mower Puts Power in Purse
9. Door to Door Salesman
10. Breaking the Bank

(NOTE: See Chapter V for more THEMES FOR CREATIVE WRITING.)

Check-Ups:

EXERCISE 15: PARAGRAPHS WITH A PURPOSE.

Three paragraphs are presented here. Read them carefully, and prepare to answer orally, giving reasons, each of these questions:

(i) Which paragraph is a descriptive paragraph?
(ii) Which paragraph is an expository paragraph?
(iii) Which paragraph is a narrative paragraph?

Following the class discussion of the answers do exercise number 18 on page 15.

(a)   A LOST BREAKFAST

One morning my mother made my cat, Puff, a delicious breakfast which she set on the floor. Very cautiously Puff walked toward it and tasted it, but she had decided that a breakfast of tender bird chops would suit her better. Just then she heard the door open and she ran quickly to get outside. She looked around until she spied an evening grosbeak. Very quietly she crept up behind the bird and pounced on it. The fight was on! Fur and feathers flew! The grosbeak pecked Puff until she was forced to leave. Later I found the bird, seriously hurt and still holding a sample of Puff's fur in its beak. I took it home. Puff still does not know that her breakfast recovered in our back porch.

—Isobel K.

(b)   SPRING IN THE FOREST

The first signs of spring in the damp dark forest would cheer anyone, even a broken-hearted lover. To make the earth warm and moist again the sun peeps in between the now-budding branches of tall majestic trees. Soft breezes play hide and seek among the bud-laden bushes, now and then lifting a shrivelled old leaf and darting back into hiding, while far above the leaf-covered soil an early robin sings his cheery song. If one kicks aside an old worm-eaten, moss-covered log, a few dainty spring beauties are seen poking their heads out, and over beside the huge maple an odd mayflower or yellow adder's tongue is enjoying the clear fresh air. Spring is everywhere, coming 'round the trees, out from the bushes, and from under the logs, always brightening even the darkest soul.

—Nancy Wood

(c)   OPENING UP

How to open a car door whose lock has frozen is a problem that many motorists have to solve in winter. With patience a key that has been heated in a match or lighter flame can usually be inserted into the ice-coated hole. Now by warming the end of the key in a similar manner heat can be transferred to the inside to melt the ice that prevents it from turning. During the process the driver remembers with gratitude the teacher whose science lessons taught him the principle that will rescue him from the cold.

—Sidney C.

Check-Ups:

Exercise 18: Writing Paragraphs with a Purpose.

(a) Write a descriptive paragraph on one of the following topics:

    (i) My Ideal Teacher
    (ii) My Favourite Relative
    (iii) The Pet I Remember Best
    (iv) A Tasty Dish
    (v) Yesterday's Weather

(b) Write a narrative paragraph on one of the following topics:

    (i) The Big Fight
    (ii) A Tall Tale
    (iii) The Deciding Game
    (iv) The Long Skid
    (v) Skin Diver's Reward

(c) Write an expository paragraph on one of the following topics:

    (i) Follow These Directions
    (ii) Bicycle Care
    (iii) Safety First
    (iv) A Good Recipe
    (v) Why I Like to Play ————
       (Fill in the blank with the name of a game.)

(Note: Chapter III of this text contains more material on "Paragraphs with a Purpose.")

Before writing more original paragraphs or stories, study carefully the material on the next seven pages. The procedures described and illustrated there will be helpful in DEVELOPING LANGUAGE SKILLS.

FOUR STEPS IN WRITING

Reports / Letters / IDEAS / Records / Stories

RECOPY FOR USE

3. COPY FOR THE TEACHER TO APPRAISE

2. REVISE OR POLISH THE DRAFT

1. FIRST WRITE A DRAFT COPY

TO BETTER WRITTEN ENGLISH

DO NOT SKIP STEPS

READ PAGES 17 AND 18 CAREFULLY

II ▲ PROCEDURES FOR BETTER WRITING

On the four pages which follow, a complete explanation of the above illustration is presented.   Read this material carefully.   Read it often.

Your teacher will discuss these four steps with your class frequently. Perhaps a drawing similar to this illustration will be made on the chalkboard or on a poster which will be placed at the front of the room.

To test your knowledge of the material on the next two pages, try to give orally all the ideas which might be written on each step of the illustration.

Four Steps in Writing

Most experienced writers follow a procedure similar to that illustrated on the previous page. In the draft stage, the main purpose is to get one's ideas on paper in sentence form. During the revision stage, each paragraph is checked. Each sentence is carefully inspected. The autobiographies of famous writers indicate that even talented writers have seldom been satisfied with the material they have produced in the first writing. One reports that he usually made so many revisions that there was hardly a spot of white left on the paper. For him, the copying was absolutely necessary.

You are not expected to become famous authors although it is hoped that some of you may. All of you should, however, learn from them that to write well you must be willing to rewrite often, to take your time in writing, and never to be satisfied with less than your best work.

Follow these four steps when you write a business letter, a story, a paragraph, a book report, or any other form of creative writing. (In writing a personal letter, which is a one-way conversation with a friend, you might not follow these steps, but you should reread that letter to correct any mechanical errors.) Use the index to find the pages on which any particular item is explained.

1. PREPARE A DRAFT OR FIRST COPY: (See page 20.)

   (a) Write on every other line.

   (b) Quickly jot down your ideas in sentences.

2. REVISE OR POLISH THE DRAFT: (See page 20.)

   (a) Check to determine if sentences have been **grouped** properly in paragraphs.

   (b) Inspect each sentence to determine—

      (i) if sentence fragments are present,

      (ii) if run-on sentences are present,

      (iii) if awkward wording has been used.

   (c) Check the order of the sentences to determine—

      (i) the suitability of the opening sentence,

      (ii) the contribution of each developing sentence,

      (iii) the effectiveness of the closing sentence.

Four Steps in Writing:

(d) Consider the possibility of improving style and structure—

    (i) by using some interrogative, exclamatory, or imperative sentences,

    (ii) by combining short sentences,

    (iii) by deliberately using short sentences,

    (iv) by changing the order of the words in the sentences.

(e) Check words to avoid the use of—

    (i) monotonous repetitions,

    (ii) carelessly-chosen words: nice, terrific, etc.,

    (iii) slang (except in reporting conversation),

    (iv) contractions, except in friendly letters and in reporting conversation.

(f) Consider the possibility of substituting synonyms for some words for greater effect.

(g) Compose a title.

(h) Read the material softly to yourself to detect omissions or repetitions, and to check *punctuation*, *grammar*, and *spelling*.

This last and careful check is sometimes called PROOFREADING.

3. COPY FOR THE TEACHER TO APPRAISE: (See page 21.)

(a) Pay attention to—

    (i) the position of the title,

    (ii) the indentation of paragraphs.

(b) Write in your best handwriting. Take pride in your work. This is your *manuscript*.

(c) Proofread again and correct errors. (See page 22.)

4. COPY, MAKING THE IMPROVEMENTS SUGGESTED BY THE TEACHER, FOR SOME PURPOSE.

Greater improvement in writing skill will be made if you concentrate on one aspect of good writing during each creative writing activity. That aspect becomes the TARGET FOR TODAY. (See opposite page.) The target may be one of the headings or subheadings from step two above. It may be to imitate the style of a model paragraph or story. The target selected will be determined by the needs of the individual pupil or of the group.

Target for Today

The wall chart shown in the illustration is made by using a sheet of fairly heavy plain cardboard which is about thirty inches long and twenty-two inches wide. The darts, or rocket pens, may be drawn entirely or made by drawing wings on large pictures of pens which have been cut from magazine advertisements. The targets, drawn on separate sheets of cardboard of the same weight, are twelve inches square. They are placed, one at a time, on the chart with the aid of thumb tacks. Five of these targets are shown. The target on the chart has a folding base which can be quickly changed to read either *according to function* or *according to construction*.

How will this chart help Grade VIII pupils in developing language skills? To answer this question think of what you do when learning to play hockey or the piano. The coach does not send you to a different position on the team each time you take a turn on the ice. Your teacher, and your parents, insist that you practise what you sometimes like to call "that same old piece" until you master it. In both activities you concentrate on one thing at a time and, if you try hard, you develop greater skill.

By concentrating on improving ONE skill during each language exercise, you will learn from that practice. The chart, by reminding you of the one skill that you are aiming to develop in each exercise, should help you to obtain better results in English more quickly.

During each composing exercise the target may be one of the items listed under the heading "Revise or Polish the Draft" which is Step 2 in the FOUR STEPS IN WRITING on pages 17 and 18. Your teacher may set as your *Target for Today* the item with which you are having most difficulty in written English.

A Good Decision
~~Unselfishness~~
~~Making a Choice~~

How delicious
this
^ ~~This~~ shiny red apple ~~would~~ might taste

~~very good~~ at recess ~~,~~! It was for

my new
~~the~~ teacher. Now, with all these questions

staring.
~~starring~~ right at me, I think I shall

Would that not
eat it myself. ~~That would~~ show her

this so much
what I think of, ^ ~~so much~~ arithmetic ~~.~~?

decision
What a ~~decision~~ to make! Let me

think. Yes, perhaps this food for

my mind will do me good. Miss

and
Smith shall have the apple ~~which~~

do it.
I ^ hope she enjoys ~~it~~ ~~very much~~.

The Transcribed Copy

A Good Decision

How delicious this shiny red apple might taste at recess! It was for my new teacher. Now, with all these questions staring right at me, I think I shall eat it myself. Would that not show her what I think of this arithmetic? What a decision to make! Let me think. Yes, perhaps this food for my mind will do me good. Miss Smith shall have the apple and I do hope she enjoys it.

The ideas for the paragraph entitled "A Good Decision" were obtained from a picture which shows a girl sitting at her desk. She has just finished doing several pages of mechanical arithmetic. She is looking longingly at an apple which is on the desk at her left elbow. She is the only pupil in the classroom.

The writer's imagination overheard the girl talking to herself. The paragraph tells what was heard in the "talking picture." The *Target for Today* was to use a variety of sentences.

Prepare to describe all the changes that the writer made during the revision step.

Keeping Written Work Neat

A person who writes a page of material which is easy to read needs to do more than just write legibly. The *arrangement of the writing on the page* is important also.

If you are using unlined paper, as you usually do when writing a letter, you must be sure to leave suitable *margins*. A margin about one inch wide should be provided on the left and right sides and at the bottom. The left margin must be kept straight, and the right margin should be kept as straight as possible. The top margin should be wider than one inch.

Care needs to be taken in placing the *title*, which often is underlined. The first and all other important words must have a capital letter. No period is used with the title.

Be sure to *indent* the first word of each new paragraph an equal distance from the left margin.

Before you leave any work which someone is to read be sure you *proofread carefully* what you have written. This proofreading can best be done by reading the material aloud to yourself. If errors are found, correct them according to these suggestions.

SOME DO'S:

1. Errors may be corᵣected like this.
2. Errors may also be ~~corected~~ corrected like this.
3. Errors may be ~~corected~~ corrected like this if detected in time. (Use only *one* line to cross out a word.)
4. Single letter errǫrs may be corrected like this.
5. Errors may be erased if time permits and if an eraser, which will do the job neatly, is available.
6. Errors should be corrected at their place in the line and not at the end of the line.

SOME DON'T'S:

1. Do *not* enclose errors in parentheses or brackets.
2. Do *not* write a small x at each end of an error and then rewrite the word.
3. Do *not* write the correct letter on top of an incorrect letter.
4. Do *not* use the symbol & for *and*.

HYPHENS:

1. This mark may be used to divide a word at the end of a line, but the word may *only* be broken between syllables.
   Examples: un-lined; character-istics; arrange-ment
2. Do *not* divide a syllable of one letter from the rest of the word. Never divide words like man-y or a-long.

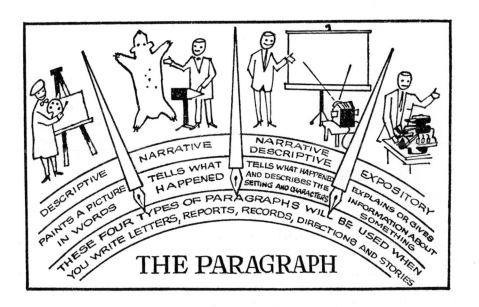

THE PARAGRAPH

III ▲ THE PARAGRAPH

From your work in other grades you have learned that a paragraph is a group of related sentences. Perhaps you have compared a paragraph to a train. In the latter, the engine, the cars, and the caboose each have special work to do, and they must be arranged in the proper order. In addition, all must be linked or coupled together, and no car that should be going east should become part of a train going west. The characteristics of the sentences that go together to form a paragraph are somewhat similar.

EXERCISE 1: After reading the introductory paragraph very carefully study the chart which follows. Be prepared to state orally the seven ways in which a paragraph is comparable to a train.

The Paragraph and Its Parts

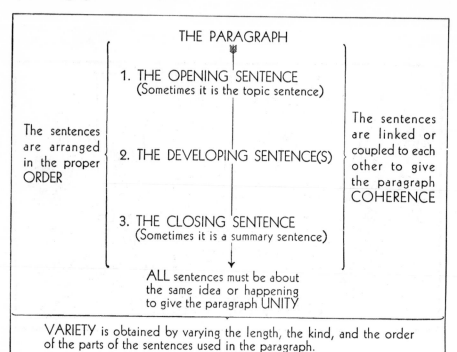

THE PARAGRAPH

The sentences are arranged in the proper ORDER

1. THE OPENING SENTENCE
(Sometimes it is the topic sentence)

2. THE DEVELOPING SENTENCE(S)

The sentences are linked or coupled to each other to give the paragraph COHERENCE

3. THE CLOSING SENTENCE
(Sometimes it is a summary sentence)

ALL sentences must be about the same idea or happening to give the paragraph UNITY

VARIETY is obtained by varying the length, the kind, and the order of the parts of the sentences used in the paragraph.

You have also had practice in recognizing and in writing paragraphs with a purpose. The illustration at the top of the previous page presents information about each of the four main types.

The exercises in this chapter will help you to develop greater skill in writing paragraphs with a purpose.

EXERCISE 2: (Oral) "A picture is worth 10,000 words" is reported to be a Chinese proverb. Discuss the merit of this statement. Is a picture better than a spoken or written description? Is it ever better? Is it always better? To how many of the five senses can a picture appeal? To how many of the senses can well-composed language appeal?

TOPIC SENTENCE DEVELOPING SENTENCE(S) SUMMARY SENTENCE

Descriptive Paragraphs

Read the following selection at least twice. Be prepared to describe what you see in each of the three pictures which the author has painted with his well-chosen words.

For two hundred miles the next day we rode south with the long chain of dunes on our right. The arid yellow of their tops, in an undulating horizon line, rose against the cloudless blue of the sky. Killdeers called from every plowed field and pastureland. Overcome by autumn wanderlust, woolly bear caterpillars humped across the concrete of the highway. All down the shore of the lake monarch butterflies drifted southward over the hayfields and orchards and fallow land now splotched with goldenrod and painted wine-red by the tinted stems of frost-touched grasses.

Beside the road black walnut trees, almost bare of leaves, were decorated from top to bottom with the green globes of their wild harvest. Green, too, was the duckweed on black swamp water, but its autumn migration down to the muddy bottom was only weeks away. Everywhere around us, from the dry fields, came the universal simmering sound of the insects, the most characteristic music of the fall.

This was fruit country, orchard and vineyard land. Roadside stands were laden. Vines were redolent with their blue burden and apple trees bent low with the weight of the autumn harvest. Mile after mile we rode among gray-barked peach trees where fallen fruit on the ground below outlined the form of the trees like shadows at noontime. All through this fruit belt this was harvest time, payoff time, the season of profit and plenty.

—From AUTUMN ACROSS AMERICA by E. W. Teale

EXERCISE 1: These questions are based on the selection above. Answer them orally.

1. From each paragraph select and read the sentence which describes the best picture.

2. Select and read the sentence which presents the greatest amount of colour.

3. Select and read the sentence which presents the greatest amount of sound.

4. In the third sentence of the third paragraph an unusual word has been used. Think of the thought expressed in the sentence and guess the meaning of this unfamiliar word. Check your ability to use the context to determine meaning by consulting your dictionary.

5. Why did the author include the phrase "at noontime" in the second last sentence of the third paragraph?

Descriptive Paragraphs:

EXERCISE 2: The following paragraphs were written by Grade VIII pupils. Read them silently. Then read them aloud. Consult the chart on page 24 and be prepared to comment orally on the effectiveness of the three main parts of each of these paragraphs, and on the four characteristics of UNITY, ORDER, COHERENCE, and VARIETY.

THE STORM

Masses of leaden clouds, being driven before a high wind, filled the sky as the thunder rolled ominously and lightning flashed viciously. The rain had not yet come, but when it did it would be hard, cold rain that would tear up the sod and beat the earth to a sticky shapeless mass. Then quite suddenly all was still. Not a leaf stirred and the sullen clouds became blacker every moment. It was almost as if mother nature was holding her breath. Without further warning the storm broke unleashing all its diabolical fury on the trees which dared to defy it. The thunder roared and the lightning flashed as the shrieking wind drove the rain before it. Muddy rivulets, swelled with the sudden downpour, emptied hurriedly into the rushing creek. Still the rain beat into the earth, ever harder, ever faster. Through the night it continued, the thunder, the lightning, the driving wind and the rain. Then, towards morning, it slackened. It stopped. At last the storm had worn itself out. At last it was over.

—Linda S.

OUR LIVING ROOM AT NIGHT

Our living room is a scene of comfort and cheerfulness at night. The soft glow of light shines on Mother's knitting which always keeps her busy. Over in the far corner comes the sound of soothing music from the radio. Curled up, looking ever so comfortable, my brother can be seen as if he were buried in his book. As if he had not a worry in the world our dog lies in front of the blazing fireplace. Only my father's hands are showing as he reads the evening newspaper. I cannot think of a more relaxing scene than this.

—Norma F.

EXERCISE 3: Write a descriptive paragraph on one of the following topics:

1. A Dish Fit for a King
2. The Hide-out
3. Weather for Me
4. It Made Me Shiver
5. My Heart Melted
6. The Hat for Me
7. Sound Asleep
8. A Word Picture of My Greatest Need

EXERCISE 4: Read the following paragraph which has been adapted from Charles Dickens' DAVID COPPERFIELD. Note how the author presents this very vivid word picture. Note also that he helps you to use two other senses as you see, with him, the scene that he beheld. What are they?

Now I gazed upon the schoolroom into which he had taken me. I considered it the most forlorn and desolate place I had ever seen. It was a long

➡

Descriptive Paragraphs:

room, with three rows of desks, and six of benches, and bristling all round with pegs for hats and slates. Scraps of old copy-books and exercises littered the dirty floor. Some silkworms' houses, made of the same materials, were scattered over the desks. Two miserable little white mice, left behind by their owner, were running up and down in a fusty castle made of pasteboard and wire, looking in all the corners with their red eyes for anything to eat. A bird, in a cage very little bigger than himself, made a mournful rattle now and then in hopping on his perch, or dropping from it. However, it neither sang nor chirped. There was a strange unwholesome smell upon the room, like mildewed corduroys, sweet apples wanting air, and rotten books. There could not have been more ink splashed about it, if it had been roofless from its first construction, and the skies had rained, snowed, hailed and blown ink through all the varying seasons of the year.

1. Select five adjectives from the paragraph above that contribute a great deal to the clarity of the description.

2. Select two verbs that have been used very effectively.

3. Listen with eyes closed as a classmate reads the paragraph aloud. In your mind's eye see the picture that is described.

EXERCISE 5: On the theme "My Home" write a description of at least two paragraphs. Select two or more of these topics for your paragraphs:

1. The setting and exterior appearance of my house
2. The interior of my house
3. My room
4. What I think of my home

Opening sentences that might be used for each of the paragraphs suggested above are presented below. They will suggest various ways in which you might begin your paragraphs. Read each group carefully before starting to write the paragraph on that topic. Use a sentence from the group *only* if it suits your particular situation.

1. The opening sentence of the paragraph on the topic "The Setting and Exterior Appearance of My House" might be one of the following:

(a) Our house is situated on a quiet street where the towering elms and a few tall pines provide welcome shade in summer and a home for numerous birds that sometimes serve as unwelcome alarm clocks.

(b) Although our house is on the main street it has many features that make it attractive to us.

(c) Our house was built fifty years ago and some people, seeing it for the first time, call it the castle.

➡ 27

Descriptive Paragraphs:

(d) My home, in an apartment over my father's store, is comfortable and conveniently located for all the members of the family.

(e) Beside a small stream and shaded by two giant willows our big old farm house stands.

(f) At the end of a long lane of poplars the Smith residence stands, reminding all who approach that great-grandfather always referred to himself as the lord of the manor.

2. The opening sentence of the paragraph on the topic "The Interior of My House" might be one of the following:

(a) As you enter our house its roominess becomes immediately apparent.

(b) In a modern home there is certainly no wasted space.

(c) On entering our hall a visitor wonders where each of the five doors leads.

(d) All our rooms are on the second floor, but they are spacious and well lighted.

(e) Mother always says that the outstanding feature of our house is the height of the ceilings.

(f) As there are five small children, a dog, and a cat living in our house, the interior is not always as tidy as we would like to keep it.

3 The opening sentence of the paragraph on the topic "My Room" might be one of the following:

(a) The appearance of my room always indicates that I share it with a younger member of the family.

(b) Small but cozy are the best words to use in describing my room.

(c) On entering my room it is evident that I am a collector.

(d) Why my mother always refers to my room as a shambles I do not know.

(e) My bedroom is a combination workshop and study.

(f) The room which my brother (or sister) shares with me bears the scars of several real battles.

4. The opening sentence of the paragraph on the topic "What I Think of My Home" might be one of the following:

(a) Now I believe that I understand the difference between a house and a home.

(b) There is certainly truth in the old saying, "Be it ever so humble there is no place like home."

(c) In our house we may not have much money, but we have a lot of fun.

(d) A house without children must be a lonely place.

(e) As every member of our family has a share of the housekeeping to do, mother has time to have fun with the family.

(f) Now I realize that I should be grateful to my parents for providing the place which I call home.

Puzzle-Pen-Portraits

The writing of puzzle-pen-portraits is a challenging exercise. It requires the writer to do some thinking, and to arrange his ideas carefully in the proper order. The easiest clues, of course, must come toward the end of the description of the character being painted in words.

The oral reading of these PUZZLE-PEN-PORTRAITS by their authors can also be an interesting activity. The most successful writer is the pupil who can keep his listeners in some doubt until the very last sentence is heard.

The ALMANAC section of this book provides the names of many famous people for whom Puzzle-Pen-Portraits can be written. At the end of each month one of these might be written about any individual who has been named in the Almanac up to that date.

Read this Puzzle-Pen-Portrait. Note that the main clue is contained in the last sentence. Can you identify the character?

When this lady, who was born in Poland on Canada's birthday, was a little girl, she often visited her father as he worked in his science laboratory at a university. As she seemed to understand so much of what was going on in that room with its tubes and bottles, the students there nicknamed her "Miss Professor." At sixteen she won a gold medal for her excellent work in mathematics and science, but was unable to continue to attend school. She worked as a governess, and in her spare time taught the country folk to read and write. Fortunately, an opportunity soon came for her to continue her studies in Paris. There she met and married a man who was also a gifted student. Working together this couple discovered the magic element, radium.

EXERCISE 1: Write a Puzzle-Pen-Portrait of a person in your classroom. Give plenty of clues to his or her identity without enabling the reader or listener to make the identification too easily. Keep the most revealing clue to include in the last sentence.

EXERCISE 2: Follow the instructions of Exercise 1 and write a Puzzle-Pen-Portrait of some historical character. The following example may help you.

This man, whose name and work are known to most people, has a day in October named in his honour. He was a daring European sailor who found it difficult to convince others that his plan was a good one. Although he had hoped to reach India by sailing westward, he reached only the western hemisphere. He is usually remembered as the man who discovered America.

29

Narrative Paragraphs

Read this selection from FROZEN FIRE by Armstrong Sperry. Note that each paragraph tells what happened. Note also the writer's skilful use of carefully-selected adjectives, adverbs, and verbs to tell about the action.

Buckling on my automatic, I followed Candido as he led the way with gingerly steps down to the moonlit shore. Bud and a few of the more venture-some camaradas trailed after us. Thomas Brown wanted no part of the business. Candido slowed his pace to a cautious, catlike tread. His gaze was fixed ahead into a shadowy tangle of vegetation. Suddenly he drew up short, pointing with a quivering forefinger.

At first I could distinguish nothing in the dappled pattern of darkness and pale light. Then my astounded gaze made out a mottled, cone-shaped coil that seemed to stand as high as a man! From the base of this coil came the neck and wedge-shaped head of the anaconda, flat on the ground, bead-black eyes glittering. Slowly we advanced until we were within fifteen feet of the monster. And so formidable was that piled-up coil that involuntarily an exclamation escaped me. Here was a serpent large enough to crush us all to death at once. We stood stock-still, staring, and being stared at in turn. Bud's sharply indrawn breath came from behind my shoulder. The camaradas were snared in a trance of fear and silence.

I have heard it argued by men that a snake has no power to mesmerize its prey. Perhaps that is true. For myself, I can only state that I felt spellbound, I was unable to take a step. I could not even think on my own initiative. It is an experience for which I could find no parallel.

The anaconda still had made no move, but in the dappled moonlight we could see its body expand and contract in breathing. The eyes seemed to give off a phosphorescent light. Curiously, I felt no fear nor any inclination to retreat. Thus we remained, scarcely moving an eyelid, for what could only have been a matter of seconds, yet they seemed to stretch into eternity.

There came a slight movement, a tension, in the snake's coils. With an effort I shook myself free of the spell. My right hand slid down to the holster. For a moment the anaconda's entire body seemed to congeal. In the split second before it struck I fired the entire chamber of soft-nosed bullets point-blank between the glittering eyes. Instantly the head raised to a great height above us, hissing in its death agony.

The wounded snake uncoiled and, writhing with pain, made for the river. Hastily we retreated beyond reach of the thrashing tail, one blow from which could have killed a man. Mortally wounded, its struggles grew perceptibly weaker, but no one of us could bring himself to a closer approach. Finally the anaconda lay inert, its head and a portion of its body submerged in the water.

Narrative Paragraphs:

EXERCISE 1: Select one of the following sentences and develop it into a narrative paragraph.

1. When bath night comes for my young brother, the whole household is in an uproar.

2. A little care and thoughtfulness would have prevented it from happening.

3. As I jumped from the dock to the deck, I remembered what I had promised to do.

4. The thirty-five-lap late-model stock car race was the feature that I really went to see.

5. Slowly she climbed to the highest board on the diving tower.

6. The players dropped their gloves and started swinging.

7. A short fat man entered hurriedly, as if blown in by a sudden gust of wind.

8. Everyone was running for the exits.

9. Up until now it had been fun lying in the hammock listening to records on the portable phonograph.

10. All the way down I kept wondering why she had told me to report to him at once.

EXERCISE 2: Select one of the following topics and develop it into a story. Select your action words carefully.

1. The Day I Flew a Jet (In My Dreams)
2. Refrigerator Raid
3. The Neighbours' Party
4. Fisherman's Luck
5. Pets on Parade
6. The Spill
7. Crayons, the Wall, and . . .
8. Meals from the Deep Freeze
9. Aching Muscles
10. By Candle Light

When you write to tell what has happened, you must aim to select action words that really reveal all the action that took place.

Narrative Paragraphs:

This narrative paragraph has a closing sentence which contains the main thought.   A sentence of this type is sometimes referred to as *the punch line*.   Note the effect of the short sentences.

I smiled a little ruefully at the recollection of one of my first discoveries in natural history made here in the fall.   I was, at the time, in second grade.   The teacher had asked us to bring in brilliant autumn leaves and I found the most brilliant of all on a slope of the gravel pit.   I knew my moment of triumph when I handed the large bouquet to the teacher.   But it was short-lived.   A few days later I was not at school.   Neither was the teacher.   The bright-coloured leaves were the autumn foliage of the poison ivy.

—From Autumn across America by E. W. Teale

Keeping the punch line at the end is a technique that one needs to use in telling or writing a funny story.

Reproducing in words all the humour that is found in a cartoon provides excellent practice in developing this skill.   The following is an example of this type of writing.

Unlimited Ceiling

The captain and his co-pilot were at the controls of the transcontinental jet liner.   Through the almost cloudless sky they flew at a height no bird had ever travelled.   All was quiet for at their speed the roar of the engines was always far behind them.   There was no vibration either, and consequently, it would have been very easy to go off to sleep.   Suddenly a wisp of cloud came into view and on it there appeared to be a youthful angel whose golden wings reflected the setting sun.   As the aircraft sped past this lone sentinel of the sky, the pilot turned to his first officer and asked, "What do you figure our altitude to be?"

—David B.

Exercise 1: (a) (Oral) Name the four people or objects that were shown in the cartoon.   What four items of information indicate that the writer knew something about jet aircraft?   Where in the story did the writer place the caption that appeared under the cartoon?

(b) Make a class collection of cartoons whose humour can be told in words.   *Maclean's* and the *Saturday Evening Post* are representative of the type of magazines in which you will find material.

(c) Select one of the cartoons from the class collection and write the story which it presents, making the closing sentence the punch line.

Narrative-Descriptive Paragraphs

> Language is sometimes used to tell what happens and also to describe the people, places, or things connected with the action that takes place. A paragraph that both tells and describes is called a NARRATIVE-DESCRIPTIVE paragraph.

Read the two paragraphs that follow. The ideas for both were obtained from one magazine picture. In one paragraph the writer has told only what happened. In the other the reader is presented with a word picture and with the story of what happened. Which is the narrative paragraph? Which is the narrative-descriptive paragraph? Which paragraph do you prefer? Give your reasons.

1. Johnny's birthday was almost over. On his way home from a movie with his friends, he suggested that they should stop at a soda fountain. He had already eaten plenty, but Johnny thought that a banana split would provide the perfect ending to a very happy day. It was less than half eaten when he suddenly realized that his eyes had been bigger than his stomach. He recalled having been told that it is always wise to know when to stop. How he wished that he had remembered that saying a little sooner!

2. Dressed in his best suit, complete with grey shirt, blue tie and pocket handkerchief, Johnny sat at the soda fountain. From beneath his small black cap which was pushed back on his head, a shock of uncombed red hair hung down over his forehead. The freckles across his nose and cheeks were like those to be seen on many ten-year-old lads. He looked to be very healthy, but at the moment all was not well. To top off his birthday celebrations, Johnny had invited his friends to have one last treat on their way home from the movie. A picture of a banana split had persuaded him to order one. He had eaten only a few spoonfuls. The look on his face seemed to say quite loudly that his eyes had been bigger than his stomach. Perhaps he was thinking that he should have remembered that it is always wise to know when to stop. What happened next to Johnny that day I do not know, but one delicious-looking, nut-sprinkled gondola of ice cream and fruit was left almost untouched as he and his friends left for home.

> To compose a narrative-descriptive paragraph the writer must select describing words and action words carefully. Details must be provided to help the reader to see a clear picture, to see the action, and to hear the sounds.

Narrative-Descriptive Paragraphs:

EXERCISE 1: Select one of these sentences as the opening sentence for a narrative-descriptive paragraph. Remember that well-chosen action and descriptive words are needed. Write the draft in pencil. Revise or polish the draft carefully. Give your paragraph a title.

1. The attendant at the gas station which we patronize always gives us service with a smile.

2. An after-the-show raid on the refrigerator is usually successful.

3. The plane was falling like a leaf, and the spectators knew that the pilot was in trouble.

4. While waiting for visitors at the station, I study the people who are going and coming.

5. It was unexpected, but there in front of me was a table laden with the foods that I enjoy most.

EXERCISE 2: Apply the directions for Exercise 1 above to the following sentences:

1. A carelessly flicked match or cigarette was the cause.

2. At the stock car races the thrills and spills keep the crowds standing most of the time.

3. In spite of the wind and the rain, Policewoman Malone waited patiently in the shadows.

4. As the sun broke through the clouds, little Mary, dressed for the party, came running out of the house toward the curb where the water was running like a small river.

5. The fireworks display at the fall fair always frightens some and entertains others.

EXERCISE 3: Each of these themes might be the topic for narrative-descriptive writing in a friendly letter. Select one of the topics and compose the paragraph or paragraphs that you might write on that topic in a letter to a friend or relative.

1. My first experience at the hairdresser's

2. Big sister gets ready for a party

3. Relatives or friends arrive in their new car

4. The neighbour's new pup

5. Answering a summons to the office

34

Expository Paragraphs

> Language that provides an explanation, that gives directions, or that presents information is called EXPOSITION. An EXPOSITORY PARAGRAPH is one which explains a process, a thing, or an idea.

Read each of the following expository paragraphs. Then answer the accompanying questions. They will help you to recognize that expository paragraphs also have the characteristics listed on the chart on page 24.

1. An author, before the invention of the typewriter, wrote each book or pamphlet in his own handwriting and sent it to the publisher. This hand-written copy was called a manuscript, a word obtained from two Latin words meaning "hand" and "write". Although nowadays most writers prepare their material on a typewriter, the word manuscript is still used in referring to the copy produced by the writer. Each of your paragraphs or stories, after the draft has been revised or polished and carefully copied, may also be called a manuscript. That word will be particularly appropriate when it refers to the material which you will submit for publication in your class or school paper.

2. To understand why very few errors in spelling and punctuation are encountered in printed material, readers should know something about one important step in the process of printing. This stage begins when the type which makes the words and lines of reading is set in a metal pan called a galley. Before the type from this galley is placed in the press to print the pages of the book, the printer inks the type with a roller. He then presses a sheet of paper over the wet type in the galley to obtain a copy of the message. This copy, called a galley proof, is read very carefully by people called proofreaders. The author also reads this galley proof. They mark any mistakes that may have been made by the typesetter in setting the type as he read from the manuscript. When errors are found the proofreaders and author mark the galley proof using symbols which the typesetters understand. The corrected galley proof is returned to the typesetter and the type is reset where necessary. This proof-reading is an attempt to produce printed material which will be free from errors.

Expository Paragraphs:

QUESTIONS FOR DISCUSSION:

1. Would you prefer to call the first sentence in each paragraph on page 35 a topic sentence or an opening sentence? Give reasons for your answers.

2. Which paragraph has the more effective closing sentence? Give your reasons.

3. Both paragraphs illustrate the characteristics of ORDER and COHERENCE. In most sentences there is a word or group of words that refers back to something in the preceding sentence. Find some of these linking words, and read the word to which they point back.

4. Read orally three sentences that open with the subject. Read three sentences in which a modifier of the bare predicate opens the sentence. Which characteristic listed on page 24 is provided by a change in the order of the parts of the sentences?

5. In expository writing the ideas must be presented in the proper order. Read paragraph 2 on page 35 again. Without referring back to it arrange the following points in a written list in the order in which they are given in the paragraph: —marking errors in galley proof; —inking the type in the galley; —resetting the type; —making the galley proof; —setting the type in the galley; —returning corrected proofs to the typesetter; —reading the galley proof. Now read the paragraph again and check the order of the items in your list.

6. Read again the opening and closing sentences in paragraph 2 on page 35. Answer these questions orally:

   (a) What 3 words in the opening sentence refer to the activity which is later called proofreading?

   (b) What two types of error do proofreaders attempt to eliminate?

   (c) Skim read page 18 in this text and find the heading of the section that contains the words "spelling" and "punctuation."

7. Compose a title for each of the sample expository paragraphs.

(NOTE: Every manuscript that you write will be free of errors if you PROOFREAD carefully everything that you write.)

Careful planning is required in order to write expository paragraphs. All the ideas needed for a clear presentation must be included. They must be presented one at a time and in the proper order. Opening and closing sentences must be carefully composed.

Expository Paragraphs:

Exercise 1: Write an expository paragraph on at least one of the following topics. Before starting to write, jot down the ideas that you want to include. Carefully arrange these ideas in the proper order before you begin to write. Strive to create effective opening and closing sentences. Compose an interesting title.

1. Decorating the Christmas tree
2. Repairing a bicycle flat
3. Building a campfire
4. Preparing a pet for a pet show
5. Assembling a plastic model airplane
6. First aid in case of fainting (*or* a nose bleed, a deep cut, or a bad burn)
7. Using the dictionary, a treasure house of information
8. Planting bulbs for indoor blooms
9. Putting baby sister (or brother) to sleep
10. What to do during fire drill

(NOTE: Sketches are often useful in connection with expository writing. See paragraph 2 on page 35.)

Exercise 2: Select one of the following sentences and use it to open an expository paragraph. Follow the draft-revise-transcribe procedure described on pages 17, 18. Compose the closing sentence very carefully. Provide an interesting title.

1. Neat legible handwriting is produced when a few simple rules are followed.

2. The Junior Red Cross provides pupils of the elementary school with an opportunity to help others who are less fortunate than we.

3. Why should I like to ride the range in the saddle of an intelligent horse?

4. To produce a composition that will provide interesting reading, follow these steps.

5. In choosing material for a dress, there are many factors to consider.

6. In selecting the kind of wood for a particular project, there are many factors to consider.

7. The climate in which people live determines the type of clothes which they wear.

8. How would people get along today if the ———— had not been invented? (Fill the blank with the name of an invention of your choice.)

Expository Paragraphs:

The following are expository paragraphs. Note that in this type of writing, the author is explaining how something is done, or the purpose for which something is used.

BLOCK BALANCING

1. Two equal teams containing any number of players are lined up side by side. The members of each team stand behind one another. Placed on the ground approximately twenty feet away from the leader of each team is a marker. At the sound of the word "Go" the leader of each team puts a block of wood, which is approximately the size of a book, on his head and proceeds to walk towards the marker, around the marker, and back to his starting point. As he reaches the starting point, he tags the next member of his team and passes the block to him. This person now proceeds to walk around the marker with the block on his head. The block of wood must not be held in position by the contestant's hands. A player must return to his starting point and repeat the procedure if the block falls to the ground. The team having all its members complete the walks first is the winner.

THREADING THE NEEDLE

2. For this game two chairs, two pairs of cloth garden gloves, two needles, and two four-foot-long pieces of thread are needed. Two teams, with an equal number of players, line up with the leaders facing the chairs which are approximately twenty feet away. When the signal to start is given, each leader walks to his chair, puts on the gloves, threads the needle to the satisfaction of the referee, and then removes the thread from the needle. All the articles are then replaced carefully on the chair. The contestants now return to their teams tagging the next member of their team as they reach the starting line. The process is continued until all persons on one of the teams have completed the threading and been declared the winner.

EXERCISE 1: Select some simple game that you play and imagine that you want to tell a friend exactly how to play it. Write the explanation that you would make.

EXERCISE 2: Select any one of the following topics and write an expository paragraph explaining its full use. 1. A carburetor; 2. The speedometer; 3. The rear-view mirror; 4. The clutch; 5. The fan belt; 6. The sun visors; 7. The distributor; 8. The glove compartment.

Expository Paragraphs:

Read the following expository paragraphs. Be prepared to tell whether each paragraph explains, gives directions, or presents information. Compose a title for each paragraph. Then turn to the exercise on page 40.

1. Did you ever notice that the names of most towns that end in "ford" are situated on rivers? Did you ever wonder how those places received their names? A ford is a shallow place in a stream where it is possible to walk or drive a wagon across. Years ago these fords were usually named after the person who owned the nearby land. For example the ford in the river close to the land owned by a Mr. Campbell was called Campbell's ford. Because a ford was a place where people would meet and do business buildings were erected there. Sometimes a village or town eventually developed. When it did, it took the name of the ford which was then usually shortened into one word.

2. The old Spanish dollar that became famous in the days of pirates and buccaneers was known as a "piece of eight". To provide small change this coin was cut into eight pieces. As two of these bits or pieces was the equivalent of a quarter of a dollar, our twenty-five cent piece has become known as "two bits".

3. Take any number from one to ten. Double it. Add ten. Divide that number by two. Give me your answer, and I shall tell you the number with which you started.

(Do as this paragraph tells you to do two or three times, using a different number each time. Can you figure out how to do it?)

4. Easter is a Christian celebration whose date can fall between March 22nd and April 25th. It comes on the first Sunday after the first full moon after the vernal equinox which occurs about March 21st and which is the official first day of spring. Why does the date of Easter depend upon the lunar timetable? It is said that the method of choosing it was worked out in the early days of Christianity so that pilgrims bound for religious shrines would have the aid of moonlight on their travels. Easter will not fall on March 22nd again until 2285. It will not come on its latest date until 2038. These last two facts assume, of course, that no progress will be made among peoples and nations by those who advocate either establishing Easter on a fixed date or reducing the range of its movability.

5. Every tree and bush and plant is, large or small, a kind of invisible fountain. Moisture rises from its leaves, given off by the vital processes of plant life. As the leaves slow down their activity at the end of summer, as they begin to lose their hold and drop to the ground, these fountains dry up. This is one of the reasons why autumn tends to be a time of dryness and dust.

Expository Paragraphs:

6. Ostrich hunting in Argentina is different. On horseback the gauchos first cut the bird they wish from the flock and then ride hard after it across the pampas. Whirling the bolas overhead, they let it fly when about thirty feet away. The rope, to which is attached the lead or stone weights, wraps itself around the bird's neck and legs and throws it. Another rhea is captured.

EXERCISE 3: Select one of the following sentences and use it to introduce an expository paragraph. Think carefully whether the paragraph is to explain, give directions, or provide information. Compose the closing sentence carefully. Give the paragraph an interesting title.

1. The person that I dislike most is the one who . . . (Complete the sentence as you wish.)

2. It is only to be expected that parents and adolescents will not always agree.

3. When I visit my father's office, I sometimes wonder why we learn to write by hand and to do arithmetic on paper and in our heads.

4. While working in the supermarket on Saturdays I learned that the manager has a variety of problems.

5. About hot rods my dad's views and mine seem to differ considerably.

6. To earn promotion into grade nine just follow my advice.

EXERCISE 4: (a) Read the following paragraphs which explain the significance of each part of Canada's coat of arms which is shown on the opposite page.

The story of Canada's rise to nationhood is told on the coat of arms. The crest, the shield, and the motto are tributes to the pioneers from four nations who carved their new country from a wilderness.

Above the arms is the Imperial crown, the symbol of Canada's place in the British Commonwealth of Nations. Below is the crest, a crowned lion holding a red maple leaf. This represents the sacrifice of loyal Canadians. On the shield are the arms of four nations: England, Ireland, Scotland, and France. They are represented by the three lions of England, the Irish harp, the Scottish lion and the three gold fleur-de-lis of old France. Across the lower part of this shield is a sprig of three maple leaves, Canada's emblem. Supporting this shield are the lion and the unicorn of the Royal Arms. The lion holds the Union Jack. The unicorn bears the ancient lily banner of France. Canada's motto, "A mari usque ad mare", which may be translated "from sea to sea", signifies the breadth of this nation which stretches from the Atlantic to the Pacific.

Surrounding the motto is a cluster of lilies, roses, shamrocks, and thistles. These are the national flowers of the French, English, Irish, and Scottish settlers who laid the foundation for Canada's nationhood and who wrote the first chapters in Canada's story.   —Adapted

(b) Rule 2 columns in your language note book. Write the headings NOUNS WITHOUT MODIFIERS and NOUNS WITH MODIFIERS. Select all the nouns in paragraph 2. If the noun is used without either a word or phrase modifier write it in column 1. If it has a modifier, write it, complete with modifier in column 2. (Do not count the articles as modifiers.)

Note that in exposition few adjectives are used. The target when writing exposition is to explain clearly and concisely.

| TOPIC | SENTENCE | DEVELOPING SENTENCE(S) | SUMMARY SENTENCE |

Three-Sentence Paragraphs

Writing a paragraph of only three sentences is more difficult than writing one of greater length. You will have to think more carefully. You may have to revise your paragraph several times.

A three-sentence paragraph has all the characteristics that are listed in the chart on page 24.   When you deliberately limit a paragraph to a length of three sentences you will produce a paragraph having all those features.   You will also develop the following skills:

(a) the ability to combine short sentences into longer sentences without using *and* or *but* too frequently,

(b) the ability to use punctuation correctly as you write longer sentences,

(c) the ability to select only the most important ideas to include in your paragraph and to discard the unimportant ideas.

Practice in writing three-sentence paragraphs is purposeful practice. Therefore frequent practice in writing paragraphs of this length is worth-while.

Before doing the exercises on page 44, read the following paragraphs. Note that each is composed of only three sentences.   Listen as they are read aloud by your classmates.   Discuss whether the writers of these paragraphs have shown that they have used the three skills listed above.

1.   STEEL TAKES OVER

In the 1850's steel took over the greatest share of Canada's transportation load from the express canoe, the early steamers, and the stagecoach.   Two thousand miles of track were laid, and by 1860 Canada had the longest trunk line on the continent, from Riviere du Loup to Sarnia.   The first train from Montreal to Toronto gave thousands of Canadians, in 1856, a thrilling vision of how, within thirty years, steel rails would bind a new nation together from coast to coast.

2.   THE WEST BEGINS

The first great westward trek of Canadian immigrants included British, Russians, and Germans who were lured, in the 1870's, by the offer of free land in a wonderfully fertile country where there were no trees to be cleared.   In two-wheeled ox-drawn Red River carts these settlers pushed westward from Winnipeg in search of adventure, independence, and security. Probably few dreamed that, by working together, they and their descendants would turn the Canadian Prairies into one of the greatest food-producing areas in the world.

3.   THE MOUNTIES

When a squad of the North West Mounted Police went to London in 1911 to represent Canada at the Coronation of King George V, the "Mounties" made their bow to a world which had long heard of their prowess. Organized in 1873 to bring law and order to the Canadian West, the men of the Mounted quickly won the admiration and the respect of pioneer settlers, trappers, and Indians. Today, as the Royal Canadian Mounted Police, the force maintains lonely Arctic patrols and wages war on smugglers, dope traffickers, and all who threaten the Dominion's internal security.

4.   THE NEW ARRIVALS

In the two decades at the beginning of this century three million newcomers from distant lands were added to Canada's population of five million citizens. From more than thirty countries they came to fill the rich, beckoning acres of the West and to claim their share in the building of a new-born nation. Since World War II Canada has welcomed a new wave of immigrants who have also been attracted by the freedom and the opportunities which this Dominion has to offer.

5.   THE FIRST CITIZEN

Canada's first settlers were of necessity farmers, no matter what their trades before they left the Old World. Despite the rapid growth of towns and cities in recent years, the farmer remains as Canada's first citizen. Twenty-five of every hundred members of Canada's working force are engaged in agriculture and produce the food which helps to feed fifteen million Canadians and millions of other people throughout the world.

6.   NORTHERN LIGHT

For three centuries the diaries of a few explorers, the reports of courageous missionaries and police, and the tales of occasional prospectors were all that we Canadians had to reveal the breath-taking wonders of our far northern territory. Today, painters, writers, engineers, seekers after gold, oil, and uranium, are tearing away the curtain of mystery that has cloaked this great unknown territory lying across the top of a continent. Now we know that this area possesses inestimable wealth which casts a bright new light on Canada's future.

Three-Sentence Paragraphs:

EXERCISE 1: Select at least three of the following opening sentences and build each of them into a three-sentence paragraph. You will probably have to revise your first or draft copy carefully to make your paragraph say what you wish it to say in only three sentences.

1. Some people when talking on the telephone do not realize that it is unnecessary to speak more loudly than when in quiet conversation with a friend.

2. There in front of me was the most appetizing strawberry shortcake that I had ever laid my eyes on.

3. Spellbound was the only word that could describe my sister as she sat looking at the gift.

4. There was proof that it does not pay to hurry.

5. Have you ever caught sunfish and cooked them over an open fire at the edge of a pond?

6. The neighbours stood around in silent amazement.

7. My little brother maintains that cakes were never baked just to be looked at.

8. Walking through the rain, penniless and hungry, he suddenly felt a piece of crumpled paper in the deepest corner of his topcoat pocket.

9. Only a blinking lighthouse pierced the chilly damp blackness at that early hour.

10. For seven miles we jolted, swayed, and pitched over a roadbed so rough that it was difficult to believe in the existence of rails.

EXERCISE 2: Write a three-sentence paragraph on the topic which any one of these groups of words suggests to you. In your first attempt to develop the paragraph you may use more than three sentences. By combining sentences, and by selecting only the important ideas, reduce your paragraph to three sentences. Give the paragraph a title.

1. barge, shadow, swim fins

2. abandoned house, cobwebs, footsteps

3. report card, father, low marks

4. parents, parties, the clock

5. monkey, mirror, banana

IV ▲ WRITING MULTI-PARAGRAPH STORIES

Dividing your writing into paragraphs is much more difficult to do when writing a story than when reporting conversation or when writing a friendly letter. In the former, each time the speaker changes a new paragraph is begun. In the latter, each new topic about which you "talk in ink" requires a new paragraph. In writing a story, however, you must often rely on your own judgment to determine if a new paragraph is required. By reading the following explanation, and by using the illustration on this page, you can develop the ability to make these decisions correctly.

Multi-Paragraph Writing

As you write, imagine that your story is being produced for a movie or for a television programme. Think of your pen as being the camera. The amount of the story that would be "shot" with the camera in *one* position is the amount which can be written in one paragraph. The illustration shows several pieces of film, each of which is made up of several frames. Each piece of film resembles a paragraph. Each frame resembles a sentence. Just as the number of frames will vary for the different scenes, so will the number of sentences vary from paragraph to paragraph.

When the thought or action of the story changes, a cameraman must move his camera to cover the new situation. Note that the camera is always mounted to make the movement easy. A writer shows these same changes by beginning a new paragraph each time a similar change occurs in his story. Both writer and cameraman must do some thinking to decide how long to make each paragraph or scene, and when to make the change from one to another.

Read the following selection from THE RAIN FOREST by Armstrong Sperry. Read it twice. Then listen as one of your classmates reads it orally. Listen carefully for the change from paragraph to paragraph, and imagine that you see the cameraman making the necessary moves. (The paragraphs have been numbered for easy reference.)

1. Chad and Natua had been carried to the edge of a lagoon, a body of water that lay smooth and glittering in the hot sunlight. Alert and watchful now, the boys discovered the pygmy village. It consisted of cunningly concealed tree houses whose supports were living casuarina trees. Somewhere, ages ago, Chad had read about such houses, but he saw them now with a sense of admiration tinged with disbelief. They looked so enormous to house pygmies! Each dwelling could accommodate several families. Perched fifty feet above ground, they were reached by means of vine ladders. The whole village appeared to be no more than two rows of houses facing each other across a strip of sand.

2. The little chief motioned toward a vine ladder, shouting angrily, indicating that they should climb without further delay. Chad ascended as best he could while Natua below him, reached upward with a helping hand. Chad collapsed on the narrow veranda of the tree house as Natua hauled himself up beside his friend.

3. The pygmy chief pulled himself up on the platform with two warriors at his heels. Unceremoniously the boys were hustled inside the tree house and a stout screen of bamboo was fastened over the doorway. This accomplished,

the three pygmies descended once more to the ground. Now the boys were prisoners indeed.

4. Before darkness settled in, a monstrous bonfire was blazing in the open space between the two rows of thatched tree houses. Stones were being heated for the cook ovens. The fires, constantly replenished, leaped and crackled toward the dark sky. Somewhere drums began to beat—a score of them in varying timbre, low and fitful at first but rising in crescendo. Those drums, heard so close at hand, seemed to reverberate with the very sound of doom.

5. Louder and louder swelled the message of the drums. Now, down the cleared space between the two rows of houses, a column of nearly naked pygmies advanced. Their bodies glistened in the light from the leaping fires. Each man carried a tubular drum under one arm and with his free hand sent forth a spine tingling rhythm. In perfect unison, bare feet stamped out the measure. Headdresses wrought from hundrds of paradise plumes swayed and dipped with every movement of the dancers.

6. Tranced with a sense of doom, the boys stared spellbound through the opening in the tree house floor. They saw the column of dancers break into quarters and revolve like the spokes of a living wheel. Dust rose in clouds mingling with the smoke from the fires—both to be whipped by the wind. The thunder of the drums grew in violence. The air hummed with sound and fury. The dancers stamped and shouted in frenzy.

7. What happened came so swiftly that the boys were momentarily confused. They saw a flaming palm leaf lifted and spun for a second in a vortex of wind. The next instant it dropped upon the thatch of the house. The roof burst into flame. The wind caught and fanned the blaze. Like fire through a field of wheat the holocaust swept the length of the village. A cry of anguish rose from the now terrorized band of pygmies.

8. From one house to another the disaster passed. Smoke billowed high above the flames, like some gigantic smoke signal reaching to the sky. Women with howling babies rushed frantically for the jungle. Children slid screaming down the firemen's poles. Dogs howled. Pigs squealed. Hens shouted in panic.

9. Clinging together, Chad and Natua watched the disaster with wide eyes. There was little danger that the houses on their side of the village would catch fire, since the force of the wind was driving the flames in the opposite direction. Desperately the pygmies tried to salvage whatever they could— household treasures, implements of war. House after house, burned to a shell, crashed from its aerial supports. Even the inevitable deluge of rain, arriving on schedule, failed to extinguish the hungry blaze. Clouds of steam now blended

Multi-Paragraph Writing:

with the smoke, to go soaring skyward. Long before dawn the entire southern half of the village had been destroyed, and a great wailing rose from the jungle where the pygmies mourned their injured and their dead.

EXERCISE 1: In the following list, a title for each of the scenes or paragraphs of the story above is presented. Arrange the titles in the order in which the paragraphs are written.

1. Escape
2. Obeying Orders
3. The Pygmy Village
4. The Aftermath
5. Locked In!
6. Fire!
7. The Fires and the Drums
8. The Dancers' Arrival
9. The Dance

EXERCISE 2: This selection from THE RAIN FOREST is a splendid example of narrative-descriptive writing. In his mind's eye the reader sees clearly what is happening and the scenes in which all the action is taking place.

Read aloud sentences, phrases, or words which match each of the following: (The numbers after each item indicate the paragraph in which the material will be found.)

1. two fear-frozen boys (6)
2. very short sentences which indicate panic (8)
3. a long sentence that suggests the passage of time (9)
4. short sentences that indicate the speed with which the fire spread (7)
5. six well-chosen words that help the reader see, or hear, or feel (5)
6. an exclamatory sentence that indicates Chad could hardly believe his eyes (1)
7. the sentence that effectively ends the paragraph (3)
8. a sentence that begins with an adverb (4)
9. a sentence that begins with an adverb phrase (5)
10. a sentence that begins with an adverb (3)

Armstrong Sperry has written several books. THE RAIN FOREST is one. FROZEN FIRE is another. Read these exciting adventure stories.

Completing Unfinished Stories

The pupil who wrote this story was given the first paragraph and the headings or topics for some of the succeeding paragraphs as is done in the exercises which follow on pages 50-52. Read the story silently at least twice.

Have the story read aloud by having a different pupil read each paragraph or by having two pupils read the paragraphs alternately. Listen carefully and note how the change of readers helps to emphasize the change in thought which each paragraph expresses.

Then turn to the exercises on the next page.

A Different Life

Billy leaned his head against the window and watched as the train rounded the curve. He closed his eyes and listened to the clicking of the wheels on the rails. Those sounds kept telling him that he was being carried rapidly to a new part of the country and to a new home.

Billy's destination was his grandparent's farm where he would stay until further arrangements could be made for him. He was full of excitement because he had never really been on a train before as his parents could not afford to let him take a train ride.

After two hours of an interesting journey Billy arrived at the small town called Fairview. He climbed off the train in time to see his grandfather tying up a horse with a buggy. "Hop in," said his grandfather as he put Billy's suitcase into the back of the vehicle.

As they rode to the farm Billy's grandfather introduced the horse as Queenie and told Billy that at the farm they all had something for him, even Queenie.

When they arrived at the farm they were met by Jim, the foreman, who took the horse to the barn. Then Billy and his grandpa went into the house. In the kitchen was Billy's grandma with her cat which he later learned, by some hardship, was called Scratchy.

Suddenly Billy noticed a box on the table. He was told to open it. Inside he found a tiny black pup which he named Tarbaby. Then Jim came in and gave him a cowboy suit complete with Roy Rogers cap guns. He put it on and, picking up Tarbaby, went outside to find Queenie nuzzling a colt which grandpa said was for him.

That night in bed he thought how different the farm was from his two-bedroom apartment in the big city. There his parents could never hear of him having a pet.

—K. I. P.

Completing Unfinished Stories:

EXERCISE 1: After reading "A Different Life" prepare to answer these questions orally.

1. What idea suggested in the fourth paragraph and which is explained in the second last paragraph adds interest to the story?

2. What does the phrase "by some hardship" suggest to the reader?

3. Suggest some suitable alternative titles for the story.

4. What sentence in the third paragraph should have been re-worded to avoid saying something which might be incorrectly interpreted? Why is this sentence unintentionally humorous? Re-word it to avoid the ambiguity.

5. In paragraph three the writer avoided the repetition of one word by carefully selecting a suitable substitute. What are the two words?

6. Why is "Tarbaby" a suitable name for the pup?

7. Select three separate words used in this story that were particularly well chosen?

8. Explain why the writer started a new paragraph each time.

EXERCISE 2: The writer of "A Different Life" was given this first paragraph and the headings for four developing paragraphs. How many additional paragraphs did the writer provide? Compose a title for each of the extra paragraphs. Using the opening paragraph and the suggestions for the developing paragraphs, write your own story.

Billy leaned his head against the window and watched as the train rounded a curve. He closed his eyes and listened to the clicking of the wheels on the rails. Those sounds kept telling him that he was being carried rapidly to a new part of the country and to a new home.

PARAGRAPH 2: Why Billy was on the journey   (expository)

PARAGRAPH 3: His arrival—what and whom he found   (narrative-descriptive)

PARAGRAPH 4: His new home   (descriptive)

PARAGRAPH 5: Comparing the past and the present   (narrative-descriptive)

The words in parenthesis indicate the kind of paragraph that will be written in each case.

Completing Unfinished Stories:

Exercise 3: After having read page 49 and after having done the exercises on page 50, select one of the following paragraphs and use it to open a story. Topics for the developing paragraphs are provided. Additional paragraphs may be included in your story. Compose a title.

1. Suddenly sitting up and looking about him, Jerry was puzzled. How long he had lain there, he did not know. He had a slight recollection of having stumbled in the darkness, and of having fallen, but he could remember no more. Then, as his eyes became accustomed to the dim light, he saw . . . (Complete the last sentence after copying the paragraph.)

PARAGRAPH 2: Remembering how he happened to be in this situation

PARAGRAPH 3: A complete description of his present surroundings

PARAGRAPH 4: A narrative paragraph to tell what he decided to do

2. In a corner of the old ruin, although it was almost concealed by a pile of stones that had fallen from the crumbling wall, Ricky discovered a small door. A massive rusty padlock looked as though it would crumble at a touch. Beside it, on an equally rusty hook, hung what appeared to be a golden key!

PARAGRAPH 2: Where was Ricky? In what country? What was the ruin?

PARAGRAPH 3: How did he open the door?

PARAGRAPH 4: Where did the door lead and what was found inside?

PARAGRAPH 5: What were the results of the investigation?

3. Sally stepped up to the post office wicket and peered over the counter. The postmaster smiled at her and carefully handed her a curiously-shaped parcel. She eyed it thoroughly. She shook it. She listened. She heard a distinct ticking sound.

PARAGRAPH 2: Sally's guesses as to the contents of the parcel judging from the shape and the sound

PARAGRAPH 3: The breathless trip home on foot

PARAGRAPH 4: Opening the parcel with the family all about

PARAGRAPH 5: Sally's reaction to the metronome

Completing Unfinished Stories:

EXERCISE 4: Select one of the following paragraphs and copy it as the opening paragraph for a story. Topics for the developing paragraphs are provided as a guide. Additional paragraphs may be included in your story. Compose a reader-catching title.

1. One dreary day Jerry was playing alone in the house. He was making a great deal of noise, and his mother, who was enjoying her favourite television programme, became annoyed. She ordered him to his room. Jerry went and flopped on the bed. As he lay there his gaze fell upon the trap-door in the ceiling. He had always wondered what was beyond that entrance to the attic. Now was his chance to explore!

PARAGRAPH 2: Jerry's efforts in getting to and through the trap-door

PARAGRAPH 3: What Jerry found

PARAGRAPH 4: What Jerry did with his discovery

PARAGRAPH 5: The result of the adventure

2. The elderly white-haired man leaned back, sinking into the soft white mass of pillows. He looked again at the brief article on the front page of the evening newspaper, and smiled. Gradually the paper slipped from his hands as he returned down memory lane, to the day when . . . (Complete this last sentence.)

PARAGRAPH 2: What had he read in the article?

PARAGRAPH 3: What were his thoughts on reading the article?

PARAGRAPH 4: What happened when he awoke from his day-dream?

3. Down, down into the murky depths of the ocean the diver was lowered. As his heavily booted foot sunk into the ooze on the ocean floor, and as his eyes became accustomed to the dim light, he saw before him the massive form of a sunken ship covered with green algae. This was his destination. Little did he know that he was not alone in this strange, silent world.

PARAGRAPH 2: A description of the creature that awaited him

PARAGRAPH 3: The diver's actions when he saw the creature

PARAGRAPH 4: The action on the surface when the danger signal was received

PARAGRAPH 5: The rescue of the diver and the harm he suffered

PARAGRAPH 6: What happened subsequently to the sunken ship

Have you read Chapter II recently?

Multi-Paragraph Stories

This is another selection from THE RAIN FOREST by Armstrong Sperry. It tells more about the adventures of Chad and Natua, about whom you have read on pages 46 and 47 of this text.

Read this selection silently at least twice. Then listen, with your text book closed, as your classmates read the selection orally. A different pupil may read each paragraph or two pupils may read alternately. If they read well, the listening audience will see the action, hear the sounds, and feel the suspense which the writer has so vividly portrayed.

Which paragraphs close with an interrogative sentence?

Select the most effective opening sentence. Give your reasons.

Select the paragraph in which the writer has produced the best sound effects. Give your reasons.

By midafternoon, far down the river and ready to turn back, Chad and Natua were startled to discover a suspension bridge of cane which spanned the river. It had been constructed quite recently, for its canes were scarcely discoloured by rain. Swaying some thirty feet above the water, it looked fragile in the extreme. Who could have built it?

Chad cast all caution to the winds. As he raced for the vine ladder leading to the footropes of the bridge, only one thing in the world mattered. Somewhere across the river was the bird his father had been longing to find. Somehow he must capture it.

Chad seized the handrope above his head and slid forward onto the swaying footrope, feeling for all the world like a tight-rope performer. Below him the river raced and boiled, dark and cold looking. But the boy kept his eyes fastened on the ropes ahead and fought to maintain some measure of balance. He knew, by the sudden sag of the bridge, that Natua was behind him. His heart leaped with gratitude.

Halfway across the bridge, the boys heard behind them a high wild shriek. So startling was the sound that involuntarily they flung one backward glance. What they beheld froze the blood in their veins. On the bank stood Kaiva. He was brandishing his bush knife and shouting in a kind of frenzy. In that instant Kaiva slashed his blade across the vines which bound the bridge to the earth. With a sound like the crack of a pistol the footropes snapped.

The boys were dropped into space like crumbs flung from a carpet. Chad struck the water with a smash. Icy-cold it drove the wind from his lungs. Buffeted, twisted, wrenched, he was forced down and down. A giant's hand was squeezing the life from his body. Terror filled his soul. Frantically he clawed his way upward, upward. . . . Natua—where was he?

Multi-Paragraph Stories:

EXERCISE 1: After having read the material on page 53, select one of the following paragraphs and use it as the opening paragraph for a story which you will complete.

Read the opening paragraph several times, and then jot down the topics for the paragraphs which you plan to write to develop the story. Use these topics as a guide as you proceed to write.

Your teacher may conduct a class discussion of each paragraph during which several suggested topics for the developing paragraphs will be listed on the chalkboard.

1. As soon as the days became longer and warmer, Jim pulled his canoe out of the shed and took it down to the water's edge. At this time of year there were rapids in the river, but Jim was not afraid of them. He was an expert canoeist. Why should he worry? He pushed away from the shore and was paddling blissfully and easily along when suddenly, to his amazement, he realized that he was being pulled down stream at a rate that he could not check. Every effort to paddle the other way was futile.

2. Silently, so that he would not waken his sleeping parents, Johnny crept out of the house. In the grey light of dawn he could see the outline of the barn. He began to wonder how he was going to get his pony, Jody, saddled and away without making too much noise. Quietly he opened the big door and stepped into the warm darkness of the stable.

3. The leafy green forest was very inviting as I picked my way through the spring wild flowers and thick underbrush. Although squirrel hunting was my objective, I had stopped to admire nature's handiwork. Suddenly the thicket ahead stirred with a deep-throated growling. What could it be? A bear? I shouldered my rifle and advanced. Then it happened!

4. The night had been dark when he set out, but now it seemed even blacker as Tom quickly made his way homeward. Not a star was to be seen. The moaning wind sifted through the pines as he approached the cemetery. He had to pass through it! Stealthily and fearfully he approached! Suddenly there loomed before him that which he had feared.

5. As Bob and Ted were pulling in the biggest catch of the day, the boat began to rock and sway just like the old green hammock. The boys had been so busy that they had not noticed that the bright summer day had become cloudy. They had not heard the unmistakable warning rumble that had come, at intervals, out of the west.

Multi-Paragraph Stories:

EXERCISE 2: After having read the material on page 53, select one of the
following paragraphs and use it as the opening paragraph
for a story which you will write.

Read the opening paragraph several times, and then jot down the
topics for the paragraphs which you plan to write to develop the story.
Discard the topics that are not needed. Add others that seem to be
required. Arrange them carefully in the order which will produce the
best story. Follow this plan as you proceed to write.

1. Sergeant Jim Hughes of the Royal Canadian Mounted Police was alone,
alone in the vast, bleak, windswept area known as the frozen north. Wearily he
plodded on. The tracks of his snow shoes vanished behind him in the drifting
snow. Somewhere in the barrenness ahead was the man he sought. Grimly,
silently, Jim stalked his prey. It would not be long now.

2. With a long birch pole my companion pushed our crudely constructed
raft into the silent river. When we reached mid-stream, an undetected current
caught us. I took the pole and frantically attempted to direct the course of the
raft toward the opposite shore. My thrust into the water was too strong. The
pole fell from my hands and bobbed up behind the raft out of reach. Far
ahead could be heard the thunder of the rapids. We were at the mercy of
the river.

3. The night was warm and balmy as David lay half asleep in the hammock behind his family's cottage. Nearby stood an old vacant shack, whose
uneven outline was barely visible in the light from the waning moon. This
place had always intrigued David. Suddenly he had an idea! Although it was
approaching midnight, he sprang quickly to his feet and ran toward the rambling
path that led to a doorway, almost obscured by weeds. On reaching the door he
placed his hand on the rusty latch with some hesitation. A loud snap in the
bushes caused him to jerk back fearfully.

4. It was Friday afternoon, four-ten to be exact, and the happiest time of
all in the life of a boy like Jimmy. He was particularly happy as he leaped over
the winding creek beside the path that took him home from school. In his
pocket he had that very special something he had been dreaming about for so
long. Excitedly he patted that back pocket. Then he stopped. He didn't
feel it there! He reached into the pocket. It was gone! What could have
happened to it? He simply had to get it back! Maybe it was in his desk! No,
he was sure that he had put it into that pocket. Who might have found it?
And where? Jimmy sat down on a big rock and began to think.

Multi-Paragraph Stories:

Study the *Henry* comic strip on this page. Then read the story that a pupil wrote when he converted each of the four pictures into a paragraph.

HENRY —By Carl Anderson

UNSELFISHNESS

That afternoon it was very hot when a boy named Harold became hungry. He went and got a tray, and took it to the inviting refrigerator. There he found some chocolate cake and milk. He put on a serviette and went to the table.

Harold sat down, pulled himself up, and was ready to enjoy his appetizing meal when he heard a whine behind him. Turning around, he saw his dog and cat, and in the window some hungry birds. He was a kind lad, so he decided that he would give them his food.

He went to the cupboard for a saucer. Now he walked to the table and poured his milk in it, and set it on the floor. The dog and cat came over and started to lap up the milk.

Harold went back to the table, got his cake and took it outside. He sat down on the step and held the cake and the birds came and ate it. When Harold came back into the room he had nothing to eat but a few crumbs, but he was filled with happiness because he had been kind to God's dumb creatures.

—John D.

Henry and other cartoon features will provide the ideas for the creation of stories of more than one paragraph. The strips in which the artist has told his story without using words should be used for this purpose. Although the picture presentation usually consists of four frames, it is not always necessary to compose four paragraphs when writing the story. Sometimes the action of two adjacent frames can be told in one paragraph. When converting these strips to stories, always use at least two paragraphs.

Make a class collection of *Henry* strips in which the artist has used no words. Use one of the strips as a source of ideas for a story of several paragraphs.

Make a class booklet of *Henry* stories. In writing each story follow the draft-revise-copy-transcribe procedure described in Chapter II.

Writing an Autobiography

Read the following selection entitled "About Myself" and prepare to discuss the questions which appear on the next page.

ABOUT MYSELF

On September 29 I shall celebrate my thirteenth birthday. Dad has promised to take me to the big football game when last year's champions will be the visitors. As my two sisters, both of whom are older than I, do not care much about sport, Mother will take them shopping in the afternoon. We all are looking forward to the big steak dinner which we shall have in our favourite restaurant as we always do when we go to the city. You can easily guess the two main topics of conversation during the meal on that occasion.

Although I was asked to write about myself, the word birthday made me forget my subject. However, now that my family has been introduced, I can proceed to describe the person I see so plainly whenever I comb my hair. It is red and usually stands straight up at an altitude of five feet five inches. Gravity and my one hundred and ten pounds hold it to the ground.

To be honest, as a scout must be, I have to say that school appeals to me only moderately well. There are other activities that I find more pleasant, although my report card never seems to displease my parents too much. My marks in arithmetic and science are often quite good, at least for me. In social studies, spelling, and reading comprehension the results are usually fair. In oral reading, language, and handwriting I admit I could, and should, do better.

Music is something I like. Some fellows seem lost when asked to explain a key signature, but I find it quite easy. Of course, after taking piano lessons for five years, a fellow should have something to show for his parents' money. Friends compare my singing voice to the croakings of the inhabitants of the ponds. The teacher makes no comment. His silence has helped me stick to the idea that I should play an instrument. I am looking forward to high school where I hope to be able to join the band as a sousaphone player. Please do not ask me to explain why I want to play that instrument.

Making things with my hands is fun. Art periods and those spent in the shops are just play to me. As I have built models of boats and airplanes since I was six, I have learned to handle tools quite well. Even with that experience I occasionally hit my thumb with a hammer.

My interest in sports is not limited to watching football. Swimming, a favourite pastime, is something I do fairly well, and this winter I hope to obtain my life saving certificate at the "Y." There my friends and I make good use of both the pool and the gymnasium. Although I like baseball and hockey, I know the big league scouts will never be interested in me.

How do I earn money? My paper route has been fairly profitable. Once a year when my customers say "Merry Christmas" in a way that really shows that they appreciate my work, I forget about the many occasions when I would have liked to have forgotten the papers and to have gone off with my chums.

Writing an Autobiography:

Then I also forgive some of them for never having the money for me on collecting days.   I am frequently told that many successful men claim to have started their business careers as paper boys.   Well, I have started!

Sidney C.

For Oral Discussion:

1. Suggest a title for each paragraph.   List the best title suggested by the members of the class on the chalkboard.

2. State whether you consider the title of the selection appropriate? Give reasons for your answer.

3. Read from the selection: (i) an interrogative sentence; (ii) an imperative sentence; (iii) an exclamatory sentence.   Does the use of these sentences help the reader feel that the writer is talking?

4. In which paragraph has the writer added a touch of humour to his writing?   How has he injected some fun into the story about himself?

5. Commas have been used carefully by the writer.   Read the third paragraph aloud as you pay close attention to each of the commas.

Exercise 1: (a) Plan a story about yourself which tells as much as the selection discussed above.   First jot down the topics for the paragraphs.   Perhaps some of the following will be included in your list:

(a) Helping around home or the store or the farm; (b) our house a community centre; (c) church activities; (d) summer camp; (e) my hobby; (f) how I learned to drive; (g) my ambition.

(b) Write the story you have planned in (a) above.   Follow the draft-revise-transcribe procedure described in Chapter II.

V ▲ THEMES FOR CREATIVE WRITING

In this chapter twenty opportunities for creative writing are presented. The descriptions are intended as suggestions and guides for both you and the teacher.

The illustration on this page shows six booklets which were prepared by pupils of Grade VIII classes. They contain the stories that were written by the boys and girls who used some of the ideas contained on the following pages.

Before attempting to write on any one of these themes, read the next two pages carefully. The information to be found there will help any class to make the preparations that will make it possible for these themes to be used more effectively. Then by following the procedures for writing described in Chapter II considerable improvement in the development of language skills will be achieved. In addition, the practice will be pleasant.

Themes for Creative Writing:

The use of one of these topics during each two-week period will provide some interesting and worth-while opportunities for creative expression in which all the writers will have something to say. Time will then be available to complete several developmental exercises that are found throughout Part I of this text. It may not be possible, however, to use all of the twenty themes during the school year.

The order in which the themes will be selected for use must be determined by your interests and by the availability of the materials needed.

Frequent reference will be made to the collecting and use of pictures which may be obtained from magazines and newspapers. The purpose of these pictures is to stimulate the growth of ideas and thereby, to provide you with something to say. Interest is added when these pictures are used to illustrate the finished writing. In many cases, however, it may be preferable, or even necessary, to make your own illustrations.

Where are the pictures to be obtained? A collection of magazines is the best source. Stress must be placed, however, on the fact that *only discarded* magazines and newspapers are to be used. Most householders welcome the opportunity to get rid of old magazines regularly. Pupils with whom the authors have worked have found many useful pictures and clippings in Canadian magazines and newspapers, and especially in the *Saturday Evening Post* which is published in the United States.

A practical method of distributing the pictures for the writing exercises has been developed. If, for example, you are about to write on the theme "Stories from Pictures," one picture from the class collection is given to each pupil. The distribution is made with the pictures held face down in order that no one has the opportunity of selecting a favourite. After examining the picture received, you are permitted to make *one* exchange, either with another pupil or with the class file, if the original is not one of interest.

A convenient and easily-obtained depot for the class's collection of pictures and clippings is shown on the next page. It is made from a cardboard box which was obtained from a grocery store. The one in the picture is fourteen inches long, ten inches wide and eight inches deep. A piece of stiff cardboard, fourteen inches by twenty, is placed at the back and on it a table of contents is printed.

The pictures and clippings are placed in letter-size filing folders which are procurable at stationery stores. One of these folders, plainly numbered and labelled, is used for each of the twenty themes for creative writing.

What does the word STIGRODEAS mean? It is a word which will not be found in a dictionary. It is a word that was coined by the authors, derived from the letters contained in the phrase "STImulate the GROwth of iDEAS." It is used as a label for the file of pictures and clippings to remind you that if the collection is made and used according to the procedures outlined in this chapter, you will be engaged in language activities which will give you ideas to write about. In addition you will have a reasonably satisfactory purpose for doing the writing.

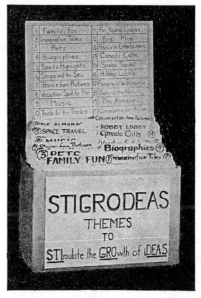

In order that you may not miss an opportunity to obtain material for your classroom STIGRODEAS box, read this chapter thoroughly. When you find material that will be useful in any one of the twenty themes bring it to school and place it in the proper file folder.

I. FAMILY FUN

1. There is much that happens around and in our own homes that is easy to write about. Stories that tell about family incidents are usually interesting to others who can then compare our experiences with theirs.

The following story is a vivid account of a little boy's action at the table. He must have given his family a good laugh.

THE VANISHING MOUNTAIN

My younger brother has a very elastic imagination. He can look upon a big piece of white angel cake covered with vanilla ice cream and think he is about to climb Mount Everest. Picking up the plastic container, he slowly squeezes ribbons of syrup up one side of the snowy mountain and down into the valley on the other. These are the ropes that will keep him from falling into the crevasses. Having arranged for his safety, as he describes it, he is at last ready for the great adventure. The conquest is complete when his eyes look contentedly upon the empty plate.

—Sidney Carter

Themes for Creative Writing:

Select some interesting incident that has happened when your family was together and write about it.   The following topics may include one which will be useful to you.   You need not select from this list.   Compose the title carefully.

Father in An Apron	Eating Out
Packing for Our Vacation	Getting Dad Ready for Fishing
Early Risers	On the Hills in the Snow
Dishes at Our House	Washing the Car
Summer Picnics	Storm Window Time Again
Birthday Parties	Moving Day
Mother's Weekly Shopping	Attending the Fair
Buying New Clothes	Visiting the Library
Painting Easter Eggs	Our Musical Tastes
House-cleaning Time	Father Loses His Car Keys
A New Pet Arrives	The Duty List
Sister Bakes Her First Pie	Mother's Easter Bonnet
The New Car	Father on Skates

2. Read this paragraph.   It was written by a pupil who used a picture obtained from a magazine for the ideas.   The words printed in italics describe the picture and the purpose of the writing.

Do It Yourself

(The writer of this paragraph used a picture showing a family busily at work assembling a wooden chair whose parts have just been emptied from a large cardboard carton.   Father, mother, brother, and the dog are on the dining-room floor.   Sister sits on a nearby chair.   The pupil's paragraph presents further details.   The writer's purpose was to describe the scene as if she were an announcer providing the commentary for a telecast of this picture.)

The Wilson family frequently works and plays together.   Here we see them all busily engaged in one of those popular do-it-yourself projects.   Even the dog is on hand to supervise the assembling of a chair whose parts have recently arrived in a huge cardboard carton complete with a quart can of liquid glue. Mother is reading the directions as she studies the illustrated instruction pamphlet which is designed to make the whole procedure mere child's play. Brother Bill hands the rungs to Dad who cautiously taps them into the legs using a wooden block to soften the blows of his hammer.   Sister Sue simply looks on with an expression which seems to say that she just bets there will be one piece left over.   All five seem to be enjoying themselves but perhaps, before they are finished with this newest piece of living room furniture, they will wish that they had let someone else do it all.

—Sharon L.

Themes for Creative Writing:

For the file folder collect pictures from magazines. These brief descriptions will indicate the type that are useful: a family of five is boarding an airliner; happy grandparents meet children and grandchildren at the station; father is the horse for two youngsters; father and son complete a model airplane; a family is cooking a meal over an open fire; all the members of the family help to paint the garden furniture; father and son are doing arithmetic homework; a family strolls down the midway at a fair or exhibition; father helps junior with his meccano or tinker-toy set.

The pictures should be of a size suitable for pasting on the sheets of paper used for writing the stories.

Distribute these pictures according to the procedure described in the introduction to this chapter. Write a commentary on the picture which you receive as if you were an announcer at a television station. Before beginning to write study your picture carefully and then reread the model paragraph "Do It Yourself." Note that the written comment tells what is happening and that it also includes some of the writer's own thoughts.

3. In almost every home there is some article that is considered by at least one member of the family as a treasure. Ask at your house if such an item exists. Obtain as much information about it as you can. Tell about it in writing. A collection of these written accounts might be made into a booklet entitled "Heirlooms" or "Prized Possessions."

The following articles are often regarded as heirlooms:

Family Bible	Musical Instrument
Watch or Clock	Chinaware
Jewellery	Furniture
Gun	Glassware
Walking Stick	Baby Shoes
Childhood Toy	Photograph Album

The following account is a sample of the selections that may be found in your class's collection of "Heirlooms."

ALWAYS FULL

On the piano at our house stands a green vase which is trimmed with gold. It is not what I would call a beautiful piece of glassware, but my father treasures it. How well I remember the day not so long ago when my brother and his friend accidentally broke its mate. On that occasion he told us once again about the days of his boyhood when these vases stood on the piano in the parlour of the village house where he was born. Attentively we listened and smiled as he explained once again, how the living-room, in what my little brother calls the olden days, was entered only on Sunday and then only if visitors were present. Now this lonely surviving twin is never used for flowers, but for my father it continues to hold many fond memories.

—Elsie C.

II. IMAGINATIVE TALES

PART A

"Sometimes when I write," explained the lad from whom the words seemed to flow most freely, "my pen seems to be filled with elastic ink. Even though I intend to write only what might possibly be true, that magic fluid produces words which convey ideas which are truly fantastic. Is it the ink? Is it the pen? Or is it my imagination?"

If we answer "Yes" to the last question we have replied correctly. All of us have this same power of forming pictures in our minds which are not related in any way to the experiences we have had through our five senses. Poets, artists and inventors have this power to a very great degree. Everyone, of course, is imaginative to some extent. The writing of imaginative tales, or of fanciful stories, provides the opportunity for everyone to use this interesting power.

The most famous beginning for imaginative stories is contained in the words "Once upon a time . . ." The tale which is printed below, "The Magic Snake," was written by a Grade VIII pupil in a rural school. He started with those popular words. Read Wayne's story. Then look at the illustration at the beginning of this chapter. The contents of the two booklets, "Spooky Tales" and "Imaginative Tales" were produced by using the ideas contained in this section.

THE MAGIC SNAKE

Once upon a time there lived a young, cruel, and heartless man. His name was James Snyder. James was said to be very rich. He also was reported as possessing a home filled with fine furniture and famous paintings. He never married, however, because of his character and because of the ugly look which he had on his face. James was a very unhappy man.

One day a new family moved into the house on the farm next to James. Immediately he fell in love with the older of the two pretty daughters, but she would have nothing to do with him. Even after James invited the girl, whose name was Amy, over to see his beautiful home she did not like him.

Themes for Creative Writing:

Sometime later James was out hunting in the woods. He came across a snake. Seeing that James was about to kill him, the snake cried, "Please don't kill me and I will grant any wish you may make."

Hearing this strange voice, James replied, "I wish . . . I wish . . . I wish I were a handsome prince."

At once he was changed into a charming young man who resembled the handsome princes of the story book tales. The snake was nowhere to be seen.

James ran all the way out of the forest and directly to Amy's door. She answered the bell and as soon as she saw James she fell deeply in love with him. As his disposition as well as his appearance had changed, Amy and James were soon married. They lived happily ever after.

—Wayne Tedford

1. Write an imaginative tale beginning with the words "Once upon a time. . . ." Be careful to begin a new paragraph whenever one is needed. Give the story a title that will attract the reader's eye.

2. Select one of the following groups of words to be used in the opening sentence of the first paragraph of a fanciful story.

(a) If I were granted three wishes. . . .

In each of the first three paragraphs tell about one of the wishes. In a fourth paragraph present your comments on the results.

(b) If I were a mermaid

(c) If I were Superman

(d) If I were the pilot of a flying saucer

(e) If I had been a member of Robin Hood's band (*or* one of King Arthur's Knights of the Round Table)

3. Select one of these titles and write the story which it suggests.

(a) At the End of the Rainbow

(b) The Night the Martians Came

(c) Haunted!

(d) Window into Yesterday*

(e) Window into Tomorrow*

*In (d) above imagine that you are looking through a window and observing a scene in the era of the dinosaurs and other prehistoric animals. In (e) assume that you are looking upon a scene which presents some of the items about which present day scientists still dream. Pictures suggesting stories on themes such as these are frequently used in magazine advertisements. Collect them for your classroom file.

PART B

Stories based on a dream are some of the most common of imaginative tales. The one printed here was written by an author who mixed his experiences in sport and at school with those he had while reading science fiction. He produced a story that has some good qualities. Read it carefully, and then use the questions which follow it to start a discussion.

WE WIN—I LOSE

The hockey game after school had been a hard fought contest, but Jed's team had won. Tired and still excited he had been able to eat hardly any supper and now he sat, or sprawled, as he attempted to watch his favourite television programme.

With a start Jed catapulted from the chair. He grabbed his books as he passed through the hall and was in his room and partially undressed before he had finished muttering to himself that he had to face a history test the next day. Without either washing or brushing his teeth he jumped into bed, propped himself up on the pillows, and began to memorize the summaries in his note book. When he closed his eyes to test his ability to recall the facts, he had the greatest difficulty remembering whether 1215 was the birthday of Magna Charta or of Maggie Carter.

Why had he not thought of it sooner? This was 1975, was it not? The Infoseat was all that he needed! What kind of seat? Why of course, the newest and most popular item in every corner store would prepare him for any test in any subject for no longer were pin ball machines and mechanical baseball games taking the dimes of those seeking recreation. This device was the favourite conditioner for any one who was going to be on a television quiz show, and everyone thought that he would be. For a quarter the knowledge-seeker could sit in the Infoseat, put on the electronic thinking cap (frequently called the cramlid), which was covered by a plastic helmet, adjust the arm clamps and dial the subject on which information was wanted. In three minutes the Infoseat did the rest!

Jed entered the Teen Town Eatery and startled a few of his friends who wondered why he was wearing a pyjama top with part of it hanging out from under his windbreaker. Hurriedly he fumbled for a coin, found it, pushed it into the slot and sat down in the chair that resembled those in a barber shop. Paying no attention to the bewildered customers he pulled on the green helmet, fastened the copper clamps above his wrists, turned and dialed "History." Sparks illuminated the surface of the plastic dome as the chair automatically tilted backward. For two minutes and fifty seconds soft lullaby music could be heard. In the background was a sound resembling that made by a rapidly-

Themes for Creative Writing:

operated typewriter. But suddenly Jed thought that workmen must be using compressed air drills to break up the hard tile floor right under his feet.

He was not in the chair, but the noise continued! He waved his arms but they were free of wires! He reached up to remove the headgear. It had gone! There was still the bright light above his head! Oh, no!

At breakfast Jed's little sister kept asking him why she had had to knock so long on the dish pan with the potato masher to make him wake up. He gave no answer. As he quietly packed his bag and started off for school he kept thinking that if only there really were an Infoseat, history would never face defeat by a hockey game.

—Percy M.

Questions for discussion:

1. In which paragraph does the reader become aware that the whole story is based on a dream? Why did the writer not reveal this fact earlier in the story?

2. What word in paragraph one suggests that Jed was sleepy? What idea in paragraph two adds to the reader's impression that Jed was a very tired boy?

3. What kinds of sentences are used in paragraph three to suggest hurry and excitement?

4. If you had been the writer of this story would you have written paragraph four as two paragraphs? The second would begin with the words "Sparks illuminated. . . ." Give reasons for your answer.

5. What do you picture Jed doing as you read paragraph five? How did the writer accomplish this effect?

6. Do the long sentences of the last paragraph suggest quietness and sadness or excitement and joy? What do the four words of the second sentence tell about Jed's behaviour that morning?

7. Suggest alternative titles for the story.

8. Write a similar story from your own imagination.

III. PETS

Most homes, especially those in which there are children, have at least one pet. Perhaps it is a dog or a cat. It may, however, be a canary or a budgie. In some it may be a rabbit, a guinea pig, or a turtle. In a few it may be a parrot or a monkey. These creatures are usually regarded with affection by both young and old. Many interesting stories can be told or written about them.

In magazines, especially on the pages devoted to advertisements for pet foods, a variety of pictures for your classroom file can be found. These illustrations will suggest many stories. In both magazines and newspapers many short interesting articles about pets can be found. Clip these for the file and use them for exercises in writing summaries. The following are examples of this type of writing.

FAVOURITE DOG

This news will be of interest to all who believe that a dog is man's best friend. Perhaps they will be surprised to learn that, in America, the friendly, flop-eared beagle hound is now the most popular of all the purebred animals. This little fellow with the tail that wags like a revolving airplane propeller has displaced the flop-eared cocker spaniel. He, whose begging eyes can melt the heart of the sternest master, is now second in popularity. Remember that this standing concerns only the purebred dogs. The all-time favourite, ahead of both beagle and cocker, is the dog who, in slang, is disrespectfully referred to as a mutt.

—John N.

POPULAR BIRDS

Shell parakeets, which belong to the parrot family, are now almost as popular as canaries. Owners prefer these cage birds, so they say, for their bright plumage and their ability to imitate the human voice. They are easily tamed and can be taught to ring bells, jump ropes and pull little wagons. In their native Australia they are called budgerigars which is derived from a native word meaning "good birds." Soon these budgies, as we call them, may move past fish and cats and be second only to dogs in popularity.

—Rosemary S.

SPANISH GOLD

The ancient tales about golden horses, although regarded by many as nothing but pleasant fables, have been read and re-read by lovers of horses throughout the world. Now, in America, the dreams of the breeders are coming true as colts are being born with coats the colour of newly-minted gold. These palominos are thought to be the descendants of the gold-coloured Spanish stallions that were lost in the desert long ago. The beauty of these animals makes them especially valuable as show horses. The most prized of all is the palomino with a coat of pure gold and a long pure-white tail.

—Harry S.

Among the following topics you will find one that is of special interest to you. Develop a story or an account on the topic which you select by following the steps in writing described in Chapter II.

A class booklet entitled "An Anthology of Pet Stories" should be prepared. An index showing the title of each story and the name of

Themes for Creative Writing:

each author should be included.　One pupil may write more than one story for the collection.

1. A Story About My Pet: Read the following story which is an account of a real experience.　Note that each of the three paragraphs presents a word picture of a different scene.

A Lost Breakfast

One morning my mother made my cat, Puff, a delicious breakfast which she set on the floor in the customary place.　Very cautiously Puff walked toward it and tasted it, but she decided that a breakfast of tender bird chops would be better.　Just then she heard the door open.　She quickly ran to get outside.

Puff looked around until she spied an evening grosbeak.　Very quietly she crept up behind the bird and pounced on it.　The fight was on!　Fur and feathers flew!　The grosbeak pecked Puff until she was forced to leave.

Later I found the grosbeak, hurt and holding a sample of Puff's fur in its beak.　I took it home.　Puff never did learn that her breakfast recovered in our back porch.

—Isobel K.

Write a story about one of your pets which will be equally as interesting as that written by the author of "A Lost Breakfast."

2. Caring for a _____ : (Fill the blank with the name of your pet.)　Write an account to tell how you care for it.　Use the heading of this exercise for the title.　The following may suggest the topics for the paragraphs:

   —a description of the pet
   —the type of shelter it requires
   —its food: kind, amount, frequency of feeding
   —its exercise
   —brushing and cleaning

3. The Best Pet: Write an article which explains why you believe a certain type of pet is the best kind to keep.

4. A Strange Pet: You have read or heard about a person who has kept a strange kind of pet.　Write an account to describe it.

5. Pets Have Odd Habits: Most pets have an odd habit that amuses their owners.　Describe one that you know.

6. Strange Friendships: Have you heard about the bunny-hugging cat?　Its owner had rescued a rabbit from a weasel and the household cat immediately befriended it and continued to do so.　They would go to sleep with the cat's forepaws around the rabbit's neck.

Write a "Strange Friendship" story which will become part of your class's collection of pet stories.

Themes for Creative Writing:

7. PET STORIES FROM PICTURES: Pictures which show a wounded pet being treated by a veterinarian are frequently found in magazine advertisements. Other pet pictures are easily obtained. Using a picture for the ideas, write a pet story. Your picture might show a worried owner holding a sad-eyed beagle on the operating table as the doctor binds the dog's right forepaw with gauze. Use three paragraphs to tell what happened, to describe the treatment, and to explain what happened later.

8. Obtain a newspaper or magazine clipping of an article about some pet or pets. Write a summary of the article. See those at the beginning of this section on page 67.

IV. BIOGRAPHIES

Lives of great men all remind us
We can make our lives sublime,
And departing leave behind us
Footprints on the sands of time.

These lines from Longfellow's poem "A Psalm of Life" tell us, in a very beautiful way, that by learning about the men and women whose work has benefited all mankind we may be inspired and encouraged to put forth the effort which will enable us to achieve equal fame. If we have ability, and use it, we may indeed leave our "footprints on the sands of time." But even though we may never make a great discovery, invent some useful device, or paint a great picture, a study of the lives of truly great people will make all of us richer by helping us to know them and by leading us to be grateful for their work. This knowledge and gratitude can be gained best by reading and by writing biographies.

For a list of the names of recommended books of biography which are available in your school or public library see page 326. To learn how to write a biography and for exercises in the writing of biographies read this section carefully. Begin by reading this story of the life and work of a famous Canadian doctor.

SIR FREDERICK BANTING
1891-1941

All over the world people would still be suffering hopelessly from the sugar sickness if it had not been for the work of a team of Canadian medical scientists. Now thousands of diabetics laugh, and work, and live long effective lives because they can use insulin. They give thanks to Sir Frederick Banting and his helpers for discovering the substance that keeps them healthy.

Themes for Creative Writing:

When Sir Frederick Banting was a boy he lived on a farm near the town of Alliston which is about fifty miles from Toronto. He helped with the chores and went to a rural school. Later he attended the high school in Alliston from which he graduated.

After completing his course in medicine at the university Frederick Banting joined the medical corps of the Canadian army for service in World War I. He was wounded while in France and was awarded the Military Cross for continuing to help others.

After returning to Canada he became interested in the sugar sickness which is a disease called *diabetes*. For over two thousand years it had been considered as incurable but Dr. Banting and his chief assistant, Charles H. Best, began the search for the cause and the cure. They encountered many hardships and many failures. At last they decided that a substance extracted from the glands of calves would help those who suffered from diabetes. They tried it on dogs and on humans. The results proved that their discovery would control the dread disease.

Many honours were bestowed upon Dr. Banting. He was awarded many prizes. He became the first Professor of Medical Research at the University of Toronto. King George V honoured him with a knighthood which gave him the title by which we remember him, Sir Frederick Banting.

When World War II broke out in 1939, this great medical scientist returned to the army. On a flight to England in February, 1941, he was killed in an airplane crash in Newfoundland. His name will live forever as one of the greatest Canadians. He will be remembered as one who fought for the health and happiness of his fellowmen.

1. From the magazines and newspapers pictures of the famous men and women of history can be found quite easily. The names of those obtained in one search are listed here in the order in which they were met:

Michael Faraday	William Tell	Sir Frederick Banting
Benjamin Franklin	Charles Goodyear	Madame Curie
Thomas A. Edison	Johannes Brahms	Cleopatra
Archimedes	Florence Nightingale	Helen of Troy
Luther Burbank	Ludwig van Beethoven	Helen Keller

Collect pictures of famous people for the classroom BIOGRAPHIES file. Newspapers, magazines, and the numerous pamphlets distributed by manufacturers are excellent sources.

During the year each pupil should write at least one account which tells about the life and work of a famous man or woman. A class book of biographies should be prepared. The quotation that opens this section might be included as part of the cover design. When illustrations are available, mount the picture on the left hand page of the book and have the written biography on the right. By using a large scrap-book of the type obtainable at stationery stores a durable book suitable for the school or classroom library can be made.

2.(a) THE STEPS IN PLANNING AND WRITING A BIOGRAPHY: Having selected, or having been assigned, a name for which a biography is to be written, consult an encyclopedia and read articles about the person which you will find in books and magazines. Here is an opportunity to apply your skill in using a table of contents and in using an index.

Copy from the source books only the words or phrases which will provide the main ideas which you may need to compose *your own story* of that person's life and work.

For example, the biography of Sir Frederick Banting was written after consulting the reference books shown in the picture on page 116 and reading a pamphlet entitled "Heroes of Health." The notes for the biography were as follows:

> . SIR FREDERICK BANTING, 1891-1941
>
> —sugar sickness, hopeless disease
> insulin to control diabetes, diabetics,
> Banting and co-workers discoverers
>
> —Alliston Ontario farm
> rural school
> Alliston High School, re-named after him
>
> —Studied medicine—Toronto University
> class enlisted medical corps
> captain
> wounded, France, Military Cross
>
> —Practiced London, Ontario
> interest in diabetes
> incurable 2000 years
> research U. of T.
> assistant Chas. H. Best
> trials and failures
> extract from glands of calves
> tried on dogs and humans
> sugar burning substance
>
> —honours
> prizes, Nobel Prize 1923
> knighthood, George V, 1934
> professor of research
>
> —World War II, 1939
> airplane crash Newfoundland, Feb. 1941
> fighter for health and happiness

Themes for Creative Writing:

After sufficient research has been done to obtain the information that will be needed to write the biography, the composing begins. For the first few biographies which you write follow this plan, making at least one paragraph for each heading.

1. The introduction
2. Childhood and early life
3. The details and results of the important work
4. A summary to describe the contribution made to human welfare

Note that the introduction may also refer directly to the importance and to the success of the work done as in the biography of Sir Frederick Banting. It may, however, be more general or refer only to the problem which the person attacked, as in the following introduction of a biography of Sir James Young Simpson, the first to use chloroform as an anaesthetic:

When we see the initials D.D.S. we know that they stand for the degree of Doctor of Dental Surgery. We know, too, that a dentist is a surgeon who operates on our teeth. Most of us know, unfortunately, that he can fill a tooth and cause very little pain as he can inject a drug to deaden that pain. None of us, however, can imagine the agony which was suffered by patients who underwent surgery a little more than a hundred years ago. Three or four men would be needed to hold the patient down while the surgeon cut and sawed. Of course the patient screamed. There were no pain-killing drugs to use.

In the biography of Dr. Banting two paragraphs have been devoted to his childhood and early life. Two paragraphs have also been written to tell about the details and the results of his work. The final paragraph tells about his unfortunate death and ends with two effective summary sentences, which refer only in a very general way to his work. Note again the introduction to his biography.

Check each item in the notes to determine if that information was used in the biography and note in which paragraph it was actually used. Was all the material collected in the notes used in the biography? In writing a biography as in building a piece of furniture or making a dress, it is always better to have more material on hand than you will need.

2. (b) WRITING A BIOGRAPHY: From the list of names on page 71 or from the names of famous people found in the *Almanac* section of this book, pages 303-309, select one name and write a biography of that person.

To avoid having more than one person writing a biography of the same man or woman follow this procedure. Have each person select a name. Have these names listed on the chalkboard. As each name can be listed only once, a pupil who has selected one that is given before

Themes for Creative Writing:

his turn comes must select another. Include in the list a number which is equal to the number of pupils in the class. When the list is complete write each name on a separate ballot. Mix the ballots in a box and draw for the name of the famous person whose biography you are to write.

Do not begin your research and planning until you have studied part 2 (a) of this unit carefully.

2. (c) Short biographies, or "Biographical sketches," as they are sometimes called can be made into interesting collections if grouped in some manner similar to the following:

FAMOUS FATHERS

1. The Father of Medicine—Hippocrates
2. The Father of Photography—Daguerre
3. The Father of the American Automobile—Henry Ford
4. The Father of the Electric Light—Thomas Edison
5. The Father of Printing—Johann Gutenberg
6. The Father of the Telephone—Alexander Graham Bell
7. The Father of Baseball—Abner Doubleday
8. The Father of the Uppercut—John L. Sullivan
9. The Father of the Steam Engine—James Watt
10. The Father of the Sewing Machine—Elias Howe

2. (d) Well chosen titles will make your biographies more interesting. Study the following:

1. The Sultan of Swat—Babe Ruth
2. Germ Detective—Joseph Lister
3. Magician with Microbes—Louis Pasteur
4. The Plant Magician—Luther Burbank
5. Trailblazers of Science—famous scientists

V. THE VACATION SPOT FOR ME

After reading the articles and the advertisements in the Travel Section of the Saturday edition of a daily paper, a young author wrote the following account on the theme THE VACATION SPOT FOR ME. Read it as an introduction to the activities in this unit.

COMING WITH ME?

The advertisements tell me that well-travelled people know that Jamaica is the place to go. If that sentence sounds like a line of poetry the following lines seem to belong in exercises on adjectives for I also read that everything in

Themes for Creative Writing:

Jamaica is refreshingly different and exciting. I learn that its foreign charm, picturesque beauty, and ideal climate are unforgettable. I really begin to believe that its scenic mountains, its superb white sand beaches and crystal clear waters will add to my delight.

Are you interested? Columbus, who was searching for gold and not for sunshine, was the first tourist to visit this colourful island. He claimed it for the Spaniards. In 1665 it was taken by the British who never gave it back.

This island, which is said to have perpetual summer for twelve months of the year, is the place that I should like to visit. I want to see its beautiful scenery and to swim in its wonderfully clear warm waters. On a native bamboo raft I should like to shoot the rapids of its biggest river, and return from my holiday with the memory of that thrilling adventure. Will you come with me?

What is the topic of each paragraph?

How has the writer made the selection sound as if he were talking to the reader?

1. From magazines and newspapers, collect advertisements that are published to attract tourists to either winter or summer resorts. Clip both the pictures and the written material that accompanies them. The latter is called the "copy" or the "text" of the advertisement.

Before placing this material in your classroom file cut the picture portion of each advertisement free. Keep the "copy" in a large envelope which will be known as the "Word and Phrase Bank." It will also be stored in the file folder.

2. (a) The following extract is a typical sample of the language used in travel folders and advertisements. Read it carefully. Listen as a classmate reads it aloud. Then discuss whether the choice of adjectives, nouns and verbs presents a true picture or an exaggerated picture of what you would expect to find there. Quote from the selection to support your opinion.

The Land of Lakes and Islands Welcomes You

Summertime is glorious in Muskoka. The life-giving sun wakens each day with golden splendour. Birds sing gaily. Waters foam over falls and rapids, velvet wavelets splash against dark grey rock, and white clouds drift across blue skies. Here is a vacation paradise that matches the beauty of the English Lake District. It is one of the enchanting natural vacation centres of the continent.

Muskoka boasts many majestic rocks. Huge chunks of granite, mountainous in their proportions, swell up from the earth with a friendly invitation to climb to their top and bask in the sun. Grey slatey rocks shelve flatly out over the waters as ready-made seats for romantic moon worshippers. Gigantic thrusts of rock—millions of years old—make the roads curve picturesquely round them, while their hoary heads support a thriving growth of dogwood or young cedars. On every side, in Muskoka, nature's unspoiled beauty gladdens the street-tired eyes of the city dweller.

Every season in Muskoka has its own charm and beauty. No time in the year finds Muskoka more glorious to behold than the autumn. The days are mellow with friendly sunshine, and the whole country dons a new dress as nature magically transforms summertime greens into magnificent autumn yellows, russets and reds. A soft haze gathers in the hollows and the crisp air is spicy with autumn scents. Birds are gathering for their southward hop, squirrels chatter as they gather nuts, and, although many of the summer activities are still in full swing, nature seems to whisper, "Take it easy." Yes, Muskoka in the autumn coaxes you into the relaxation which clears your mind and rests your body.

2. (b) Distribute ten or more items from the "Word and Phrase Bank" to members of the class who will then read them, after adequate preparation, aloud.

Listen carefully as each item is read for words and phrases which will help you to write effectively about THE VACATION SPOT FOR ME.

3. Select a picture from the VACATION SPOT FOR ME file and write an article similar in style to the selection entitled "Coming with Me?" which is found at the beginning of this unit. Plan your paragraphs equally as well as its writer did. Include an explanation of why you would like to make that particular spot the scene of your holiday.

4. Select a picture from the VACATION SPOT FOR ME file and write a single paragraph which would attract tourists to that place. Compose an appealing title. Before beginning to write, read the following advertisement and note that it resembles a paragraph in a personal letter.

HAVE FUN IN THE SUN

Getting weary of winter? Come on down and let Florida's magic sunshine put new pep in your step and new colour in your cheeks. Wherever you go in Florida, you'll find superb bathing, fishing, golf, and other outdoor sports. You'll find spectacular attractions and scenic wonders. Above all, you'll find splendid accommodations to suit your taste and your pocketbook.

Themes for Creative Writing:

Attractive booklets can be made using the products of items 3 and 4 above. Keep the written material on the right hand pages and mount a picture for each account on the opposite left hand page. Covers of original design should be made for these booklets. See the sketch. If they are taken home by the pupils, for one night each, parents will have the opportunity to become acquainted with the school's language programme. They may also get some ideas for their next summer's vacation.

VI. BEHIND THE NEWS

News items that appear in the daily papers can often be used to provide the ideas for writing interesting paragraphs. Read the short article reproduced below.

This clipping was brought to a classroom and read to the pupils. They were then requested to name the people who were directly concerned with this event. As the replies were given the teacher wrote the following list on the chalkboard:

Bulldozer Moves Seven-Foot-High Omelet on Road

SOUTH BRUNSWICK, N.J., Dec. 17 (AP).—A huge omelette was cooked on the New Jersey Turnpike early today when a truck loaded with eggs overturned and caught fire near here. Police said the omelette was so well done that a bulldozer had to be brought to scrape up a seven-foot-high pile of it that blocked the highway for nearly an hour.

1. the bulldozer operator

2. the truck driver

3. a passing motorist

4. a policeman

5. an unbroken egg

Number 5 above was included because, in this type of writing, it is possible to report the comment of inanimate objects. One pupil thought that this one fortunate egg, that had rolled to the shoulder of the road, might have something to say.

The pupils were then advised that they would be asked to write what one of the people (or things) in the list might have said immediately

Themes for Creative Writing:

after the accident happened. The following are the paragraphs that the pupils wrote:

1. The truck driver speaks:

GETTING FIRED

The truck's wheel hit an eight inch rock just as I was turning the corner. In a flash the truck turned over with me inside the cab. When I hopped out, it was a mass of flames and right in the middle of the highway. Before I knew it there was a seven-foot-high omelet. How I dread meeting the boss after this! What am I afraid of? Right now *I'm* afraid of getting fired! —Franklin D.

> NOTE: What is the humour in the last sentence? Why is sentence five a particularly good one?

2. A passing motorist speaks:

SOME FUN

What in the world is causing all that smoke ahead? Why don't the cars move faster? That looks like a fire right in the middle of the road! What could be burning? I think I smell eggs, but it must be my imagination. The flames seem to have died down now but something seems to be still blocking the road. What! I overheard those fellows say that a truck loaded with eggs overturned and caught fire, and now it's an omelet seven feet high. It will take a bulldozer to remove it. What a silly thing to happen! It's a shame that the children aren't here. Wait until they hear about it at home. They'll think it's a big joke. Don't you?

—Joan P.

3. A policeman speaks:

WRONG TURN

This is the call of all calls! In all my thirty years on the force I've never had to make arrangements to have one of my favourite dishes removed from the highway. I've heard of food being cooked *to* a turn, but this mass, or mess was cooked *on* a turn. In fact it was one turn that the driver failed to make. He would have to jackknife right in the middle of the road! Delays, confusion and more trouble are the result. All right, George, see if that cat of yours can push this delicacy aside and leave the pavement clean.

—Robin C.

> NOTE: The word "cat" is used to refer to a particular kind of bulldozer.

4. An egg speaks:

FORTUNATE TEMPORARILY

Am I lucky! That omelet almost had my goose, or should I say my yolk, cooked! What a foolish and unfortunate driver he was. He must have thought himself at the wheel of a racing car. The way he was driving down the

78 ➡

highway I had a feeling in my shell that upset me. Well, it's over and not much can be done about the loss. A crowd of passing motorists is gathering. Here comes a human my way right now. He's coming right toward me! If only I could roll! Ouch!

—Elaine K.

5. The bulldozer operator speaks:

FOR THE BIRDS

Can you imagine a seven-foot-high omelet? That truck driver had no business going eighty-seven miles per hour around that curve. Now it's my job to clean up the mess. He'd better have a good explanation for his boss, and for the police. They say they're going to leave it in this field so the animals can try his cooking. No one will ever be able to say it wasn't well done. It was burnt to a crisp. I wouldn't eat any of it because of the egg shells, and besides it is really for the birds.

—Brian W.

Examine each of the five paragraphs again. Listen as each is read well orally to the class. Note that the writers followed these instructions:

(i) to write as if they heard the person (or thing) speaking

(ii) to avoid the use of slang

(iii) to avoid the use of quotation marks

(iv) to use a variety of sentences (assertive, interrogative, exclamatory and imperative)

In situations like this the use of a variety of sentences is quite normal. The people concerned are usually excited. As they talk they ask questions. They give orders which they expect no one to carry out. They also utter exclamations. Therefore the *Target for Today* (see page 19) is one which calls for the writing of paragraphs in which all these types of sentences are used.

After the names of the persons concerned were written on the chalkboard, each pupil selected the one whose comments he or she wished to write. Some exchanges were then made voluntarily in order that an equal number of pupils would be writing the remarks of each person.

The writing procedure followed the STEPS IN WRITING described on pages 17, 18. After several sets of paragraphs were read orally to the class, each set was made into a booklet for which a suitable cover was prepared.

Themes for Creative Writing:

Now you are ready to write your own BEHIND THE NEWS stories. Read the article that is reproduced on this page. Listen as one of your classmates reads it aloud.

Boy 13, Lands Plane Safely, No Experience

ROCKY MOUNT, N.C. (AP)— A 13-year old schoolboy without piloting experience flew a private plane Saturday while dozens of fear-frozen spectators—and an ambulance—waited below for a crash.

But Tony Hammond put the plane down with only minor damage and no injury to himself or his horrified passenger, Richard Floyd who was on his first plane ride.

As related by L. P. Broadfield, manager of Rocky Mount airport, Hammond was at the controls of the Piper cub with his foot on the brakes while the pilot, William Gaither, was outside twirling the propeller to start the engine. Suddenly the engine caught and the plane, apparently with the throttle stuck, raced down a runway and took to the air.

SETS DOWN SAFELY

The youngster circled the airport for a quarter hour while a crowd gathered below and an ambulance was called. Then he pointed the nose down for a landing. The plane struck a landing light but settled safely on the field.

Hammond, asked by a reporter if he wanted to fly again, replied, "Sure."

Floyd, 20, the nervous passenger, commented, "I let the boy do all the flying. I didn't know anything about it at all."

With your teacher's help make a list of the people who are involved in this piece of news.

Your list may include the following: (i) Tony; (ii) the passenger; (iii) the pilot; (iv) a spectator; (v) Tony's mother; (vi) Tony's father; (vii) the waiting ambulance driver.

Have the four rules that are listed on the preceding page written on the chalkboard.

After the class has been organized so that the comments of each of the persons listed will be composed, proceed to write your BEHIND THE NEWS stories.

Note that in order to appreciate all the meaning which the writer puts into any one of these paragraphs, it must be read very carefully. Listen well during the oral reading of these BEHIND THE NEWS paragraphs.

Two clippings are reproduced on the next page. Use one or both according to the procedure outlined above.

Be on the lookout as you read the daily papers for news items which will be useful in writing more BEHIND THE NEWS articles. Bring them to the class and file in the STIGRODEAS box.

Trail of Pickles Stops Traffic

HAMILTON, July 29 (CP).—Provincial police were in a pickle four hours yesterday.

It all happened after a truck loaded with pickle jars headed down No. 2 Highway west of Ancaster.

The truck's tail-gate was apparently opened and hundreds of jars of pickles—sweet and sour—bounced on to the roadway.

OPP, Waterdown detachment, closed the road from Ancaster to Duff's Corners and began a mass sweeping job.

Four hours later they managed to clear the highway of glass—and pickles.

Load of Butter Litters Highway

DUNNVILLE, Jan. 18.—John Purich of Dunnville escaped injury today when his truck, loaded with butter, was struck by a Toronto, Hamilton and Buffalo Railway freight train here. Purich said he could not stop on the icy road.

Top grade butter littered No. 3 Highway at the scene of the crash. The truck is owned by the Dunnville Dairy which is operated by Highways Minister Allan.

Frank Foster, engineer, and Gordon McMillen, conductor, both of Hamilton, said the train was travelling 10 mph with the whistle sounding.

Use one or both of the news items printed above and write BEHIND THE NEWS paragraphs or stories. Follow the procedures described on the previous page. Make booklets of your stories. Prepare decorative covers similar to those shown below.

VII. HOBBY LOBBY

Most people agree that a hobby provides fun and enjoyment. One definition of a hobby states that it is a form of play that exercises our hands as well as our brains. Writing about hobbies can also have these same characteristics.

Read the following exposition of a hobby which any grade VIII pupil can enjoy. With it you will use both your hands and your brain.

A Heavenly Hobby

Do you want to explore the mysteries of the skies? Then let me give you a few suggestions to help you launch your hobby of star hopping. It will take you into the realm of astronomy which will teach you a great deal about a science that has fascinated many people for thousands of years.

No expensive equipment is required. All you need is good eyesight and a book on stars that contains simple charts of the constellations. A pair of inexpensive low-power field glasses will be useful but they are not essential. A star box will make your outfit complete.

The star box, which is a miniature planetarium, is the item you can easily make by following these directions. Obtain a shoe box, or any other kind of equal size, which has a removable lid. Measure and mark a ¾ inch margin around the top of the box cover. Cut along this line, leaving a ¾ inch frame. Cut ten slides from pieces of thin cardboard. Each of these slides has the same dimensions as the inside of the box cover frame. Apply one coat of black paint to the outside of the box and frame, and to both sides of each slide. At one side of the box cut a hole just big enough to let you insert the head of your flashlight.

Start with a star group which you probably already recognize, the Big Dipper, and then work your way around the sky. To be certain that your first slide is accurately made follow a constellation chart in your book as you punch a hole in one of the sheets of black cardboard for each of the stars in the Big Dipper group. Insert this slide into the cover and place them on the box. When lighted by the flashlight, your box now shows the star pattern seen in the nighttime sky.

There are eighty constellations, but you will be kept busy through the seasons searching for the nine or ten best known groups and making your slides. Little Dipper and Cassiopeia are also visible all-year-round. Leo, Hercules, and Scorpio can be seen only in spring and summer. Big Dog, Mighty Hunter, and the Bull, as they are known by their English names, appear only in winter. Make these and other star groups the targets which you will capture as you pursue this heavenly hobby.

Themes for Creative Writing:

1. For the HOBBY LOBBY file collect pictures, and newspaper and magazine articles, that deal with hobbies. Often you will find cartoons which have hobbies as their themes. Bring these along too. The class collection will soon contain many illustrations of hobbies like the following: model making, painting, stamp collecting, wood collecting, coin collecting, bird watching, gardening, and butterfly collecting.

Read the articles in the HOBBY LOBBY file to develop an interest of your own in hobbies, and to get ideas in order to be able to write about hobbies to interest others. (Read again "A Heavenly Hobby.") The pictures can be used for bulletin board displays, and for illustrating the stories and explanations which you will write.

2. (a) Make a list on the chalkboard of the hobbies of the pupils in your class under the headings shown below. It may include some or all of these:

DOING	COLLECTING
photography	stamps
model airplanes	hockey pictures
model ships	miniature horses
raising hamsters	Canadian coins
cooking	rocks
knitting	butterflies

2. (b) Write an account of your favourite hobby. Tell what it is, how you carry it on, how much time you spend at it, why you enjoy it, and what special interests or talents anyone should have before deciding to make that hobby his own.

Compose a carefully-worded opening sentence that will persuade any reader to continue reading. Use one or more paragraphs, and construct each carefully. Provide a title that attracts.

2. (c) If you have no hobby write a story using one of the following as the opening sentence:

(1) My friend, Bill, says that the only hobby he will ever have will be that of making money.

(2) Recently I have learned that many famous and busy people find time to enjoy at least one hobby.

(3) Collecting birds' eggs is a hobby which should be forbidden by law.

(4) A boy on the farm has little time to think about the need of a hobby.

(5) Whenever I pass a hobby store I always begin to dream.

VIII. CANADA CALLS

The pamphlets shown in the photograph on this page advertise the Canadian vacation areas and tourist attractions that are to be found from coast to coast. The messages in these booklets are informative. They are written in a style which makes them interesting to read. Each of the pictures tells a story of a thousand words, and some of them, particularly those in the Nova Scotia Camera Tour, are breathtakingly beautiful.

Obtain pamphlets similar to those shown in the illustration from your local travel agents, from railway company ticket offices, or by writing to provincial government travel bureaus. (See: Letters—page 163.) Read them, and you too will realize that CANADA CALLS.

In preparing to write on this theme, CANADA CALLS, read the publicity booklets and the newspaper advertisements that are prepared to attract tourists. Note the choice of words and the picture-making phrases which their writers have used. The following paragraph is an example.

Themes for Creative Writing:

A HUNTER'S PARADISE

Picture a brace of partridge being flushed from a woodland thicket. See in your mind's eye a flight of wild ducks winging through the early-morning mists of a reed-strewn marsh. Those are some of the challenges awaiting the hunter in the Maritimes. There are many more. Newfoundland promises mighty moose and caribou. Nova Scotia has wild cat and wolves, and the black bear is everywhere. Accessible territory, excellent guides, and some of the best scenery in North America combine to make your hunting memorable in Canada's Atlantic provinces.

From newspapers and magazines collect advertisements that are published to attract tourists to Canada's holiday resorts. In the same publications find pictures for your "CANADA CALLS" file. Use this material, along with the pamphlets referred to on the previous page, in carrying out the following activities.

1. Find at least one advertisement for a Canadian holiday centre which appeals to you. Read its content orally to your class. Explain why you might like to visit that particular place.

2. Select one of the following topics and write a one-paragraph advertisement that would attract holiday seekers to some part of Canada to enjoy that particular sport.

mountain climbing	skiing	horseback riding
hunting	camping	swimming (salt water)
fishing (fresh water)	rodeos	sailing (fresh water)
fishing (salt water)	golf	sailing (salt water)

Use a picture from the file, or your own coloured sketch to illustrate your advertisement.

Prepare a booklet of the advertisements written by the members of the class. Compose some suitable title such as "Canada Calls: Fun in the Sun." Provide an attractive cover illustration. See the illustration for this topic in the preface to this book.

3. Select one of the following topics and write an advertisement of one or more paragraphs that would attract tourists to come to some part of Canada in order to enjoy that particular attraction.

orchards in blossom time	for painting or photography
historic landmarks	(i) seascapes
friendly wild animals	(ii) mountain scenery
one of nature's oddities	(iii) autumn woods

A title such as "Canada Calls: See the Best in the West" would make a booklet of stories on the attractions of western Canada look interesting. Use a picture to illustrate each advertisement.

85

IX. ON A MUSICAL THEME

For the class file collect pictures of musicians and of instruments. You will be able to use those of the famous composers, of prominent musicians of today, and of instruments of all kinds. Use them effectively to illustrate biographies (See Theme IV) which each pupil can write, or to illustrate the class booklets which may be compiled with the material produced in the following activities.

1. Select one of the following opening sentences and complete the paragraph which it introduces. If you wish, more than one paragraph may be written. Compose an eye-catching title.

(a) Everyone tells me that in a few years I will be grateful that my parents kept me at my music.

(b) My sister (or brother) recently joined the school band and was given a clarinet (or any other instrument).

(c) Of the instruments of the orchestra I like the strings (or woodwinds, or brass, or the percussion group) the best.

(d) The instrument that I should like to play is ————.
(Fill in the blank with the name.)

(e) Some people think that a rhythm band produces music.

(f) If I were ———— this is what I should do.
(Fill in the blank with the name of any prominent musician of today.)

(g) No one knows the problems connected with music making better than I do. (Imagine you are writing as one of the instruments which is relating the inner secrets of the musicians and the instruments.)

(h) Some of the best instruments are found only in a hillbilly band.

(i) Why most adults dislike modern popular music is something I just cannot understand.

(j) If I were the director of music for our schools these are the changes that I would make.

2. Select one of the following titles and develop a story of several paragraphs which would be suitable for publication in your school or classroom paper.

(a) Those Piano Lessons
(b) Why Popular Songs Don't Last
(c) My Favourite Music
(d) My Favourite Musician
(e) Music in Nature

(f) The Mad Musician
(g) First Public Performance
(h) Magic Fingers
(i) Our Record Player
(j) The Piano Next Door
(or any other instrument)

X. SPORTS HIGHLIGHTS

There is just one thing better than winning
and that is taking defeat like a man!

—Ralph Connor

"All the world loves a winner" is a well-known phrase. As everyone cannot be a winner, even in a school-yard foot race, the truth of the quotation printed above should be accepted, and remembered.

Because of the universal interest in the best in sports, this theme on "SPORTS HIGHLIGHTS" is presented. It will give you the opportunity to write about important sporting events, to describe some sports which are unknown or unfamiliar to Canadians, and to create some memorable sports stories of your own.

To obtain illustrative material for your writing on this theme, collect pictures that represent SPORTS HIGHLIGHTS of all kinds. These will include those of "Deadeye with the Dibs," the marble champion; of the winner of the annual Trappers' Festival Dog Derby in The Pas, Manitoba, a team of huskies; and of the Stanley Cup. *Note that you are not collecting ordinary pictures of sporting events. You are gathering pictures of* SPORTS HIGHLIGHTS.

Clip news articles from magazines and newspapers that tell about strange or unfamiliar sporting events. Bring them to the classroom file. These will have headings such as: "Campbell Aims at Faster Speedboat Mark" and "Gliders Ride the Thermals." These news items will enable you to compose interesting accounts like the following:

BAT-MEN OF THE SNOWS

When Tyrolean skiers take to the air the visitor thinks he is watching a flying circus. High on the peaks of the Austrian mountains these intrepid sportsmen strap a sail-like cape to their wrists and ankles. As they race down hill the capes are hugged tight. On approaching a crevasse they lean forward and throw open their fabric wings. The rushing updraft of air sends them soaring. Some, if they straighten up too soon make a crash landing after rising to a height of only five feet. Others, who are more experienced, make sky-flying look like child's play. These experts, keeping an eye on the smoke from blazing torches they have placed in the valley below, take advantage of the needed headwinds. Taking off from a hillock, they glide a hundred feet or more, pick up ground speed after landing, and take off again. Thus these skiers wing their way into the valley below. A fledgling, it must be admitted, experiences many a bruising disappointment as he attempts to imitate these skiers who really fly.

Themes for Creative Writing:

The writer of "Bat-Men of the Snows" read the captions on a series of pictures very carefully. The account was then written without referring to those pictures or captions for ideas.

1. Select one of the following sentences and use it to open the first paragraph of an article on that topic. More than one paragraph may be written. Compose a title.

(a) Last night I dreamed that I was the second man in history to score my first goal within fifteen seconds of stepping on the ice in my first NHL game.

(b) To be the winner of the North American figure skating championship is my ambition.

(c) Swims across Lake Ontario and the Strait of Juan de Fuca make the headlines, but at our cottage the champion is the first to touch the island and return.

(d) Parents and some teachers often wonder why the sports pages are the second most popular part of a newspaper.

(e) The sports figure I admire most is ————.
(Fill in the blank with the name of your choice.)

2. Select one of the following titles and develop a story based on it.

> Never Say Die!
> Friendship Through Sports
> Stanley Cup Thrills
> Coach Supreme
> Grey Cup Fever
> Little League Baseball (or Hockey)
> Dressing Room Gossip
> Women Too Are Good Sports
> How Important Is Winning
> House Leagues vs. Inter-School Competitions
> The Most Popular Sport in My Community

3. The following are suggested as activities in which the enthusiastic sportsmen in the class may be interested. They should be carried out voluntarily.

(a) Prepare a booklet which is entitled "Great Events in Sports." By using reference books and by talking to adults, obtain information which will enable you to write descriptive accounts of the *history* of one or more of the following:

The Olympic Games	The Allan Cup
The British Empire Games	The Mann Cup
The Grey Cup	The Davis Cup
The Stanley Cup	The Harmsworth Trophy
The World Series	The Memorial Cup

➡

Themes for Creative Writing:

The last paragraph of your account should describe briefly the last game or event.

(b) In pioneer days ice hockey was played on the frozen rivers, ponds and lakes. Now this lightning-fast game has moved, for the most part, indoors and has become a national sport. It presents a challenge to the skill and stamina of all who play it. It presents a dream of some day being a Stanley Cup finalist to almost every school boy. Hockey is truly a great Canadian game.

Write a description of the hockey player you admire most. He may be in the N.H.L. or on a team which plays in your own home town.

(c) Prepare a booklet entitled "Sports Hall of Fame" by writing descriptive accounts of the sports personages who deserve to be included under this title. Use the pictures from the classroom file to illustrate your articles.

Include in this booklet the stories of the last winners of the following trophies: (i) The Vezina Trophy; (ii) The Lady Byng Trophy; (iii) The James Norris Memorial Trophy; (iv) The Art Ross Trophy; (v) The Frank Calder Trophy.

(d) Sports Oddities: Prepare a collection of sports stories that deserve a place under the title Sports Oddities. The story "Bat-Men of the Snows" would be included here. Descriptions of games like *el-pato* which is played in Argentina would also find a place in this group.

XI. SHIPS AND THE SEA

The little cares that fretted me,
I lost them yesterday.
Among the hills above the sea,
Among the winds at play.
—Anonymous

Although we do not know who wrote the four lines printed above we do know that most people enjoy reading, talking, and thinking about Ships and the Sea. The activities in this unit will provide opportunities for you to do some writing on this popular theme.

From old magazines and newspapers collect pictures of ships of all kinds. These will include Hawaiian outriggers and Chinese junks, Eskimo kayaks and modern ocean liners: You will also find interesting illustrations for this theme, such as those showing an elderly sailor talking to a youngster as both look dreamily out to sea. Place all these

Themes for Creative Writing:

in your classroom file, and use them to make your written work more attractive to the reader.

1. Select one of the following sentences and develop it into a sea story of one or more paragraphs. You may need to do some reading in reference books before you proceed to write. When you are ready, follow the four steps described on page 17. Compose an appealing title. Illustrate your story with a picture or your own sketch.

(a) Sailing vessels of old had a variety of names.
(b) After being a member of John Silver's crew for three years, I welcomed his order that I should immediately walk the plank.
(c) Do you want to buy a famous silver ship for a dime?
(See the Canadian ten cent piece and do some research on the *Bluenose*.)
(d) My friend and I were determined to obtain some information about the submarine that we had seen off the eastern coast.
(e) If I had my choice of occupation, I would like to be in charge of entertainment on an ocean liner.
(f) A trip around the world in a tramp steamer would be more enjoyable than a luxurious cruise on a big liner.
(g) Deciding that it was time to get away from it all, my partner and I put our life-time savings into the purchase of a submarine.

2. Select one of the following titles and develop a story for which it is suitable.

1. A Visit to Davy Jones's Locker	6. Sea Sick
2. The Ship That Never Returned	7. Sea Rover's Dream
3. Rescue at Sea	8. An Old Mariner's Tale
4. Sea Monster vs. Ship	9. It's the Navy for Me
5. Ghostly Galleons	10. A Freight Boat's Story

3. The following topics should be used for research. Consult reference books to obtain information for either oral or written reports.

(a) Some famous ships:

(i) The Mayflower	(iv) The Queen Elizabeth
(ii) The Golden Hind	(v) The United States
(iii) The Titanic	(vi) The Flying Cloud
	(vii) The Nautilus

(The first Nautilus is described in Jules Verne's 20,000 Leagues Under the Sea; the second Nautilus is an atomic-powered submarine.)

(b) The Travels of the St. Roch   (See page 303.)
(c) The Mystery Ship—Mary Celeste
(d) The Flying Dutchman
(e) The Blue Ribbon of the Atlantic

4. MAKING A DICTIONARY OF NAUTICAL TERMS: As a co-operative class activity prepare a list of words, with their meanings, that are used in connection with ships and the sea. The girls will be interested in learning the difference between a gunwale and a keel. The boys may already know how to describe a companionway or a bulkhead. Can you describe a coracle, an umiak, a brigantine and a stern-wheeler? Arrange the list in alphabetical order. (See SHIPS AND LIFE AFLOAT in the book list, page 328.)

5. Compile a scrapbook bearing some such title as "Our Mariners' Museum" which will include: (a) copies of your favourite sea poems; (b) pictures and sketches of ships and boats; (c) the vocabulary of ships and the sea prepared under (4) above; (d) stories of the seven seas; (e) pictures, sketches and stories of lighthouses and lightships. If a plywood cover is made for this book in the industrial arts shop, quarter-inch rope might be used to "write" the title which would be glued to the surface to give a real nautical air.

XII. TOOLS FOR THE TRADES
(For Boys)

Read the following account which was written about a very common tool. Then complete the exercise.

FOR USE NOT ABUSE

My father often says that the screwdriver is the most abused tool in any man's kit. As its name suggests it has one main job to do, but it is used for a variety of tasks. With it a lid can be pried off a paint can quite easily, or a stuck window can be forced open. By hammering it, some people use it to split wood. After being used in these ways, however, the blade is usually so chipped and dulled that its owner finds that it is no longer useful for driving screws.

When most people hear the word, they think only of the standard screw-driver. An electrician needs one with a long thin blade and a shock-proof handle. A radio-T.V. repairman usually carries a vest pocket or midget screwdriver which also has a shock-proof handle. Auto mechanics sometimes use a stubby screwdriver which may have a plastic or amber transparent unbreakable handle.

How do I know so much about this tool, which every mechanic and carpenter uses properly? I read the descriptions and studied the illustrations in a catalogue that came to our house from an auto supply store.

A well-equipped home workshop will have a variety of screwdrivers. The Phillips fits those screws with the star or "X" type slot which are commonly used in automobiles. The Robertson screwdriver has a square point and is used with the screws that have a square slot which are frequently used in the manufacture of furniture.

There are also ratchet, magnetized, and combination screwdrivers. The book said that the last type is absolutely indispensable. Remembering my father's actions when he wanted to remove a mirror from a dresser and could not find a screwdriver to fit the square slot screws, I certainly agree. My brother and I will give him a kit containing Robertson, Phillips and regular screwdrivers for his next birthday.

—Sidney Carter

EXERCISE 1: (a) Comment upon the suitability of the title "For Use Not Abuse." Does it arouse interest? Does it well represent the ideas that are presented in the paragraphs which follow? Compose another title for use in part (b).

(b) In your language exercise book complete this outline of the account entitled "For Use Not Abuse." After composing a suitable alternative title, provide a word or phrase as the topic of each paragraph.

Title: _____

    1. _____

    2. _____

    3. _____

    4. _____

As the writer of "For Use Not Abuse" stated, descriptions and illustrations of tools of all kinds can be found in catalogues. More pictures of tools and instruments may be found in magazines. Collect these, along with their captions, for your classroom file. Use this material as a source of ideas for writing on this theme, TOOLS FOR THE TRADES.

The following is another example of the type of writing that a Grade VIII boy can do when he uses the material referred to in the preceding paragraph. Note the title.

SEVEN SHARPS

My father often says that a boy should always carry a piece of string, a jackknife, and a dime in his pocket. When I was in search of a suitable picture to illustrate what I might write in developing that quotation into a story, I came across one entitled "Which One Belongs in a Sailor's Dungarees?" The seven types of knives shown there certainly increased my knowledge of this very useful tool.

The handy pocketknife which every small boy longs for is really a folding tool chest. It may have one or more blades, a screwdriver, a bottle opener, an awl, a nail file and, perhaps, even a small pair of scissors. Its proud owner will find more uses for it than the knife has gadgets.

There are two other types of folding knives. One is used by the growers of citrus fruit and one is always found in a sailor's dungarees. The former is a long thin pocket knife whose single blade can cut through an orange or grapefruit with one swipe. The fruit man then knows whether the crop is ripe and juicy. The rigging knife has a strong sharp blade for cutting rope. Equally useful is its marlin spike for splicing rope and for loosening tight, water-soaked knots.

Perhaps you have seen the ringknife which is used by packing clerks. Its blade, which reminds me of a parrot's beak, snips off a cord with the flick of a finger. Two other interesting knives which do not fold are the budding knife and the farrier's knife. One is used by a nurseryman to insert buds under the bark of seedlings. The blacksmith uses his to trim the inside of a horse's hoof before putting on the shoe.

The seventh knife in the picture was a handleless semicircular blade which is used by cigar makers to clip the ends of newly-rolled cheroots. Today this knife will be put to a new use. It will bring this account to an end. In my next article I shall tell you what I intended to write this time. Read it to find out why a boy always needs a string, a dime, and a jackknife in his pocket.

—Roger S.

EXERCISE 1: In your exercise book write the title "Seven Sharps."

    Below, list the figures 1-5 and state the topic of each paragraph in a word or short phrase.

EXERCISE 2: Write a story or an explanatory article on this theme TOOLS FOR THE TRADES. Reread "For Use Not Abuse" and "Seven Sharps," and proceed to write on a topic of your choice. If you prefer, select one of the following sentences and use it to introduce your story.

1. Girls certainly know little or nothing about tools of any kind.

2. Did you ever watch a very small boy use a hammer?

3. In our basement workshop there hangs a motto, "A Place for Everything and Everything in Its Place."

4. My young brother never replaces the tools.

5. In the industrial arts shop we learn much that is both interesting and valuable.

6. My mother says that dad has spent five hundred dollars on his workshop in order to build a cabinet that we might have bought for twelve dollars.

7. Whenever dad sets out to repair a leaking tap the family gathers for some entertainment.

8. A favourite trick of some workmen is to send their inexperienced helper for a left-handed hammer.

Themes for Creative Writing:

EXERCISE 3: FOR INDIVIDUAL OR GROUP RESEARCH: Make displays of the tools and instruments used in the trades and professions. Use pictures from the classroom file, or sketches, or, if possible, the real objects. Arrange for oral reports to be made to the class during which the use of each instrument or tool in a particular group will be explained. The following list includes only a few of those which might be made:

medical doctor	draftsman	plumber
veterinary doctor	auto mechanic	electrician
tinsmith	surveyor	carpenter
gardener	welder	mason and bricklayer

XIII. SPACE TRAVEL

Stories of space travel, of rocket riders, and of flying saucers are not the invention of the mid-twentieth century. Tales of imaginary adventures on the moon and other planets have been written for many years. Old or new, these products of imaginative minds never lose their appeal for those of any age who are young at heart.

The following selection has been adapted from a book written more than a quarter of a century ago. It tells of some of the adventures of Dr. John Dolittle and his odd companions after they have reached a heavenly body.

Read the selection carefully. (The paragraphs have been numbered in order that you may refer to them easily.) Then prepare to answer orally the questions on page 96. They have been provided to help you use this selection in order to develop more skill in writing your own stories of many paragraphs. There is the possibility, of course, that you may become a writer of science fiction.

1. John Dolittle's prophecy that the animal kingdom would not delay much longer in getting in touch with us was surprisingly and suddenly fulfilled. I had a piece of yam smeared with honey half-way to my mouth when I became conscious of an enormous shadow soaring over me. I looked up and there was the giant moth that had brought us from Puddleby! I could hardly believe my eyes. With a graceful sweep of his gigantic wings he settled down beside me— a battleship beside a mouse—as though such exact landings were no more than a part of the ordinary day's work.

2. I could see that poor Chee-Chee was simply scared out of his wits. And little wonder! Insects of this size gathering silently about one were surely enough to appall the stoutest heart. Yet to me they were not entirely terrible. Perhaps I was merely taking my cue from the Doctor who was clearly more interested than alarmed. Beside that, the manner of the creatures did not appear unfriendly. Serious and orderly, they seemed to be gathering according

to a set plan. I felt sure that very soon something was going to happen which would explain it all.

3. A few moments later, when the ground about our camp was literally one solid mass of giant insects and birds, we heard a tread. Usually a footfall in the open air makes little or no sound at all—though it must not be forgotten that we had found that sound of any kind travelled much more readily on the Moon. But this was something quite peculiar. Actually it shook the ground under us in a way that might have meant an earthquake. Yet somehow one *knew* it was a tread.

4. Chee-Chee ran to the Doctor and hid under his coat. Polynesia never moved, but just sat there on her tree-branch, looking rather peeved and impatient although evidently interested. I followed the direction of her gaze with my own eyes for I knew that her instinct was always a good guide. I found that she was watching the woods that surrounded the clearing where we had established our camp. Her beady little eyes were fixed immovably on a V-shaped cleft in the horizon of trees away to the left.

5. It is curious how in those important moments I always seemed to keep an eye on old Polynesia. I do not mean to say that I did not follow the Doctor and stand ready to take his orders. But whenever anything unusual or puzzling like this came up, especially a case where animals were concerned, it was my impulse to keep an eye on the old parrot to see how she was taking it.

6. Now I saw her cocking her head on one side, in a quite characteristic pose, looking upward towards the cleft in the forest wall. She was muttering something beneath her breath (probably in Swedish, her favourite swearing language) but I could not make out more than a low peevish murmur. Presently, watching with her, I thought I saw the trees sway. Then something large and round seemed to come in view above them in the cleft.

7. It had taken, we suddenly realized, a whole day for the creatures to gather. As it was now growing dusk, one could not be certain of his vision. I noticed the Doctor suddenly half rise, spilling old Chee-Chee out upon the ground. The big round thing above the tree-tops grew bigger and higher. It swayed gently as it came forward. With it the forest swayed also, as grass moved when a cat stalks through it.

8. Very soon we could hear other sounds from the oncoming creature besides his earth-shaking footfall. Giant trees snapped and crackled beneath his tread like twigs under a mortal's foot. I confess that an ominous terror clutched at my own heart too. I could sympathize with poor Chee-Chee's timidity. Oddly enough, although this was the most terrifying moment in all our experience on the Moon, the monkey did not try to conceal himself. He was standing beside the Doctor fascinatedly watching the great shadow above the trees.

9. Onward, nearer, came the lumbering figure. Soon there was no mistaking its shape. It had cleared the wood now. The gathered insects and

waiting birds were making way for it. Suddenly we realized that it was towering over us, quite near, its long arms hanging at its sides. *It was human.*

10. We had seen the Moon Man at last!

> —From Doctor Dolittle in the Moon by Hugh Lofting

Exercise 1: After reading the selection on the preceding two pages do the following:

1. Listen carefully, with your textbook closed, while two of your classmates read the ten paragraphs of the selection aloud alternately. As the voices change and a new paragraph is begun think of the writer's reason for starting that new paragraph. If you imagine the author is taking a moving picture of the events as he tells the story you can often see him change the position of the camera between paragraphs. Sometimes, though, as in paragraph five, he seems to stop the camera to explain his own actions.

This listening practice will help you to develop *paragraph sense.* You will need this ability to know when to start a new paragraph when writing your own stories.

2. A title for each of the paragraphs in the selection is provided in this list. Arrange the titles in the proper order in your language book.

(a) Depending on Poly	(f) The Arrival
(b) Fearful Sounds	(g) Interrupted Lunch!
(c) The Tread!	(h) The Approach
(d) Identified!	(i) Polynesia's Gaze
(e) Gathering of the Giants	(j) The Stranger Detected

3. How many sentences are in the longest paragraph? How many sentences are in the shortest paragraph? What is the average number of sentences used in the ten paragraphs?

4. Read aloud the sentence or sentences:
   (a) that allows the reader to use his sense of feeling;
   (b) that helps the reader to hear sounds;
   (c) that helps the reader to see movement;
   (d) that gives the reader goose flesh.

5. Read aloud the sentence in which the writer has used dashes. Note that between these dashes are words which tell the reader what the author thought at that moment. They interrupt his telling of the story. Watch for the use of dashes in other stories but do NOT attempt to use them in your own writing. Only experienced writers can use them correctly.

6. Be prepared to declare each paragraph as belonging to one of the following classifications: (a) narrative; (b) descriptive; (c) narrative-descriptive; (d) expository.

7. What effect does the writer produce by using short sentences in paragraph nine?

Themes for Creative Writing:

The material written on this theme may be bound in a booklet similar to the one illustrated here. If you are particularly interested in this theme, perhaps you would prefer to make a booklet of your own. Otherwise you may contribute to a class booklet.

Each booklet should have a cover with a title and an illustration or suitable design.

A table of contents should be prepared.

In writing material for the book-lets follow the draft-revise-transcribe procedure described on pages 17, 18.

By reading some of the science fiction books to be found in your school or public library, you can acquire some useful vocabulary and ideas for writing on this theme. Encyclopedias and other reference books will provide useful information about the planets.

1. Select one or more of the following sentences and use each as the opening sentence for a paragraph which introduces a story of several paragraphs. Illustrations, which you make yourself, will add interest to your stories.

(a) As the flashing interplanetary computer indicated we were within sixty seconds of our destination, Captain Eight-o took over from the robot.

(b) Insulating passengers from the extreme temperatures created by the rockets' propellants was a problem that I helped to solve.

(c) When we arrived the interplanetary rocket was in the firing pit ready for blast-off.

(d) Ignoring the signs and the warnings that I had been given, I pulled the lever.

(e) Getting into my space cadet suit made all other problems seem comparatively easy.

(f) Back in 1960 I remember the airlines boasting of being able to travel from Vancouver to Halifax in seven hours.

(g) When I tried to explain to our visitor from Mars that earth-men had been flying for only a few decades, he looked astonished.

(h) If you were the captain of an interplanetary rocket, what would you do when you found a stowaway?

Themes for Creative Writing:

(i) As we came within range, the disto-vision screen showed us that molten lava from an erupting volcano maintained a sea of glowing fire on the planet on which we had been ordered to carry out our investigations.

(j) Our television set has a special channel selector labelled "From Outer Space."

(k) My first visit to a space station on the rocket route to Mars has given me an experience I shall never forget.

(l) When I first looked from the observation window of the rocket ship I could hardly believe my eyes.

(m) Never, as long as I live, shall I forget my first inspection of Leader Seeglo's space machine.

2. Write a story on one or more of the following topics:

      (a) Hitchhiking to Mars

      (b) Pirates in Interstellar Space

      (c) The Interconstellation Cruiser

      (d) Visiting a Spaceport—A.D. 2050

      (e) Our Town's Saucer Scare

      (f) The Lost Planet

      (g) The Day the Earth Stood Still

3. Additional material for an "OUT OF THIS WORLD" booklet may be written on one or more of the following themes:

(a) An advertisement inviting tourists from our earth to enjoy the attractions on some other planet.

(b) An advertisement for the clothes and equipment needed for safe and comfortable space travel.

(c) An advertisement that seeks recruits for an interplanetary police patrol.

(d) An advertisement to attract young ladies to train for positions as stewardesses on rocket ships.

(e) A speech delivered by the leader of the EXIANS to the members of your community whom he meets on his first visit to earth.

XIV. PARAGRAPHS TO PERSUADE

Wanted for Publication

Many interesting projects are carried out in your classrooms, on the school grounds, or in the community. Perhaps you have developed a sanctuary for birds, or an exciting nature trail. Whatever it is, be a writer and let us hear about the new discovery. This will help others to explore the out-of-doors. Share your joys with others, and assist your school or club in its work.

THE CANADIAN AUDUBON SOCIETY

46 St. Clair Ave. E.   —   Toronto 5, Canada

The above advertisement is an example of a paragraph that was written to persuade the reader to do something. Note the use of imperative sentences.

The written material in advertisements is known as the "copy." The illustration may attract the reader's eye, but the written material persuades him to act. To write advertising copy, one must be clear, concise, and persuasive.

1. From a newspaper or magazine obtain an advertisement for some article of clothing, some piece of furniture, or of some household appliance. Bring it to class and be prepared to read it orally.

2. Compose an advertisement for some piece of furniture, some article of clothing, or for some household appliance, which you would insert in a magazine or newspaper in order to persuade customers to buy that item. Use a picture or a sketch to illustrate your advertisement.

3. Imagine that you are one of the following people and compose the advertisement which you would use:

(a) a tourist resort owner: to attract tourists to your establishment

(b) a farmer: to sell some plump geese or turkeys prior to Thanksgiving or Christmas

(c) a dog breeder: to sell some purebred puppies

(d) a theatre owner: to attract patrons to see a new type of film presentation

(e) a real estate salesman: to sell a well-wooded lot as a site for a house.

99

XV. FOODS, FASHIONS, FABRICS, AND FURNITURE
(For Girls)

Man's work is from sun to sun,
But a woman's work is never done.

Girls, after repeating the above quotation to their mothers, would certainly be able to obtain much material to prove the truth of it. It might, therefore, serve as a topic for a debate. It is used here, however, to introduce topics about which all girls should have something to say without having to do any research and without conducting any interviews. Perhaps in your writing you will be able to convince the boys that women do make a greater contribution to all homes than do the men.

For the classroom file, collect interesting pictures of items that will help you illustrate your writing on this topic of Foods, Fashions, Fabrics, and Furniture.

1. Select one of the following sentences and use it to introduce an article on food. If you prefer, you may write on any other food topic which interests you. Compose the title carefully.

Follow the four steps in writing that are described on page 17. When the articles have been completed compile an illustrated booklet for the boys to read. Can you help to make their mouths water? The booklet might be entitled "Kitchen Comment."

(a) This is the way that I prepare my favourite dish.

(b) Diet is a small word with a big meaning.

(c) Take my advice and follow the Canada food rules.

(d) An after-school snack provides the best-tasting food of the whole day.

(e) What is my favourite food?

(f) If I could order as much as I wanted of just what I wanted this is what it would be.

(g) What happens at meal time when mother is away or is ill?

(h) The can opener is the modern cook's best friend.

(i) Let me tell you about one of the useful lessons we have had in home economics classes.

(j) My grandmother says that her cookbook is in her head.

2. Select one of the following sentences and use it to introduce an article on "Fashions and Fabrics." You may, if you prefer, write on any other topic on this theme. Compose the title carefully.

Compile an illustrated booklet using the articles which the girls

Themes for Creative Writing:

in your class have written on this topic. The boys, and your parents, will be interested in your opinions.

(a) To buy clothes wisely you need a knowledge of fabrics.

(b) What do I look for when buying clothes to get the most for my money?

(c) My father says that the hem line of ladies' skirts is like an elevator, up this year and down next.

(d) Ladies' hats and shoes are, we must admit, topics over which men can have some real laughs.

(e) Some boys say that a girl's best friend is her hairdresser.

(f) The use of cosmetics can easily be overdone. (or) Both taste and caution need to be exercised in using cosmetics.

(g) Little girls take delight in dressing up in their mothers' clothes.

(h) This is my opinion of school uniforms.

(i) Women certainly are slaves to fashion.

(j) There are many reasons why I should like to be a model.

3. Apply the instructions provided with activity 1 and 2 above to the following sentences.

(a) Modern furniture is certainly more practical than the overstuffed variety that was common when my grandmother started keeping house.

(b) A visit to a furniture store gives a girl much to start dreaming about.

(c) To have a completely modern kitchen is the dream of every homemaker.

(d) This is a word picture of my favourite living-room (or kitchen, bedroom, school room—real or imaginary).

(e) Perhaps the people of the western world do not have the right idea about how to furnish their homes.

4. Each of the following names has a special connection with furniture. Prepare to make a brief oral report on each by consulting reference books in your school or public library.

Queen Anne; Louis XV; Chippendale; Hepplewhite; Sheraton; Duncan Phyfe; the Adam brothers

In using the reference books look up the names that are given under the general heading "furniture."

XVI. BIRD MEN

Thoughts of flying like the birds have been running through the minds of men for centuries. The story told by a Roman poet who died in the year A.D. 12 proves that statement. It is retold here by a writer who consulted two reference books to obtain the facts. After reading the paragraph carefully discuss a suitable title for it.

A Greek myth tells the story of a skilful sculptor and architect who, about 1500 B.C., was refused permission to return to Greece after completing several buildings for the king of Crete. Determined to escape to his homeland with his son Icarus, Daedalus made two pairs of immense wings with feathers and wax. With the wings fastened to their shoulders, father and son took flight from the island and headed across the sea. Icarus ignored his father's warning that the sun might melt the wax. He flew too high, the wax softened, and he fell into the sea, where he drowned. Daedalus completed his journey safely and continued his work of building temples and carving statues in his native land.

In the 15th century, Leonardo da Vinci designed an airplane which would have flown, but there was no satisfactory power to drive it. He also maintained that if a man had a tent made of linen he would be able to throw himself down from any height without sustaining injury. He thus foresaw the use of the parachute.

The airplane as we know it had its birthday on December 17, 1903. On that date, at Kitty Hawk, North Carolina, Orville and Wilbur Wright raised the curtain on the air age. Since that time rapid progress has been made in air transportation.

Whether of the past, present, or future stories of air travel are interesting. Most boys and girls enjoy reading them. May you find these activities in which you will be writing about air travel to be both interesting and helpful in developing your language skills.

1. For the classroom BIRD MEN file collect pictures of aircraft of all kinds. Include pictures of balloons, zeppelins, dirigibles, and gliders. Use these pictures to illustrate the stories which you will write. Sketches will also be useful for this purpose. A booklet of stories, entitled "From Flying Berry Box to the Flying Blow Torch" or "A History of the Airplane" might be prepared by the class or a group of pupils. Another booklet might be entitled "The Blue Highway—Stories of Air Travel."

2. Select one of the following opening sentences and use it to introduce a paragraph. More than one paragraph may be written to complete your story. Useful information for most of these topics will

be found by reading the section entitled "airplane" in one of the reference books. Compose a reader-catching title.

(a) My sister, like almost any other girl, knows so little about airplanes that she thinks a pilot needs money when he banks his aircraft.

(b) Let me explain the difference between a seaplane, a flying boat and an amphibian.

(c) In their relentless quest for speed aircraft engineers, having conquered the sound barrier, are now concentrating on overcoming the thermal barrier.

(d) Pilots who fly modern military planes wear suits that make them resemble the comic book rocket riders.

(e) Mother tells me to keep my feet on the ground, but the job of a stewardess for an airline appeals to me.

(f) By making model planes a fellow learns a lot about the principles of flight and about the equipment of both fighter and transport aircraft. (At least three paragraphs are needed here.)

(g) The cockpit of a man-built bird is where my office is going to be.

(h) My first airplane ride is one I shall never forget.

(i) The mechanics who keep the machines airworthy have a big responsibility.

(j) In spite of some accidents, few people hesitate to travel by air.

3. Discuss in class or in a group the topic—Uses of Aircraft in Peace and War. Make a list of the uses mentioned. It might include: weather reporting, spraying crops, rainmaking, preventing frost from damaging fruit crops, rescue services, photography, troop carrying, submarine hunting, bomb carrying, refuelling long range planes, glider towing. Many more items can be added to this list.

Write the name of each use on a separate slip of paper. Mix the slips in a hat and conduct a draw. Each pupil will prepare a brief oral or written report on each topic that he or she has drawn.

The following is an example of the type of story that might be written on one of the themes entitled "Uses of Aircraft in Peace and War."

Wolf Hunt

As the sun rose over the pine trees fringing Minnitaki Lake, we bumped to a takeoff across the frozen ski tracks of bush freight planes. Half an hour later we spotted fresh wolf tracks close to the west shore of Pickerel Arm, and while looking these over we almost missed seeing the animal that made them.

Directly down sun, the wolf blended into the surrounding snow, and not until we were almost above it did a shadow betray its presence. Our plane pounced, and in an instant we were pulling in behind the animal, now streaking for the shore one hundred yards away. Then fifteen feet above the ice, the pilot grasped the control column between his knees and cradled his shotgun in a dent that countless recoils of the gun had hammered in the aluminum window frame.

Guiding the plane with feet and knees, he sighted down the gun barrel, and when the line of sight had crept up to the tip of the wolf's tail, he fired. The wolf collapsed in mid-air, and spun to a stop.

Aerial wolf hunting had its start in the late 1940's. War-trained pilots were dreaming up all sorts of uses for small aircraft, and this one stuck. Although the originals probably had ideas of making money shooting wolves and collecting the Ontario government bounty of twenty-five dollars, the uncertain returns have made it appeal more as a sport. It is a beneficial one, for the wolves prey on deer.

—Jack Macfie

CIL Oval, April, 1957

4. Here are topics for the budding aeronautical engineers who want to do research: (a) Pilotless Aircraft; (b) Aircraft Blind Landing Systems; (c) Navigational Aids; (d) The Future of Transport Aircraft.

XVII. STORIES FROM PICTURES

Many pictures can be found in magazine advertisements that will provide the ideas for interesting stories.

A picture of a forest through which a fire has swept and in which a lonely fawn stands helped a writer begin a plea against carelessness with this paragraph:

Once the trees stood proudly here, tall and green, roofing the shadowy coolness of the forest floor. Now they are stark and fire-blasted, in a desolation of scorched earth. Not only their beauty but their usefulness is gone.

Here are brief descriptions of pictures in full colour that were obtained from magazines such as the *Saturday Evening Post* and *Macleans:* (1) A fourteen-year-old boy and two younger children sit on the tailgate of a truck loaded high with furniture as it drives away from a now-abandoned farm house which appears to be located in a sea of sand: (2) Rain is falling on a crudely-constructed dog house labelled "Spot." A forlorn pup looks out. Nearby is a toy wagon in which is a hammer, a saw, and a small pail of nails. A few scraps of lumber are scattered about. (3) Sleeping peacefully and apparently noisily an elderly gentleman relaxes on a garden lounge. From the bushes nearby a tramp, on his knees, is beckoning to a small dog. The tramp already holds one of the sleeper's shoes. The pup holds the other. (4) A flood scene shows a roadside rural mail box on its tilted post which the swirling mucky water almost covers. On the box sits a small kitten.

Themes for Creative Writing:

Collect pictures-that-tell-a-story for your class file. Use them to obtain the ideas for a story of one or more paragraphs.

The transcribed stories may be placed in class booklets. Write the stories on the right hand side of the pages, and paste the picture which inspired each on the left hand side. Make a table of contents for each booklet. Provide a decorated cover for the booklet.

In some classes, each pupil may paste the picture for his story at the top of a piece of foolscap. The story is written beneath it. The illustrated stories are placed on the bulletin board or on the classroom reading table.

XVIII. FAVOURITE ENTERTAINERS

1. From magazines and newspapers collect pictures of well-known entertainers who perform in the movies, on radio, on records, or on television. Keep them in the classroom file.

2. Write a paragraph which names your favourite entertainer and which explains why that person is so regarded.

3. Make a class booklet entitled "Our Hit Parade" which will contain illustrated accounts of favourite programmes, songs and entertainers.

Begin by writing each of the following names on a separate slip of paper: TV comedy programme; TV educational programme; TV musical programme; TV sports programme; TV variety programme; TV dramatic programme; song; singer; actor; actress; animal performer; movie; comedian or comedienne; band or orchestra; sportscaster; disc jockey; ventriloquist.

Provide a slip with a name on it for each pupil in the class by making two or more of each item until the required quantity is available. Mix the slips in a hat or box. Then each pupil draws one slip.

Each pupil will name his or her favourite in the category named on the slip and write an explanation for his choice.

Use pictures from the class file to illustrate your explanations. If pictures are not available, make your own sketches.

4. Express in writing your comments on one or more of the following topics:

(a) The Programmes my Parents Like
(b) The Programme I Would Like to Sponsor
(c) The Give-away Shows
(d) The Hit Parades
(e) Radio and Television Commercials

XIX. CONVERSATION FROM PICTURES

1. Obtain a picture from a discarded magazine or newspaper which shows two characters who are, or who might be, engaged in conversation. The size of the picture should make it suitable for mounting on a sheet of writing paper. The picture might be of two people, of a person and an animal, of two animals, or even of two inanimate objects such as a bowling pin and a bowling ball. Of course, if your picture is one of the last three, you will have to imagine that a conversation could take place between the two.

Using the picture as an illustration, write the dialogue that might take place between the two characters. Remember to provide an introductory paragraph which describes the setting and introduces the characters. The conversation need not be long. Each time the speaker changes a new paragraph must be begun. Be careful with the use of quotation marks, and avoid using the word *said* too often. Finish your story with a well composed concluding paragraph which indicates what happened to the characters when the conversation was over.

Review the methods of paragraphing and punctuating a story with conversation before you begin to write. Turn to Exercise 10 on page 10 and to Exercise 11 on page 11.

Use the draft-revise-transcribe procedure in writing. These steps are described on pages 17, 18.

Submit the transcribed story, with the illustration attached, to your teacher for appraisal. When the stories have been returned, each pupil should obtain a piece of paper of uniform size. At the top of this sheet mount the illustration for the story. Then carefully copy the story, making any changes or corrections which the teacher has indicated are necessary. The stories can now be bound into a booklet, an index can be prepared, and a cover designed. (The art lesson might be devoted to a cover design contest.)

These booklets are prepared in order that the stories may be read. In some classes each pupil takes a booklet home for one night. Parents and older brothers and sisters enjoy reading the works of Grade VIII authors. Booklets of this type can also be exchanged with other rooms and other schools. A letter should be written to accompany the material sent on exchange.

2. Bring pictures that are suitable for writing CONVERSATION FROM PICTURES for the classroom file. Use them in the manner suggested in the fifth paragraph of page 60.

XX. THE ALMANAC

This theme presents many opportunities for language activities of many kinds, but it cannot be limited in its use to any one period of the school year. The oral or written activity should be carried out in the classroom on the day when the topics are most meaningful.

Because of its importance to the Grade VIII classroom, a section in the Appendix has been devoted to this topic. Read pages 301 and 302 which introduce THE ALMANAC, and plan to make frequent use of the information and suggestions which appear on pages 303 and 309.

VI ▲ IDEAS

Look carefully at the illustration on this page. Then read the following selection silently two or three times. The author had the experience of which he writes while on a leisurely two thousand mile journey across North America during the autumn. He travelled from Cape Cod to the "Land of the Windy Rain" which is across the Strait of Juan de Fuca from Vancouver Island.

As I walked back over the ridge and slowly descended the farther side my foot scuffed in the gravel. A pebble rolled away down the incline before me. What vast stretches of history were encompassed by the span of that tiny stone! Lying there since glacial times it had been warmed by the springs and cooled by the autumns of aeons of time. How much human life and plover life and grasshopper life had passed away while its insensate existence had gone on and on? Yet, surely, it is better to be able to enjoy the glory of the senses, if only for a single moment of life. Surely it is a thousand times better to know, to feel, and to appreciate the sunshine, the dry smell of autumn, and the dust-born clouds above than to possess the epoch-long unconsciousness of a stone.

Cheered somewhat by so simple a thing as the roll of a pebble, I returned to the car. We drove away, south and west, across the rich cornlands towards the Great River, that age-old flyway of the autumn birds, the Mississippi.

—Adapted from AUTUMN ACROSS AMERICA by E. W. Teale

Ideas:

EXERCISE 1: After reading the two paragraphs on the preceding page prepare answers to the following questions. Use your dictionary to be sure of the meanings of some of the new words.

1. Read the sentence that records the author's exclamation when he thinks that all the memorable events of many centuries have passed unnoticed by the stone which his foot sent rolling down the hill.

2. Quote three phrases from the selection that are used to emphasize the fact that the stone had lain there undisturbed for a very long time.

3. Select two words, each from a different sentence, which are used to indicate that the stone had lain there for centuries without being able to use any of the senses which living things possess.

4. Quote the phrase used by the author to refer: (i) to people; (ii) to insects; (iii) to birds.

5. Which of the following statements best summarizes the thoughts which came to the author during this experience on a hillside in the country.

   (i) Stones and pebbles have a lengthy and lonely existence.

   (ii) A short life during which constant contact with nature is maintained by using all the senses is better than a long existence without such rich experiences.

   (iii) When people keep all their senses alert they are able to observe all the wonders of nature quite easily.

6. From the following titles select the one which you think is best for this selection. Give reasons for your choice.

   (a) THE GLORY OF THE SENSES

   (b) THE ROLL OF A PEBBLE

   (c) A ROLLING STONE GATHERS NO THOUGHTS

   (d) MAKE THE BEST USE OF YOUR TIME

   (e) KEEP YOUR SENSES SHARP

   (f) THE REAL MEANING OF THE WORD "OBSERVE"

Ideas:

"Sense experiences are the raw materials of thought." That sentence says very briefly that all our ideas are acquired by listening, by seeing, by feeling, by tasting, or by smelling, and that we use these ideas when we think. When a person expresses his thoughts for others, either orally or in writing, language is used. Therefore a person who speaks and writes easily and well is one who has much to think about. That person is one who uses all his senses to gather a wealth of ideas.

A few people must use all their senses in their daily jobs. Others like to use all their senses, even imaginatively, on a particular occasion. To realize more fully the usefulness of all the senses read the following selections. Each was written as an exercise on the topic "Using the Five Senses." Read each carefully, and answer the questions that follow.

1.   A RECIPE FOR SLUMBER

Let me tell you how a pleasant memory from each of the senses may be used to help you relax and go quickly off to slumberland on those occasions when sleep evades you. The recollection of the soothing strains of Brahm's Lullaby will provide the ingredient of sound. For sight, think of a painting in full colour of Lake Louise. In your mind's eye see the blue of its water and the colourful poppies along its edge in the foreground while from the opposite shore the glistening Victoria Glacier rises majestically. The fragrance of lilacs or of the nicotine in the border of the garden will return if you think deeply of a summer's eve. Remember next the cool refreshing waters of the pond or pool in which you have enjoyed a swim. In make believe walk again through an orchard at harvest time picking and eating tree-ripe peaches. Round and round you stir these memories from the senses—tasting, feeling, smelling, seeing, hearing. Soon you slumber peacefully.

1. Discuss the title of this selection. What are the ingredients of this recipe?

2. Compose alternative titles for this selection.

3. Read a sentence from this selection which refers to the use of each of the five physical senses.

4. Read five imperative sentences that are found in this selection. Why are imperative sentences used in writing a recipe?

5. Read the sentence that suggests by its shortness that the writer does not wish to disturb the sleepy user of this recipe. What soft sound is heard three times in this short sentence?

Ideas:

2.   FIVE OR SEVEN

(Note: Rapid developments in aircraft construction may have made the facts of this story obsolete. They were accurate at the time the exercise was written. THE AUTHORS*)*

How difficult it must be for the flight engineer of a large transoceanic airplane to be responsible for over four hundred instruments and controls during a flight! To look after all of these properly he has to use all five senses, both hands, a slide rule, numerous charts and tables, and a highly developed sixth sense called intuition. In addition he must be an accomplished toe wriggler, for during busy take-offs and landings he sometimes slips off a shoe and reaches with his foot to flick a hard-to-reach switch.

The engineer of a large transoceanic or transcontinental aircraft must be ready to use all his senses, as well as his common sense, with split-second speed. The needles on the numerous dials and the signal lights on the instrument panel must be watched carefully. The engineer must be alert to detect any unusual smell which would tell him that fuel was leaking or that fire might be threatening. Any leaking liquid must be quickly tasted to determine if it is gasoline, oil, hydraulic fluid, or just plain water. Knowing a change in the tone of the plane indicates trouble, as when it begins to ice up, he listens carefully for any unusual sounds from the air frame or from the engines. Feeling the controls that regulate the fuel supply will tell him whether the engines are performing satisfactorily, or whether the engines need a change of fuel mixture or more heat. In fact, the vibration of his seat may cause him to look around and perhaps to discover that a nose-wheel door is not completely closed. Yes, indeed, a flight engineer uses every one of his senses to carry out his very important tasks.

1. Discuss the title of this selection. Quote sentences or phrases to justify the use of the word "seven" in it.

2. Compose alternative titles for this selection.

3. Compose a sentence which uses the word "tables" with the same meaning that it has in this selection.

4. For each of the following senses read a sentence from the selection to indicate that it is used by the flight engineer: sight; hearing; taste; smell; feel.

5. Which of the seven senses is being used when a person says, "I have no other reason for thinking this way except that I just feel it in my bones?" Be careful!

This question is for class discussion: In what ways, other than through language, do people express ideas?

Use all your senses, all the time, to gather ideas.

111

Ideas:

EXERCISE 1: This is a test to determine how well you have been using your five senses. From the following groups of words select those which remind you of an experience which you have had. Use each of the selected groups of words in a sentence. On the first line beneath each sentence write the name of each sense which you did use, or which you might have used, on that occasion. Under each word list the words that name or describe the ideas that might come to you through that particular sense.

Example: On my first magic carpet ride I travelled in a turbo-prop Viscount airplane from Toronto to Winnipeg.

SIGHT	HEARING	TASTE	FEELING	SMELL
postage-stamp fields	engines	dinner	ascending	food
ant-like cars	flaps and landing gear	—chicken	descending	newness of the plane
ribbon high-ways	stewardess's comments	—pie	touch-down	exhausts
snake-like streams		—salad	bumps	
			air-conditioning	

1. on an airplane trip
2. on a canoe trip
3. in a delicatessen shop
4. at the stock car races
5. at a birthday party
6. at a cottage or a camp
7. our kitchen before a big meal
8. at a children's playground
9. lunch time at school
10. in a doctor's or dentist's office
11. at a super market
12. autumn clean-up time outdoors

EXERCISE 2: Select any one of the twelve items listed in the exercise above and use that item as the topic of a story or article on the theme "Using the Five Senses." Read again the two selections on pages 110 and 111. Your aim is to make your writing show how each of the senses is used in that particular situation to gather ideas. The lists which you have completed in Exercise 1 will help you.

EXERCISE 3: Select one of the following topics and write a record of either your real or imaginary experiences. Make your account resemble that which might be found in a diary or log book. Date the records for each day carefully.

Limit your account by recording only the most important ideas which came to you by using your five senses.

1. Visiting a Farm at Harvest Time
2. Around the World in Eight Hours
3. Five Days with My Favourite Explorer
4. Chief Cook and Bottle Washer for a Week End
5. Relatives Come for a Week End

Gathering Ideas

Read this selection carefully at least twice. Then turn to the exercises on the next page.

READING AND WRITING

Authors and journalists, when asked by boys and girls to describe the best way to become a good writer, always include the same item in their answers. Their advice always states that if anyone aspires to be a great writer that person must first become an avid reader.

Real experiences provide the opportunities for us to use all our senses to acquire ideas. But most of us cannot go wherever we wish and do whatever we should like to do. We can, however, learn quite easily from the experiences of others. We can do so by reading books.

A reader is able to use the great stock of ideas which he finds in books. A reader will also use, even though he does not make any real effort to do so, the vocabulary, the phrases, and the sentence patterns of the books that he has read. This is true because much of our language ability is acquired by imitation. In fact, some people maintain that reading will do more to develop language skills than all the exercises in all the language texts. The quality of the material that is read is, therefore, of great importance, but it need not all be of the same kind.

Francis Bacon, a famous English writer and statesman who lived between 1561 and 1626, said, "Some books are to be tasted, others to be swallowed, and some few to be chewed and digested." He was saying, in fanciful language, that there are many kinds of books that should be read, but that all books should not be read with the same amount of care and concentration. Animal stories, science fiction, and detective stories are only tasted when read quickly for pleasure. Stories about historical events, or biographies, for example, are to be read more carefully in order that interesting and useful facts may be remembered. Text books, whose contents need to be discussed, thoroughly understood, and remembered, are books of the type that need to be chewed and digested.

The advice given in the preceding paragraph should be applied to the reading of the various parts of a newspaper. The comic pages contain the material to be read quickly, or tasted only. The news sections will be read more carefully, with attention being given to the reports of events that are of some importance and which people will be discussing. The editorial page contains the type of material which will be chewed and digested. The thoughtful reader proceeds slowly, and tries to decide if the editor has put up a convincing argument on each of the topics.

Book readers become better writers.

Gathering Ideas:

EXERCISE 1: After having read the selection entitled "Reading and Writing" on the preceding page, prepare to answer these questions orally. Refer by number to the sentence or paragraph in which your answer may be found. This will help your classmates to follow your explanation.

1. Read the sentence which suggests that, almost without exception, all great writers and journalists read a great many books of all kinds when they were young.

2. Read the sentence that states that a person picks up most of his language habits by listening and reading.

3. Read the sentence or sentences which state that inability to travel and do things is really no handicap to the person who seeks experiences of all kinds.

4. Why is it important that most of the material that a person reads should be in language that he would be proud to use?

5. In which of Francis Bacon's three categories would you place each of these: (a) comic books; (b) adventure stories; (c) movie magazines; (d) the sports pages; (e) a newspaper column entitled: Answers to Teenagers' Problems; (f) a handbook of first aid; (g) an encyclopedia.

EXERCISE 2: Make a class chart on the chalkboard or on the bulletin board with the three headings: (1) Books for Pleasure; (2) Books for Information; (3) Books for Study These sub-headings might be added: (i) For tasting; (ii) For swallowing; (iii) For chewing and digesting.

In each list place the names of at least ten books that are found in your classroom, school or public library.

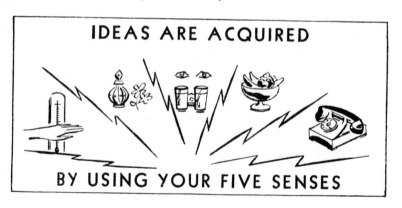

IDEAS ARE ACQUIRED

BY USING YOUR FIVE SENSES

Book readers become better writers.

The Parts of a Book

To get the most out of a book a reader must be able to use all of the content.   A book may have all or some of the parts described in this list. Examine the book now in your hands to find the answers to most of the questions that appear on this page.   Prepare to answer the questions orally.

1. The dust jacket — This is the name given to the removable paper cover that is sometimes found on new books to protect the cover.   Collect some dust jackets to discover what information is contained on their flaps.

2. The cover — What information is contained on the front and back cover?   What do you find on the spine of the book?

3. The end papers — This is the name given to the sheets pasted on the inside of the covers.   Find at least one book in which the end papers contain printed information. Describe or show them to your class.

4. The title page — Who are the authors of this book?   Who prepared the illustrations? What company published the book?

5. The copyright page — What information is found on the back of the title page?   Why is it important to know the date when some books were printed?

6. The preface — What was the authors' purpose in writing the preface? Sometimes a "foreword" or an "introduction" is also provided.   Note the spelling of the former word.

7. The illustrations — Where is a frontispiece located?   Often a list of all the illustrations used is given at the beginning of a book.

8. The table of contents — This section lists in order of appearance the main topics presented in the book.   In what chapter will you find help in verse writing?

9. The body or text — How many pages are devoted to this section?

10. The glossary — This section is a small dictionary which gives the meaning and pronunciation of the new or unusual words introduced in a book.

11. The appendix — This section contains material which will be referred to many times as the book is being used.

12. The index — Here you will find an alphabetical list of all the items to be found in the book.   On what page in this text will you find: (i) biographies; (ii) figurative language?

Reference Books

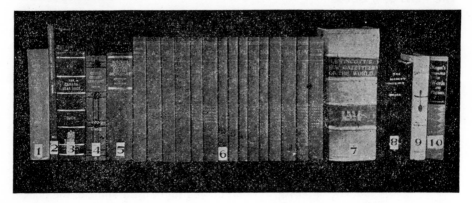

Reference books which everyone should learn to use are shown in the picture above. They are:

1. An Almanac
2. An Atlas
3. The Canada Year Book
4. A Concordance
5. A Dictionary
6. An Encyclopedia
7. A Gazetteer
8. A Reader's Handbook
9. A Cook Book
10. A Thesaurus

EXERCISE 1: Read each of the following items. Prepare to explain which of the reference books shown in the above picture you would select in order to carry out the instructions or to answer the questions.

1. What is a lapidary?

2. To which country does Canada export the greatest amount of commodities each year?

3. What is the name of the strait between the Malay Peninsula and the island of Sumatra?

4. In which book would a brief summary of the various uses of copper be found?

5. On what map would Kilimanjaro be found?

6. In what book and verse in the Bible would you read,
   "Judge not, lest ye be judged?"

7. Explain how to prepare rice croquettes.

8. What was the pen name of Charles L. Dodgson and what well-known book did he write?

9. Find a proverb on the subject of waste.

10. What is the precise time for the beginning of autumn during the year you are in Grade VIII?

Reference books are storehouses of useful knowledge.

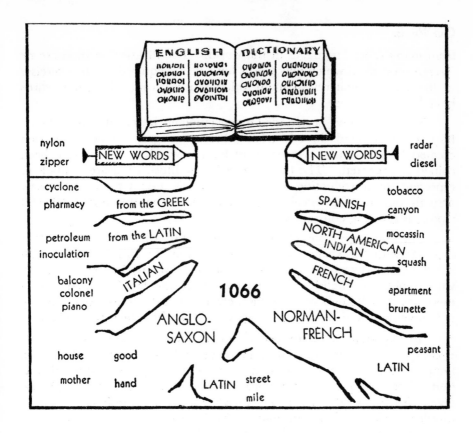

VII ▲ OUR WORDS

The illustration on this page shows, in a very simplified way, the origins of many of the words to be found in an English dictionary. The two main roots indicate that many of the words that appear on the leaves of the dictionary have been obtained from a combination of the language used by the Norman-French with that used by the Anglo-Saxons. This mingling began when William the Conqueror came to England in 1066.

The illustration also shows that most of the Norman-French words came originally from the Latin language of Italy, and that some Latin words had been added to the Anglo-Saxon language before 1066. These Latin words were left by the Romans who had remained in Britain from 55 B.C. to A.D. 410.

The English language continued to grow, however, after 1066 by absorbing more words from both the French and the Latin, as well as

➡ 117

from many other languages in the world. The illustration shows some foreign roots from which new words have been acquired. The exercises in this chapter will reveal many other sources from which our words have been borrowed.

New words have been added to our language in recent years. Some have been adopted directly from other languages. Some have been created by combining two or more foreign words. A few have been coined or invented. The two needles in the illustration are symbols to represent the introduction of these new words. As a result of the new arrivals our English vocabulary, which now contains about 600,000 words, is growing constantly.

Our language is sometimes compared with a healthy oak tree that expands with the years. Records reveal that the Bible contains only 5,000 different words, and that Shakespeare knew only 15,000. In 1850, we are told, the English dictionary contained only 50,000 words. Now there are 30,000 kinds of butterflies, each with a different name. Every new invention and discovery brings with it a whole new vocabulary.

An explanation of the origin and history of a word is called its *etymology*. In larger dictionaries a brief etymology of most words is to be found. It usually is presented in square brackets preceding the definition. For example, for the word *neighbour* this information might be given: AS. *nēahgebūr*, lit. a near-dweller, from *nēah, near* and *gebūr*, a dweller. The explanatory notes at the front of the dictionary help the reader to understand the abbreviations. Using them he learns that the word *neighbour* is derived from two Anglo-Saxon (AS.) words which literally (lit.) mean *a person who dwells nearby.*

"Words have wings" is a saying that is often heard. A study of the etymologies of some words proves that they have been great travellers. For example, a dictionary will show that the word *magic* was adopted into the English vocabulary from the French; that the French acquired it from the Latin; that the Latin borrowed it from the Greek. This word has travelled down through the centuries, from language to language, and is now used by English speaking boys and girls, and adults, to explain how rabbits can be made to jump out of hats and how water can be poured from empty jugs.

Everyone is familiar with the word *sandwich*. It came into use sometime after 1800. About that time, the Earl of Sandwich, unable to take time from his entertainment to go for his meals, used to have his servant bring him a piece of meat between two pieces of bread. Now, even though the two pieces of bread may have various kinds of filling, the name *sandwich* is still used for this form of food.

➡

Our Words:

Our English words *sincere* and *sincerely* come from the Latin *sine cera* meaning *without wax*.

In Roman times it was common practice to conceal flaws in pottery with wax. The honest manufacturer, who wished to guarantee that his product had no imperfections which he had covered with wax in order to deceive the buyer, labelled his wares with a sign which read SINE CERA. These words meant that this pottery was "without wax."

In English we now use the words *sincere* and *sincerely* to indicate that we are not pretending, that we are honest, or that we are not trying to deceive.

In letter writing, *sincerely* is frequently used as part of the complimentary closing. What are we actually saying to the reader when we use that word to end our letters? When we know the meaning of the word *sincerely* what must we be careful to include in our letters?

Over some words, there is a difference of opinion regarding the origin. Some philologists maintain that *good-bye* resulted from a contraction of the phrase *God be with ye*, which people often said to one another as they parted. Others point to our greetings *good morning*, *good day*, and *good evening*. They say that the original parting remark was *good be with ye* or *good abide with ye*, and that from one of these phrases our word *good-bye* has come. There seems to be no argument, however, that the parting wish *may you fare well* has become our single word *farewell*.

QUESTIONS FOR ORAL ANSWERING:

1. What is the most important date mentioned in the introduction to this chapter? What historical event took place at that time?

2. What language used in Italy, and now studied by many students in secondary schools, contributed many words to both French and English?

3. What word is used as a synonym for *created* to describe a word like *radar* which was made from the letters of the phrase "*radio direction and range*"?

4. Why is the statement "Words are good travellers" a true one?

5. Which of these words was derived from a man's name: *sincerely*, *sandwich*, *farewell*?

6. Read again the questions that are posed in the paragraphs about the word *sincerely*. Answer these questions.

7. In comparing our language with a tree why is the oak the tree that is mentioned?

8. Which origin of the word *good-bye* do you prefer? Why? Which origin does your dictionary support?

119

Word Origins

EXERCISE 1: Rule two columns in your language note book and write these two headings: (a) Anglo-Saxon Words; (b) Latin Words.

By consulting a dictionary, determine the origin of each of the following and list in the proper column:

father	camp	house	table
day	tent	hope	uniform
life	disciple	land	bishop

The words in list (b) were borrowed by the Anglo-Saxons from the Latin that had been used by the Romans in early Britain.

EXERCISE 2: Rule two columns in your language note book and write these two headings: (a) Anglo-Saxon Words; (b) Norman French Words.

By consulting a dictionary, determine the origin of each of the following words and list them in the proper column.

begin	avenue	ship	parliament
meadow	curtain	road	vessel
cow	barley	watch	battle
board	beef	commence	bench
champion	gentlemen	water	night

EXERCISE 3: Rule two columns in your language note book and provide the headings as in Exercise 2 above. One of each of the following pairs of words is Anglo-Saxon, and one is of French origin. By consulting a dictionary, list each word in its proper column. From these lists, note that the fusion of the two languages has provided English with a wealth of synonyms.

ask	—demand	savage	—wild	luck	—chance
shore	—coast	outsider	—stranger	work	—labour
difficult	—hard	help	—assist	arrive	—come
fountain	—well	perceive	—see	residence	—home

EXERCISE 4: Prepare or obtain an outline map of the world on a sheet of paper that can be inserted in your language note book.

Consult a dictionary to determine the country in which each of these words originated. Print each word neatly on the map as close as possible to the country from which it came.

alphabet	boomerang	bungalow	calendar
calico	gorilla	wagon	guinea pig
sky	igloo	tepee	egg
gingham	toboggan	cocoa	banana

Word Origins:

catsup	kindergarten	khaki	tea
shawl	gypsy	seersucker	skin
raccoon	ballet	umbrella	poodle

Be prepared to use each word in a sentence and to point to its country of origin on a wall map.

EXERCISE 5: Many English words that name inventions and discoveries are derived from the Greek language. The word *telephone* comes from *tele* meaning *distant* and *phone* meaning sound or voice. *Thermostat* is derived from *thermo* meaning *heat* and *stat* meaning *to stand*, and names the instrument that controls the temperature so that the heat will stand at the degree which is set.

Consult a dictionary to obtain information which will enable you to explain the meaning of the following words in a manner similar to that used above to explain *telephone* and *thermostat.*

phonograph	telescope	automobile	photograph
thermometer	speedometer	thermos	television
microscope	telegraph	metronome	photo-electric

EXERCISE 6: Many words that are now heard frequently were unknown at the beginning of this century. Some have been adopted from other languages. Some are old English words to which new meanings have been attached. Some have been created by combining two or more words from Latin of Greek root words. Others have been coined or developed from English sources to represent new ideas.

(a) Consult a dictionary to find the meaning, and the origin of each of the following words. Be prepared to give an oral explanation to your class.

camouflage	prefabricated	zipper	Technicolor
stokers	insulin	caterpillar	nylon
radar	commando	fluorescent	kitchenette
smog	diesel	lipstick	cellophane

(b) Make a heading in your language notebook, *Recent Immigrants to the English Language.* Talk to adults and ask politely to be introduced to more words that are new arrivals in our language. List them in your notebook. Learn about their origin.

Family Names

Were any of your ancestors craftsmen? There is a way you may be able to tell.

During the early Middle Ages, before A.D.1000, only a few families had surnames, family names or last names. Most people had only what we call first names. As many people had the same first name, a method had to be found to tell them apart.

One way of doing this was by adding the father's name. If in any village or district there were three boys, each with the name of Harold, people would distinguish them by referring to the boy whose father's name was John as Harold John's son. Another might be called Harold William's son; another might be called Harold Eric's son. As time passed the additional name, the over name or surname was combined and the three Harolds became known as Harold Johnson, Harold Williamson and Harold Ericson.

Some surnames were attached to people because of the location of their homes. It is easy to guess where John Townsend lived, or where the home of William Hill was located.

Many surnames were obtained by using the occupation of the person. Jack the smith became Jack Smith and Thomas the miller became Thomas Miller.

The custom of using surnames grew as it helped to refer to people more easily. Later laws were passed requiring people to have surnames. The names referred to here are all of English origin. If your surname comes from the language of another country, it probably has an origin similar to those of these English names.

EXERCISE 1: Consult a telephone directory, or ask adults, to obtain names to add to this list which should be labelled "Surnames Derived from Occupations."

Baker	Brewer	Butcher	Carpenter	Mason
Miller	Potter	Shoemaker	Tanner	Smith

EXERCISE 2: Consult a dictionary or an encyclopedia to find the type of work done by the first people who had each of the following surnames:

Currier	Cutler	Fletcher
Glover	Goldsmith	Webber
Turner	Glazier	Fuller
Wright	Webster	Chandler

Meeting New Words

Advertisements in the daily papers often present messages which give their readers new ideas, and which also make them acquainted with new words. Read the following message silently. Then listen carefully, with your text book closed, as your classmates take turns reading it, paragraph by paragraph, orally. After that turn to the exercises on the next page.

This Land of Ours . . .

Look about you. Look thoughtfully at the world in which you live. In the centre of this wide and stirring stage there stands a nation newly come to greatness.

It wears its new mantle well. Already, its reputation stands high and its voice is heard respectfully. It is a ringing voice, speaking with vigour and clearly sounding a call of progress and achievement to all men of enterprise.

This is a nation that symbolizes freedom in action—and its accomplishments today merely foreshadow what is to come.

The products of its fertile fields, its vast forests and wind-whipped seas indicate, in their abundance, the potential of a land which is only just beginning to reach its full stature.

This is a nation of industry and commerce—of progressive people working hard and willingly to create all those things which enrich our living and typify, in themselves, the rewarding pattern of existence to which all men aspire.

This is a nation of peace-loving people, of friendly and hospitable people who cultivate those attitudes of heart and mind that tend toward horizons ever brighter—ever greater—ever more inspiring.

This is a happy land, a land without fear, without hate—a land of many peoples united in a deep and timeless love of all that their country represents.

It is a youthful land, a hopeful land—and its name is Canada.

Courtesy of General Motors Products of Canada

Meeting New Words:

EXERCISE 1: From the selection on the preceding page select a word or phrase that matches in meaning each of the following. Use your dictionary, if necessary.

1. cloak or dress
2. strength
3. courage and energy
4. are symbols of *or* stand for
5. look forward

6. represents
7. development or size
8. moving forward
9. willing to welcome
10. a way of thinking or acting

EXERCISE 2: Find in a discarded magazine or newspaper an advertisement whose message uses language effectively. Bring the advertisement to class. Read it orally. Be prepared to explain the meaning of any strange words.

EXERCISE 3: The selection on the preceding page says that Canada is a "land of many peoples." The names of many Canadians indicate the country from which they or their ancestors have come.

(a) John is a popular first name for boys in this country. In early England it was Johannes. It became shortened to the familiar John at the time of the Crusades.

Each of the following are first names which are the equivalent of the English word John. By consulting books or by making polite enquiry of adults, find the country from which each comes.

(a) (i) Jean or Jan (Watch the pronunciation.); (ii) Hans; (iii) Ivan; (iv) Ian; (v) Jock; (vi) Owen; (vii) Jon; (viii) Sean or Shawn; (ix) Giovanni; (x) Juan.

(b) There are several girls' names which are the equivalent of the boy's name John. They are: Anna, Hannah, Giovanna, Juanita, Yvonne, Jeanne, Jeanette, Ivanna, Jeannie, Joan, Jane and Janet.

Match the girls' names with their language of origin: English (3 of the above); Scottish (1); Russian (1); French (3); Italian (1); Hebrew (2).

(c) The surnames in Exercise 1 and 2 on page 122 are all of English origin. With the help of the New Canadians in the class or the community build up a list of the more popular surnames of people from other lands. Find the origin of as many as possible.

Enlarging Your Vocabulary

Here are some suggestions to help you build a larger vocabulary.

1. LISTEN TO GOOD SPEECH: Your vocabulary grows when you pick up words by imitating the talk of other people. Therefore you must learn to listen attentively. All the language that you will hear is not worth repeating, but if you take advantage of the many opportunities that you do have to listen to good speech your vocabulary will certainly grow.

2. READ A VARIETY OF BOOKS: Comic books are interesting to many boys and girls, but they are not much help to you in building a bigger and better vocabulary. Develop the habit of reading a variety of books. Use your public library, your school or classroom library, and, if possible, start a library of your own. Good books make permanent friends.

3. PRACTISE USING NEW WORDS: A bookmark that is easily made of light cardboard is sketched at the right. As you read, jot down on it the new words which you meet that you think you may find useful. After the reading is completed, practise using these words in sentences. In addition make lists of new words that you meet in your study of literature, social studies, science, and health. Do not forget those that you hear in school radio broadcasts and in the films shown by your teacher.

4. USE A DICTIONARY: Although you want to develop a large vocabulary, your aim is not that of being able to use big words. A large stock of words will enable you to use the proper word in the proper place.

Language is acquired by imitation.

The Value of a Well-Stocked Vocabulary

The following paragraph was written by a Grade VIII pupil. The writer is a person who reads a great deal. Her extensive vocabulary enabled her to create a word picture that is the equal of a beautiful oil painting. Read the paragraph carefully two or three times and then do the exercise that follows.

REFLECTIONS

The landing place on the lake at our summer cottage was a dreary spot on the winter's day that I revisited it. Feathery white drifts surrounded the dock, glistening palely in the wan sunshine. Farther along the shoreline, dark rocks jutted out in sharp contrast to the monotonous tone of an almost unbroken blanket of snow. Stretching out in front of me was an expanse of dull gray ice, shattered only at length by the dark patch of evergreen forest on the opposite shore. Bright patches of colour, reflecting from the roofs of cottages, seemed strangely alien in this atmosphere of winter at its worst. The bitterly cold wind whistled bleakly in the limbs of the unadorned trees, reaching their bare branches to the steely gray of the sky above. Involuntarily I shivered, and decided it was time to depart and leave the beloved lake-front to the fate of the winds and the weather.

—Marlene H.

EXERCISE 1: Select one of the following topics, or any other theme that is based on one of your own experiences. Write a descriptive paragraph. Work carefully during the revision stage to make your language paint a vivid word picture.

A SUNSET OVER WATER

A SUNRISE OVER WATER

CLOUD FORMATIONS

AN AUTUMN SCENE

A FISHING CAMP

AT THE STOCK CAR RACES

A PARADE

THE FALLS

EXERCISE 2: Test the size of the vocabulary you possess to name the parts of an automobile, the parts of a ship, articles of jewellery, and household electrical appliances. Rule four columns in your language notebook. Write one of the four headings on each. Write as many nouns as possible in each column. Start with these: tiara, distributor, rudder, humidifier.

Literal and Figurative Language

Look carefully at each section of the illustration, then read the following expressions.

1. May I put a word in your ear?

2. That fellow just ate up arithmetic at school.

3. Please keep an eye on my bag for me.

The illustration shows what would have happened if the exact meaning of the words was used in each sentence. The words would then have been used as *literal* language, that is, according to the letters.

Compare these three sentences with those that are numbered above.

1. May I say something to you?

2. That fellow found arithmetic very easy at school.

3. Please watch my bag for me.

In this latter group no imagination or exaggeration has been used to express the ideas. A speaker or writer, however, may often use a considerable amount of both to add force or beauty to his language. When he uses words which have other than their original or literal meaning, he is using *figurative* language.

In literature lessons you will become acquainted with several figures of speech that are used by both poets and writers of prose. The following exercises will show that everyone uses figurative language. By doing so, we can express our ideas more forcefully, more colourfully, and sometimes more concisely.

Literal and Figurative Language:

Many words that name parts of the body are used with meanings different from their original or *literal* sense. These exercises show how plentiful and common these *figurative* expressions are.

EXERCISE 1: Write the numbers from 1 to 10 in a column in your language book. From the sentences in the right hand column, find one that best expresses in *figurative* language the thought of the literal expression on the left. Write the equivalent figurative expression beside the proper number.

1. Help me.
2. Nothing frightens him.
3. He made a blunder.
4. She was disappointed.
5. Do not interfere.
6. Do not get excited.
7. He is in too many activities.
8. She is very kind.
9. They owe much money.
10. He looked disappointed.

1. Keep your head.
2. He put his foot in it.
3. Lend me a hand.
4. His face fell.
5. He has nerves of iron.
6. She has a heart of gold.
7. Her nose was out of joint.
8. They are knee deep in debt.
9. He has a finger in too many pies.
10. Keep your nose out of it.

EXERCISE 2: (Oral) Express the thought of each of the following sentences in *literal* language. The figurative language in each sentence has been printed in italics.

1. Everyone *put his shoulder to the wheel* in order that the job might be finished on time.

2. Even when angry it always pays to *keep a civil tongue in your head*.

3. Whatever you attempt, do *with all your heart*.

4. Even though your first model does not fly, *keep a stiff upper lip*.

5. The invader *brought* his enemy *to his knees*.

6. The old boxer *had no stomach* for a rematch.

7. The contestant had a wealth of knowledge *at his finger tips*.

8. When I asked the way to the post office I was told to *follow my nose*.

9. Mother says that my little brother and sisters are too often *under foot*.

10. When father found out, I was *rapped over the knuckles*.

Literal and Figurative Language:

Expressions in which words do not have their ordinary or literal meaning are called *figures of speech*.

1. A *simile* is a figure of speech in which a comparison, made between two unlike things, is introduced by *like* or *as*.

2. A *metaphor* is a figure of speech which suggests a comparison between two things   The words *like* and *as* are NOT used.

3. *Personification* is a figure of speech in which something which is not alive is spoken of as if it were a living thing.

EXERCISE 1: Read each of the following items.   Select and name the figures of speech that have been used in each.   The number in parentheses after each item indicates the number of figures of speech to be found.

1. At the sale of baked goods, the old bachelor ploughed through the crowd to make sure he bought the chocolate cakes.   (1)

2. As we approached the hill, the tail lights on the cars ahead twinkled like the lights on a Christmas tree.   The headlights of the oncoming cars sparkled like tree-top stars as they came over the crest.   (2)

3. The leaves danced a jig on the ground as the wind shook their lonely friends from their summer home.   (4)

4. In the water he swam like a fish.   On the track he ran like a hare. At his desk he reminded everyone only of John Brown.   (2)

5. The drizzle and the freezing temperature had glass-coated the trunks, the branches, and every twig of all the trees.   (1)

6. Her teeth were like stars.   They came out every night.   (1)

7. His fists were as hard as iron.   They pummelled his opponent like a triphammer.   (2)

8. The thirsty land greeted the rain as a desert wanderer would welcome the sight of an oasis.   (2)

9. She is a walking dictionary although no one calls her a bookworm.   (2)

10. The billowy clouds floated across the sky like an armada.   (1)

EXERCISE 2: Designate a period of a week or two as FIGURES OF SPEECH COLLECTION PERIOD.   Collect examples of similes, metaphors, and personifications that are met in your reading.   Place them in your language notebook after labelling a page for each.   Compare your collection with those of your classmates.

Language for the Occasion

The illustration represents a fact that every Grade VIII girl and boy accepts. Clothes are selected to be appropriate for the occasion on which they are worn.

The garb that is worn for Saturday morning recreation, for chores, or for sport is not usually that which is worn to school. The clothes that are worn to a party, to church, or when you go visiting with your parents are commonly known as your Sunday best.

What have the illustration and the opening paragraphs to do with language? They should help you to realize that the words you use, and the manner in which they are expressed will also change with the situation in which you will be using them. Language, like clothes, must be appropriate for the occasion.

In talking with your friends on the playground or at the snack bar you will frequently use incomplete sentences, contractions, and perhaps some slang which, it is admitted, may help you to express some ideas quickly to those who understand it. In the classroom, in conversation with adults, and in much of your writing you will use language which is similar to that used by educated people when they talk. On some occasions you will want to be able to use very carefully chosen English. When writing a business letter, an article for your school or community paper, or a speech your language will resemble that which is found in textbooks.

Slang has been described as streamlined language. It is picked up quickly, especially by young people, because it is fun to find a word or

Language for the Occasion:

phrase that expresses an idea briefly, in a new way, and in words that have life and sparkle.   One of the chief characteristics of slang is that the expressions are usually popular for only a short time.   Others quickly take their place.   Only a few slang words stay and enrich the language.

Study this table which is a summary of the characteristics of each type of language.   Do the exercises which are designed to help you to be able to use the language that is appropriate, just as you like to be able to select the clothes that are appropriate, for each occasion.

"Colloquial" or its abbreviation "Colloq." is a word you will meet in many definitions in the dictionary.   A *colloquial* word is one that is

TYPE	WHERE FOUND AND USED	CHARACTERISTICS
Special occasion or formal English	—in textbooks —in business letters —in articles for school or community papers —in written records and reports —in essay contests —in platform speeches —on examinations	—always grammatically correct —words carefully chosen —no words omitted *Example:* I know that we had it. *Not:* I know we had it. —no contractions *Example:* I shall be there on that date. *Not:* I'll be there on that date. —sentences sometimes long
Everyday or informal English	—in the speech of educated people —in friendly letters and notes —classroom story writing	—always grammatically correct —some omissions —some contractions, especially in friendly letters and in speech —colloquial words accepted —easier to read and to listen to than formal English —no slang
English for your age group	—in talking with friends of your age —not in writing except in reporting conversation	—always grammatically correct although sentences may be incomplete —slang, in small doses may add colour to language —many contractions —colloquial words common

➡ 131

Language for the Occasion:

appropriate for use in informal speech and in the type of writing that is done in friendly letters. *A colloquialism* should never be used in special occasion or formal English.

Short forms such as exam, maths, photo, auto and phone are colloquialisms often heard in conversation. Words such as kid (a child), guy (a person), jiffy (a moment) and contraption (device), and the contractions, isn't, couldn't, you're, also belong to this group.

EXERCISE 1: Label a page in your language notebook COLLOQUIAL WORDS AND PHRASES. On this page make a list of common colloquialisms that you hear. Use your dictionary to obtain a formal language definition. Start your list with the colloquial words from these sentences:

1. Everyone laughed when the clown took a header into the empty tank.

2. As the new sailor walked on deck the captain said, "I like the cut of your jib."

3. I'll go out on a limb and buy that car, hoping that it is as good as you say it is.

4. When the owner of the orchard found us we were in a jam.

5. Plenty of elbow grease will be needed to remove that old paint.

EXERCISE 2: Label a page in your language notebook SLANG. Divide the page in two equal parts. Place the heading "Today's Slang Expressions" on one part. On the other write "Slang of Former Years."

Make a list of the slang expressions currently in use under the first heading. By making polite enquiry of adults build a list of slang expressions, with their meanings, that were popular in former years.

EXERCISE 3: State orally the type of language that would be appropriate for use in each of the following:

1. a letter of application for a position

2. a pupil interview with the police chief of your community

3. the introduction of a judge who is to address a school assembly

4. a newspaper editorial   (See page 174.)

Language for the Occasion:

5. an essay type answer on an examination paper

6. reporting a sports event orally to your classmates

7. a sermon

8. a dialogue between two comedians

9. a discussion of a favourite television programme

10. a discussion with your teacher to plan an excursion

EXERCISE 4: In each of the following groups, one sentence belongs to each of the three types of language described on pages 131 and 132. Identify the type of language used in each sentence.

1. (a) I should like to have you attend our conference.

   (b) I should like to have you with us when we put our heads together.

   (c) Come on over and chew the fat with us.

2. (a) He goofed on that one.

   (b) By doing that he certainly made a blunder.

   (c) By doing that he put his foot in it.

3. (a) Before I had been there an hour, I had spent every cent.

   (b) Before I had been there an hour, I hadn't a dime to my name.

   (c) Before I had been there an hour, I was broke.

4. (a) Who owns the crate in the drive?

   (b) Who owns the car parked in the drive?

   (c) Who owns the automobile that is parked in the drive?

5. (a) If you think that I did it, you are accusing the wrong person.

   (b) If you think I did it, you're barking up the wrong tree.

   (c) If you think I did it, you're blaming the wrong guy.

Use slang and colloquial expressions
ONLY on suitable occasions.

Titles That Attract

EXERCISE 1: A title does for a story what the package does for many articles of merchandise. The latter attracts the eye of the person who is about to buy. Consequently manufacturers spend considerable sums of money to present their goods in eye-catching containers. Somewhat similarly a well-composed title captures a prospective reader who might otherwise ignore the article or story. Therefore the wording of a title is important. It is short, interesting, and it does not tell too much about the story.

Read the titles listed below and the brief descriptions of the material for which they were the headings. Prepare to state orally reasons why the title appears to have been carefully chosen.

1. ALL EARS - - - - - - A story of Canada's wheat crop bore this title. It described the characteristics of top quality grain, the conditions that produced the grain, and its uses.

2. ONCE UPON A SHEEP - - - This title was used for a story of wool.

3. BEETS FOR SWEETS - - - - A description of the sugar beet industry was presented under this heading.

4. LAND OF MILK AND MONEY - The story of Canada's dairy industry was told.

5. SEALS AHOY! - - - - - Under this title an account of Newfoundland's sealing industry appeared.

6. THE SHIRT TALE - - - - An account of the history of shirt wearing and making was given this title.

7. GASOLINE GYPSIES - - - - This story told about a family motor trip during which they tented each night and cooked all their meals in the open.

8. DEADEYE WITH DIBS - - - A newspaper article reporting an annual marble derby bore this heading.

9. PADDLE AND PALETTE - - - This story told of the life and work of Tom Thomson, famous Canadian painter of northern scenes.

10. POWER IN A PACKAGE - - - An exposition to tell about the construction and use of dry batteries was given this title.

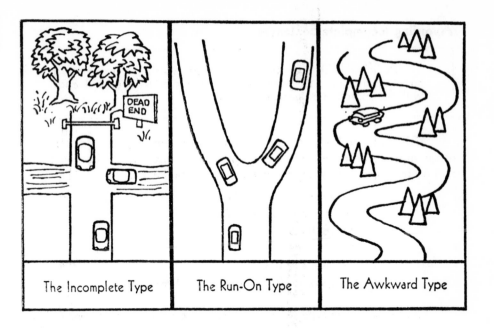

| The Incomplete Type | The Run-On Type | The Awkward Type |

VIII ▲ THE SENTENCE

Motorists use roads on which to travel from place to place. The driver of a car becomes annoyed when he unexpectedly finds himself on a dead-end street. He is in a dangerous situation if the road leads into another thoroughfare and no signs whatever have been erected to indicate who has the right-of-way. He is delayed on his journey if he has to take a road that twists and turns, and on which he must proceed slowly because he is not sure of what lies ahead.

Language is used to convey ideas. Readers or listeners will probably have trouble in understanding written or spoken language if the sentences resemble one of the three types of roads illustrated above. The use of incomplete sentences, of the run-on type of sentence, and of awkward sentences should be avoided.

The explanations and exercises in this chapter will help you to learn to write better sentences in order that you may communicate your ideas to others more easily, more accurately, and more pleasantly.

Develop your sentence sense.

Avoiding Incomplete Sentences

> A SENTENCE is a group of related words that expresses a complete thought. It always starts with a capital letter and ends with the appropriate punctuation mark.

Although you know the definition of a sentence, you do not always use complete sentences. For example, in a conversation between you and a chum the following expressions might be heard.

Go away for the holidays?
Spent two weeks near Calgary.
Travel by car?
No, flew by TCA.
Get as far as Lake Louise?
Camped not far from there for three days.

Language of this type may be appropriate on some occasions. You should not use this type of language, however, when talking to adults, especially strangers, or in your writing. If you are recording conversation, you must include in the quotations the exact words of the speaker.

A motorist dislikes running into a dead-end street. A reader is equally disturbed when he meets an incomplete sentence. Therefore inspect your sentences carefully when making revisions and while proofreading to *avoid the use of incomplete sentences and of sentence fragments.*

1. Look for words that have been carelessly omitted.

Example: The new boat tied securely to the dock.

2. Look for phrases that are unattached to any sentence.

Example: Paul's cottage is just west of the village. In a grove of cedars on the left side of the road.

3. Look for subordinate clauses that may be separated from the sentences to which they belong.

Example: Carl is going to teach me to water ski. As soon as the new motor arrives.

If the teacher's appraisal of your written work indicates that you are using incomplete sentences, review the exercises on pages 198 and 199.

Careful proofreading will detect incomplete sentences.

Avoiding Run-On Sentences

Read each of the following expressions.   Each is an example of the *run-on* or the *run-together* type of sentence.

1. The counsellor in our cabin put up with no nonsense, she was well liked by every girl.

2. We were ready for bed but the counsellor had not yet come in so we were able to find her pyjamas and sew them up and put them back where she would expect them to be and we pretended to be asleep and waited for her to return.

It is easy to imagine the trouble that motorists would encounter if all stop signs and other warning signs were removed.   When speakers or writers allow their thoughts to run together, readers and listeners have trouble also.   Read the following expressions and compare them with the examples above.   Which do you prefer?   Why?

1. (a) Although she would not put up with any nonsense, the counsellor in our cabin was well liked by every girl.

1. (b) Although the counsellor in our cabin would put up with no nonsense, she was well liked by every girl.

1. (c) The counsellor in our cabin put up with no nonsense.   She was well liked by every girl.

2. As the counsellor had not yet come in when we were ready for bed, we found her pyjamas and sewed them up.   After putting them back where she would expect them to be, we pretended to be asleep while we waited for her to return.

Note that the run-on type of sentences has been improved in one or more of the following ways:

1. By using punctuation correctly.

2. By combining two sentences into one sentence.

3. By breaking one long sentence into more than one sentence.

4. By making some principal clauses into subordinate clauses.

Watch for *run-on* or *run-together* sentences when you revise or polish your writing.   Before leaving any composition exercise, *read the material aloud to yourself* in a manner which does not disturb others.   In this way sentences of the run-on type are easily detected.

Turn to page 200 for an exercise on this type of sentence fault.

Avoiding Awkward Sentences

Roads may have many curves and sharp turns. Their surfaces may be bumpy. Along roads of this kind, drivers must proceed with caution.

Readers may encounter difficulties if sentences are poorly punctuated, or if the words are carelessly selected and arranged. Readers may then have to back up and re-read a sentence slowly in an attempt to get the real meaning. Sentences of this type may be called clumsy or *awkward* sentences.

Each of the following is an awkward sentence. Read each carefully and state why a change needs to be made to remove the difficulty which the reader encounters.

1. While sister put the soup on father set the table.

2. Paul found a quarter walking to school.

3. There were several cakes on the table which we ate.

4. Eric lost a dollar on the road which was all folded up.

5. At the age of eight my parents took me on my first airplane ride.

To obtain the real meaning of each of the above sentences, the reader must think carefully. Well-written sentences, however, enable the reader to proceed easily and quickly, and with complete understanding.

EXERCISE 1: (a) Rewrite each of the numbered sentences above and make the changes that are needed to produce a sentence whose meaning is quite clear.

(b) Add a comma to each of the following sentences to help the reader avoid a temporary misunderstanding.

1. I ate all the cookies and my spaniel looked very disappointed.

2. Mother grabbed the dog and the porcupine ambled off.

3. The girls washed the dishes and the boys removed the tables and chairs.

4. When John had finished his report on wall-papering the teacher said that he should make that his trade.

5. The pupils noticed the new map coming in after recess.

Proofread carefully and remove awkward sentences.

Using the Comma

Read each of the following sentences aloud in two ways. First read carefully, and group the words according to the position of each comma. Then read as if all commas had been removed.

1. Yes, the comma is an important punctuation mark.

2. When you are writing, boys and girls, use the comma carefully.

3. Use commas when doing written work in social studies, science, health and arithmetic, as well as in English activities.

4. Although a few commas may be necessary, pupils sometimes use them carelessly.

5. Too many commas, to be sure, hinder rather than help the reader.

6. Miss Martin, our teacher last year, warned us not to be comma shakers.

7. Miss Martin advised us to use a comma whenever necessary, but she emphasized that we should use them with great care.

8. After the teacher read, the pupils wrote the sentences to test their comma sense.

9. For information on the use of the comma in letter writing, consult the index of this book.

10. To intelligent boys and girls, suggestions are always helpful.

Does the use of commas make reading easier? Do commas sometimes help to make the writer's meaning clear? Read sentences 2 and 8 again rapidly, paying no attention to the commas.

Exercise 1: (Oral) Select and read the sentence or sentences from the above group which illustrate each of the following uses of the comma:

1. to separate words or phrases in a series

2. to set off introductory words such as yes, no, please, etc.

3. To set off the name of a person or persons spoken to

4. To set off expressions such as *however, for example, indeed,* etc.

5. to set off words of explanation

6. to prevent reading together two parts of a sentence that must be separated for clarity

7. to set off an introductory modifying phrase or clause

8. to separate the clauses of a compound sentence that are joined by *and* or *but*

Develop and use your comma sense.

Using the Comma:

EXERCISE 1: Write the following complex sentences and insert the commas that are needed after the introductory subordinate or dependent clauses.

1. Whenever I go to the library I always meet new friends.

2. Although these friends never speak I learn much from them.

3. After they have been my visitors for two weeks they return to their big home.

4. When they report to their housekeeper a card is placed in their back pocket.

5. As they rest on their shelves these books must look forward to their next outing.

(*Note:* The comma may be omitted between clauses which are short if no difficulty arises in the reading of the sentence.) Study these examples:

1. Between principal or independent clauses:

(a) Father punished the children, and the neighbours were happy.

(b) Father had to punish the children or he could expect more complaints.

2. Between an introductory subordinate clause and the principal clause:

(a) After Jim had eaten, Tim said he was hungry.

(b) After Jim had eaten we called for Tim.

EXERCISE 2: A phrase which is a modifier and which begins a sentence is usually followed by a comma. Write the following sentences and insert a comma after each opening phrase.

1. Looking into the bakeshop window John began to feel hungry.

2. By putting his hand in his pocket the lad realized that he could buy nothing.

3. On seeing a sign his face broke into smiles.

4. Without thinking a moment he applied for the job.

5. After washing dozens of baking tins this ambitious fellow was too tired to eat.

The pause that clarifies

A comma represents the pause that a speaker makes to help make his language clear.

A writer can easily determine where commas are needed by reading what he writes softly aloud.

Conciseness in Written Language

While proofreading your written work, look for opportunities to replace two or more words with one word without changing the meaning. Before making the possible change, consider which expression is more suitable. Sometimes the sound may be more natural if several words are used. At other times it may be desirable to be concise by using a single word.

EXERCISE 1: Practice this skill by replacing the italicized words in each of these sentences with one word. Do not change the meaning. State whether you prefer the longer or the shorter expression.

1. *At this time* I shall tell you what happened to the hero.

2. He made up his mind to investigate when the Indians *came in sight.*

3. They *made a sign* to him that they wished to talk.

4. He learned that they had *gone to look for* food without success.

5. *Before long* he was telling them that his food too was *in short supply.*

6. Attentively he listened as they slowly described everything that had *taken place.*

7. All of a sudden a brave *uttered a high pitched cry.*

8. A tornado was approaching *at great speed* across the plain.

9. Fortunately the storm *passed along the edge of* the area where the encampment was located.

10. How astonished they all were to see that the buffalo bones that had been *placed in a huge pile* for soup making had completely disappeared!

EXERCISE 2: Sentences may sometimes be improved by removing unnecessary words. Careful proofreading will detect and remove words which are not needed because other words in the same sentence convey the same meaning.

Prepare to read each of the following sentences orally with all unnecessary words deleted. Explain the changes you make.

1. On the day I arrived at camp I found everything that I had expected to find at camp.

2. Modern airplanes of today go faster than man ever expected to travel, in the past.

3. When I awoke from my sleep, it was broad daylight.

4. A variety of horses of all kinds were in the stables at the fair grounds.

Conciseness in Written Language:

5. By combining perseverance and concentration together, every pupil can achieve success according to his ability.

6. A fortnight had passed and yet no word had been had from the patrol that had been out for two weeks.

7. The search party continued its quest further until it reached the scene of the crash.

8. Although he was a clumsy awkward fellow, everyone was his friend.

9. A young London youth won the highest award at the festival.

10. By careful proofreading he was able to eliminate the errors completely.

11. Before the examinations I am going to study up on my social studies.

12. Last night I went to the community centre hoping to meet up with my friends.

13. Please fill the container full as I shall need as much as I can carry.

14. A capacity crowd that packed the auditorium was on hand for the school concert.

15. I am going to write an autobiography of my life.

16. The stranger, after looking carefully in all directions, crossed the street to the other side.

17. His unfinished project was left incomplete on the teacher's desk.

18. The girls spent many anxious hours eagerly awaiting the telephone calls.

19. She looked in the mirror while putting her hat on her head.

20. He took his shoes off his feet before lying down.

BE ON GUARD!

In both written and oral language, the following expressions are commonly used:

1. This *here* is the one I want.

2. That *there* is the dress I like.

3. Will you please repeat that *again*?

Avoid the unnecessary words by saying or writing:

1. This is the one I want.

2. That is the dress I like.

3. Will you please repeat that?

The Non-Lazy Sentence

A Grade VIII class was asked to write a sentence using the word *philatelist*. Many pupils had to consult their dictionaries before writing. When the teacher examined the results, she found that many pupils had written sentences like these. She copied them on the chalkboard.

1. Ted Brown is a philatelist.
2. Some famous men are philatelists.
3. Are you a philatelist?
4. There is a philatelist.

"Each of these four sentences," the teacher explained, "is what some books have called A LAZY SENTENCE." As she wrote the next sentence, she said, "This is a good example of A NON-LAZY SENTENCE because it indicates what the word *philatelist* actually means. The lazy sentences give us no idea."

5. By studying the stamps that come from all over the world, a philatelist learns a lot about geography.

The teacher said that she would ask the class, occasionally, to write non-lazy sentences, especially in connection with the words in the spelling lists. To help the pupils remember the characteristics of a non-lazy sentence, she placed a poster above the front chalkboard. It contained this message:

A NON-LAZY SENTENCE
avoids the use of
1. the introductory word "there" and "here"
2. pronouns
3. the words: man, woman, boy, girl, cat, dog, and their plurals
4. proper nouns

EXERCISE 1: Write a non-lazy sentence for each of these words. Refer to the poster to avoid the use of prohibited words. Use the dictionary.

Example: When the pupils saw the movements of the sun, moon, planets and stars projected by lights on the sky-like dome of the *planetarium*, interest in the study of astronomy was increased.

relinquish	adequate	optician	unintelligible	circulate
genuine	extravagant	carnival	auxiliary	juvenile

As your classmates read their sentences aloud, listen for violations of the non-lazy rules. Here is an opportunity for oral reading practice and for purposeful listening.

Does the writing of non-lazy sentences make you think?

Sentence Patterns

Following a pattern is common practice in home economics classes and in the industrial arts shops. Using sentence patterns provides an exercise in language that will develop the ability to use a greater variety of sentences.

Read each of the following sentences silently. Then listen as they are read orally by a classmate.

1. The game being over, the crowd quickly dispersed.
2. The food being ready, the hostess called the guests.
3. The dog being asleep, the boys stole into the orchard.
4. The lights being out, mother thought that we were asleep.
5. The store being closed, we returned without the material.

Note that in each sentence the phrase that precedes the comma might be reworded to begin with "as."

Example: 1. As the game was over, the crowd quickly dispersed.

EXERCISE 1: (a) Compose, and give orally, five sentences that follow the pattern of the group above.

Example: The door being open, Rover entered the kitchen and ate all the pork chops.

(b) Read orally the sentences at the top of this page and add suitable words to describe some of the nouns.

Example: The appetizing food being ready, the nervous hostess called the hungry guests.

(c) Write five sentences that follow the pattern of the group in the answer to part (b) of this exercise.

EXERCISE 2: (a) After reading the following sentences silently, compose five sentences that follow the same pattern and give them orally.

1. To have laughed then would have spoiled the story.
2. To have turned back would have been cowardly.
3. To have followed his advice would have brought better results.
4. To have worked harder earlier would have been wise.
5. To have written more carefully would have prevented the errors.

(b) Write five sentences that follow the pattern of those in 2(a).

(c) Read orally the sentences in 2(a) and add modifiers to some of the nouns.

Sentence Patterns:

EXERCISE 3: Use these sentences as directed in parts (a) and (b) of Exercise 2 on the preceding page.

1. Seeing that the results were good, he tried again.
2. Feeling that the wind was right, the crew set sail.
3. Realizing that the enemy had fled, the soldiers relaxed.
4. Knowing that the cake had fallen, the cook felt disgusted.
5. Believing that practice makes perfect, she repeated her scales.

EXERCISE 4: Use these sentences as directed in parts (a) and (b) of Exercise 2 on the preceding page.

1. After grabbing a cookie from the jar, the lad rushed from the kitchen.
2. After holding a match near the gasoline tank, the motorist took an unexpected journey.
3. After finding a quarter under the cushion, the boy felt wealthy.
4. After making a careful investigation of the accident, the appraiser completed his report.
5. After overhauling the tractor with extreme care, the hired man asked for a day off.

EXERCISE 5: Use these sentences as directed in parts (a) and (b) of Exercise 2 on the preceding page.

1. "Please let me go," he pleaded as he replaced the cookies.
2. "You should never have taken them," mother advised as she turned him over her knee.
3. "I'll never do it again," he promised as he squirmed to freedom.
4. "You have said that before," she sighed as she replaced the hairbrush.
5. "But this time I mean it," he shouted as he dashed off to play.

EXERCISE 6: (Oral) Compose at least five sentences that are similar in pattern to each of these. Note that each sentence in this group has been made according to a different pattern.

1. It was foggy and the warning bells were ringing.
2. When the reports were distributed, some pupils were very unhappy.
3. Having replaced the supercharger, the mechanic waved to the driver.
4. While setting the table, the guest broke a piece of fine crystal.
5. After mending the harness, the lad drove back to the field.

Use a variety of sentences for effective writing and speaking.

Sentence Variety

Examine each of the following pairs of sentences carefully. Then answer the questions that appear below them.

1. (a)—We had a wonderful day at the fair.
   (b)—What a wonderful day we had at the fair!
2. (a)—Quietly down the long dark hallway crept the cat.
   (b)—The cat crept quietly down the long dark hallway.
3. (a)—We shall plan the party after our homework is done.
   (b)—After our homework is done, we shall plan the party.
4. (a)—I caught the snake and my friend received the money for it.
   (b)—Although I caught the snake, my friend received the money for it.

Name the pair which illustrates the use of one of the following methods of obtaining sentence variety: (i) changing the order of the subject and predicate; (ii) using a complex instead of a compound sentence; (iii) using a kind of sentence which is different in function; (iv) changing the position of the modifiers.

> By referring to the index, you can find the pages in this text on which each of the above methods of obtaining sentence variety is presented more fully.

Now examine each of the following pairs of sentences. Prepare to analyse each sentence orally.

1. (a) The puck hit the referee.
   (b) The referee was hit by the puck.
2. (a) Joan made that cake.
   (b) That cake was made by Joan.
3. (a) The little boy broke that big window yesterday.
   (b) That big window was broken by the little boy yesterday.
4. (a) My aunt sent all these gifts for Christmas.
   (b) All these gifts were sent by my aunt for Christmas.
5. (a) The pupils complete all their work during the spare.
   (b) All their work was completed during the spare by the pupils.

Note in sentence (a) of each group that the subject is the doer of the action expressed by the verb. Note in sentence (b) of each group that the subject is the receiver of the action expressed by the verb phrase, and that the former subject or doer is named in an adverb phrase introduced by the preposition *by*. Practice changing sentences from type (a) to type (b) by completing the following exercises.

Sentence Variety:

EXERCISE 1: Analyse each of the following sentences mentally. Then rewrite each sentence and make the word which is now the object of the sentence the subject of the new sentence.

1. My teacher assigned all this homework.

2. Scholarly monks made copies of the first books.

3. An Austrian built the first bicycle in 1784.

4. The intrepid climbers reached the peak of Mount Everest.

5. The youngest competitor won the biggest prize.

When the subject of a verb represents the doer of the action, the verb is an ACTIVE verb. When the subject represents the receiver of the action, the verb is a PASSIVE verb.

EXERCISE 2. Compare the two paragraphs that follow. Note the use of passive verbs in the revised or second paragraph to obtain variety.

(a) I made this cake for you last night. I bought these new gloves for you in the city. I picked up this parcel for you at the post office today. As you can see, I want this birthday to be a happy one.

(b) I made this cake for you last night. Your new gloves were bought in the city. This parcel was picked up for you at the post office today. As you can see, I want this birthday to be a happy one.

EXERCISE 3: The passive verb can be used to make statements when it may be desirable not to name the doer of the action. Note the following:

(a) Father broke this plate when he was doing the dishes.

(b) This plate was broken when the dishes were being done.

In sentence (b) above the phrase "by father" was intentionally omitted.

Use the PASSIVE verb occasionally in both written and spoken language: (i) to obtain variety
(ii) to avoid naming the doer of the action.

The Imperative Sentence

An imperative sentence is one that gives a command or makes a request. The terminal punctuation mark is the period. In writing to give advice the imperative sentence is sometimes used very frequently as in the following paragraphs.

Read these paragraphs silently. Be prepared to read orally each of the imperative sentences.

Prize Your Eyes

Follow a few simple rules and you will insure your sight. If you have been provided with glasses, wear them. In your pocket they are of no help to you. When reading keep the light focussed on the page, not on your eyes. Consult your doctor if you have even the tiniest eye injury. Serious damage may result if it is not treated quickly.

Good health means good sight. Proper diet, exercise and sleep help you to see well. Headaches and listlessness can mean poor vision. Ask to see your doctor when these danger signals appear.

Bows and arrows, air rifles and darts are fun, but that fun can be spoiled if a blind eye is the result. Be careful. Aim only at targets when the path to them is clear. Have your friends stand well behind you until after you have finished shooting. One careless move can cost an eye.

Exercise 1: Consult your science and health textbooks, and the reference books in your classroom, school or public library to obtain information about the structure and the care of the eyes. Then select one of the following sentences and use it as the opening sentence in a written paragraph. Some paragraphs will require the use of several imperative sentences.

1. Your eyes are among your most valuable possessions.

2. To preserve your sight the following rules should be followed when *on the playground (or in school, at home, working with some tools)*.

3. The structure of the eye is as complex as any man-made instrument.

4. By being thoughtful all of us can be helpful to our blind citizens.

5. "Be wise! Take care of your eyes!" is, indeed, a good slogan.

IX ▲ PARAGRAPHS WITH A POINT

Before reading beyond this opening paragraph, study the illustration at the top of this page. If you were asked to put on paper the ideas which it suggests to you, what would you write? Would you attempt to include everything that you see there in a word picture? Does the sketch suggest a particular idea that you would like to comment upon? Think carefully before you read further.

The ideas for each of the four paragraphs that are printed on the next page came from the illustration above. Read the paragraphs and prepare answers to the questions that follow them.

Paragraphs with a Point:

1. Four tramps have just finished an evening meal. They have probably been riding a freight train all day and have stopped for the night. They are very poorly dressed. The biggest fellow has propped himself against a tree, and from the look on his face he must be having pleasant dreams as he has his after-supper nap. Another leans comfortably against a log as he whistles. A tall thin character is playing a mouth organ and the fourth appears to be singing. They look like a happy bunch.

2. Beneath a spreading willow tree, four shabby hoboes had just finished supper. Instead of doing the dishes immediately like good housekeepers, one fell happily asleep while the others filled the evening air with music. They certainly proved on that occasion that contentment does not depend upon the possession of wealth.

3. Good music is heard in a variety of places. It thrills large audiences in city auditoriums, and it makes the cowboy on the range less lonely. It can also help to make poor, homeless, but well fed hoboes feel that they are, indeed, "Knights of the Road."

4. Are expensive clothes and accessories really necessary? A rope will do for a belt. Safety pins will serve as buttons. Holes in shoes, even in the soles, will provide better ventilation. Some people still believe that comfort is more important than style in making us happy.

QUESTIONS:

1. To which of the four paragraphs might each of the following titles be applied: Music Magic, The Four Hoboes, Comfort or Style, Knights of the Road, No Housekeeper, Done Worrying, Just a Song at Twilight, Camped for the Night.

2. In which paragraph does the writer attempt to tell almost everything that is presented in the scene?

3. Which paragraph indicates that the writer was interested mainly in telling about the happiness that the scene suggested to him?

4. Which paragraph indicates that the writer was impressed most by the sounds which he imagined that he heard?

5. Which paragraph reveals that the writer used this opportunity to make fun of the fact that many people are slaves to fashion?

Paragraphs with a Point:

Paragraph number one on the previous page is an example of the type in which a writer attempts to tell as much as he can about a topic. The term FLOODLIGHT may be used to describe this type of paragraph. A floodlight is used to cast some light over a wide area. A FLOODLIGHT PARAGRAPH attempts to cover the topic by presenting brief comments on as many items as possible. The FLOODLIGHT type of paragraph is often useful.

Paragraphs 2, 3 and 4 on the previous page show that a writer may select one idea which a topic or theme suggests and that he will develop that single idea into a paragraph. This type may be called a SPOTLIGHT PARAGRAPH. A spotlight concentrates its light on one point. A small area only is very well illuminated. In a SPOTLIGHT PARAGRAPH all the sentences help to express the writer's ideas on one particular item. A SPOTLIGHT PARAGRAPH may also be called a paragraph *with a point of view*.

EXERCISE 1: Each of the following sentences might be used to introduce a paragraph. Read them carefully.

Note that the first sentence indicates that the writer may continue to add any number of different ideas about the evening meal. He may not be able, however, to say very much about any one of them. Will this sentence introduce a FLOODLIGHT or a SPOTLIGHT paragraph?

Each of the sentences from 2 to 7 might be used to introduce a SPOTLIGHT PARAGRAPH. Prepare to read to the class the words from each sentence that indicate the particular feature of the evening meal that the writer will tell about in that paragraph.

1. The evening meal at our house is the one time during the day when all the members of the family eat together.

2. Sometimes even father seems to be in a hurry to finish the evening meal.

3. During the evening meal, our family has a good discussion on the events of the day.

4. Oral games are a feature of the conversation at our house during the evening meal.

5. During the evening meal the whole family relaxes and watches television.

6. At the evening meal mother usually keeps the family guessing what the dessert will be.

7. Except on Saturday and Sunday, the evening meal at our house is a grab and run affair.

Paragraphs with a Point:

EXERCISE 2: Select one sentence from Exercise 1 on the previous page and develop it into a SPOTLIGHT PARAGRAPH. If you prefer, compose an original opening sentence and use it to introduce a spotlight paragraph on the theme "Our Evening Meal."

EXERCISE 3: Write a FLOODLIGHT PARAGRAPH on the theme "Women and Fashions." Use one of the following sentences to introduce your paragraph, or compose your own opening sentence.

1. To be in style a girl really has to keep busy.

2. The average girl's interest in fashions amuses the boys.

3. The magazines, movies and television make most girls very conscious of fashions.

EXERCISE 4: Select one of the following sentences and use it as the introductory sentence for a SPOTLIGHT PARAGRAPH on the theme "Women and Fashions."

1. Women do like to be in style, but some of the fashionable hats make them look a bit ridiculous.

2. Unfortunately many girls spend most of their allowance money at the hairdressers in order to keep in style.

3. Dad says that shoes are really to protect your feet, but when I look at women's fashionable footwear I begin to wonder if he is right.

4. Most girls seem to spend a lot of time and money to keep their nails in style.

5. My older sister's collection of cosmetics leads me to believe that some women must spend fortunes to have a fashionable face.

EXERCISE 5: Select one of the following topics and compose an introductory sentence for a SPOTLIGHT PARAGRAPH on that topic. Develop the introductory sentence into a paragraph. Compose a suitable title.

1. Music	3. Entertainment
2. Sports	4. Hobbies

152

Models to Examine

The following paragraphs were written by Grade VIII pupils on the theme "The First Snowfall." Read them silently. Then listen as each is read orally by a classmate. After the oral reading of each be prepared to quote sentences which are particularly effective. Discuss whether the writer painted only a word picture or conveyed a message which the experience brought to his mind. Paragraphs of the latter type are paragraphs with a point of view.

FAMILY THOUGHTS

The first snow had fallen throughout the night, and a glistening world awaited everyone. First, Tommy jumped out of bed onto the cold bare floor, ran to the window, and shouted with delight as he thought of the round hard snowballs he would make. His shout awakened his older sister who began visualizing the skiing parties which would soon take place. Mother's immediate reaction to Tommy's noise was to begin meditating whether last year's overshoes would fit and to figure out how many new ski-pants were absolutely necessary. As father sat listlessly looking at the white world he wondered whether the car needed new snow tires for the coming winter. I began to wonder how many other people had similar thoughts as they too viewed the first snow fall.

—David B.

TEMPORARY SPLENDOUR

As I walked in the softly falling snow which drifted lazily to its destination I noticed how fragile and lacy it looked as it floated downward to cover everything in sight with its downy flakes. Soon it lay there sparkling, clean and white, and as a ray of sun shone on it the brightness was dazzling. As I gazed at this wonderful white blanket I regretfully realized that by evening its beauty would have vanished.

—Catherine S.

MILES OF BEAUTY

Miles of glistening scenery could be seen ahead of me as I stood on the village bridge. Along each side of the rocky river banks the sparkling, silver-white, and downy snow covered the barren trees and bushes and shone brilliantly against the unclouded sky. Tiny cakes of ice covered with flossy snow bobbed gently up and down in the rippling river, like fairies dancing on flowers. They made a peaceful, pleasant, fantastic-like scene. This beautiful sight stretched on for miles until the sky seemed to swallow up the river. I will never forget such beauty which only nature could create.

—Jessie M.

Paragraphs with a Point of View

Read the following paragraphs which were written by Grade VIII pupils on the theme "An Autumn Scene." Note that each writer has done more than just write a word picture.

ALL TO ONE'S OWN

Deep in the forest, in God's haven for animals, is where you will find it. This inspiring place of poems and stories is among the tall majestic trees set in glorious autumn colours of red and yellow trim. There it is waiting. It may be beside a little field with a stream flowing by, or deep in a shady little nook. Wherever you come upon it, you will know that you have found peace of mind.

—Ross Dean

THE ARTIST'S PALETTE

Nearby, the rustling leaves were floating gently down onto a russet carpet. Still resting on the almost bare branches were a few beautifully painted leaves. In the background I saw the scarlet maples silhouetted against the dark evergreens. There was a flash of blue as a jay flew swiftly over the red sumacs into the forest. I shall never forget the beauty of that autumn hillside which made me realize how great was the power of nature to create such an awe-inspiring display.

—Janet W.

AUTUMN SPLENDOUR

What is the most beautiful autumn scene that you have ever looked upon? Probably it was in the woods when you beheld mother nature's display of fall colours. There the reds, yellows, browns, greens and oranges were pleasing and delightful to the eye. There are many places where you can go to enjoy the ecstasy of autumn grandeur. Going on hikes is one relaxing, enjoyable, and memorable way of witnessing this splendour. Why not try it some Saturday?

—Fay W.

EXERCISE 1: Write a paragraph on the theme "Rain." Let your paragraph have a particular point of view. Do you regard rain only as something which makes outdoor activity either impossible or unpleasant? Perhaps your paragraph could be written to show how one of the following reacts to rain: (i) a sportsman; (ii) a farmer after a long period of drought; (iii) the chairman of the picnic committee; (iv) a forest ranger; (v) the water works commissioner; (vi) rural residents who depend on wells and cisterns for their water supply.

X ▲ LETTER WRITING

Letter writing is not a modern custom. Long before the time of Christ, letters were being written in Babylon and Assyria on clay tablets. Letters written by people unknown to fame have been found among the papyrus discoveries in Egypt. The Romans, some of whom were in Britain from 44 B.C. until A.D. 400, developed the art of letter writing. From the letters written by the Roman governors of the distant provinces to their superiors in Rome much of the history of that period has been learned.

"Has the mail come yet?" is a question that young and old ask almost daily, for the receiving of mail is usually a joy at any age. Whether received at the post office, or in a box at the side of the road, or delivered by the postman, the mail is awaited expectantly. But do many people realize that the only sure way of keeping the replies coming is to send letters? Conversation by mail, as letter-writing is sometimes called, can only be carried on when the receiver of today's letter becomes the writer of tomorrow's.

In the encyclopedias we can read about the famous letter writers who have been remembered for the quality of the pen conversations which they carried on with their friends. None of us may ever write that well, but whenever we do sit down to compose we should remember that we shall be judged by our letters. If the order of the ideas that we present flows smoothly, we shall be known as clear thinkers. The absence of mechanical errors will indicate that we are careful. If the words are well chosen and the sentences carefully constructed, the letter will sparkle, and the reader will hear us speaking in a pleasant conversational tone.

Friendly letters enable us to carry on a conversation with friends and loved ones far away. We may be telling them about our day to day activities. We may be sending or answering an invitation. We may be expressing thanks for a gift, or for the hospitality of friends whom we have visited. If we are applying for a job, our business letters should present a clear and favourable word picture of ourselves. This will be done both by what we write and by the manner in which we write. Other business letters will be written to make inquiries, to convey complaints, to order goods, or to accompany remittances. Thus we see that letters play a very important role in our lives, and that the ability to write letters is one language skill that will always be used. Everyone needs to be able to write all kinds of letters well.

Letter etiquette is a term used to describe the rules that should govern the writing and handling of letters. A letter is always the private property of the person to whom it is addressed. It should never be read by another without permission. Good manners also demand that we should try to use the proper kind and colour of paper, to write legibly and neatly, and to use a form of letter which suits the occasion.

Now that almost everyone between the ages of six and sixteen attends school there is little need for the services of public letter-writers, the professional scribes who once did a flourishing business. The writing of love letters was one of their chief tasks. In the writing of those flowery courting letters, as in every other type of letter, they endeavoured to make the style and appearance of the letter suit the sender. A firm hand was used to indicate the handwriting of a young man, and a feeble scrawl to convey the message of a very old woman. The few public letter-writers that still exist are hired chiefly to write business letters that deal with such topics as taxes and the law. As education has become more universal the need for those who practise this ancient profession has almost disappeared. Seldom is a sign seen which reads: PUBLIC LETTER-WRITER—If you are in difficulty with any kind of letter, come in.

Letter Writing:

Anyone who can write can write a letter, and everyone has someone who would be pleased to receive it. To invent excuses for not writing is easy, but, by sitting down frequently and deliberately writing, talking-on-paper becomes easier and easier. Remember that letter-writing is one hobby that anyone can learn to enjoy, and that it is one that brings much pleasure to others.

EXERCISE 1: After reading the introduction to this chapter prepare to answer these questions orally.

1. Prepare to point out on a map the places named in the first paragraph of the introduction.

2. What is included in the envelope address of letters that are delivered "in a box at the side of the road"?

3. What word in the introduction is derived from the same root word as is the word "scribble"?

4. Read the phrase from the introduction that refers to the type of letter commonly known as "a bread-and-butter letter"?

5. List on the chalkboard the characteristics of a person who writes a letter which is pleasant to read and free from errors.

6. Explain the difference between a letter, a note, and a memorandum. Use your dictionary.

7. On what materials have letters been written down through the ages?

8. What phrases have been used in the introduction as synonyms for the words "letters" or "letter-writing"?

9. Which of the two main types or forms of letters would you write in order to invite the member of parliament for your area to a school activity?

10. Collect samples of "Letters to the Editor" from your daily paper. Why do newspapers publish letters of this kind? What is a pen-name? What is a pseudonym?

For further study: Consult any of the following reference books to obtain information about the history of letters and letter-writing.

1. THE BOOK OF KNOWLEDGE

2. BRITANNICA JUNIOR ENCYCLOPEDIA

3. COMPTON'S PICTURED ENCYCLOPEDIA

4. WORLD BOOK ENCYCLOPEDIA

Study the letter writer's guide—pages 159 and 160.

Letter Writing:

The following letter was written by a pupil who was about to enter Grade VIII. Following it is a reproduction of the list of letter topics which the writer made before composing the letter.

Read both the letter and the list of topics. Then read "Hints for Better Letters" on pages 159, 160. Discuss whether the writer followed the suggestions that are made in this section.

Cave Springs Camp,
Beamsville; Ontario,
August 7, 19 ...

Dear Daddy,

Yesterday when you left I didn't know if I would get homesick or not. So far I haven't had time to feel that way as there is so much to do. Usually the girls in our cabin are together. We all get along well. I like them very much.

We have a very nice counsellor in our cabin. Her name is Lynn Forester. We aren't sure yet what her camp name will be, but we think we shall call her "Ducky" because she's the swimming instructor. She seems to like that name.

Last night we had a camp fire. The leaders helped us to play several get-acquainted games. Soon we were all friends. There we learned a secret from Ducky. Tonight at the campfire we're going to have a corn roast.

Today we went swimming for the first time. I passed the test so I can swim in the deep end. As the water in the pool comes from a pond the sides are slippery.

Please tell that little brother of mine to remember to feed the hamster, the minnows, and the snails. You'll have to keep telling him because I know how he forgets.

I would like to get a letter very soon. I will write back during our rest period.

Love,

Lena May

Hints for Better Letters

① not homesick   3 the campfire

2 our counsellor ⑥ of cabin mates

4 swimming   5 feeding my animals

~~double bunks~~   ~~food~~   .

BEFORE WRITING: Many people find that their letters are easier to write if these steps are followed. By doing so, they usually have no need for a "P.S."

1. Make a list of the things you wish to talk about in your "one-sided visit."

2. If writing a reply, read your correspondent's letter again. Add to your list the topics in it which you wish to comment upon and the questions which you wish to answer.

3. Go over your list. Cross out the items that are not of importance. Number the remainder to indicate the order in which you wish to write about them.

WRITING THE LETTER: Picture in your mind's eye the position on the page of the five main parts of the friendly letter: (i) the heading; (ii) the salutation; (iii) the body; (iv) the complimentary closing; (v) the signature.

1. Remember that margins are needed on all sides, and that neatness gives the reader of your letter a friendly smile.

2. Write plainly and punctuate carefully in order that your letter may be easily read. You wish your reader to hear you speaking plainly and pleasantly.

3. (a) The HEADING includes your complete address and the date. Either slant or block form may be used. Block form is recommended.

(b) The SALUTATION says "Hello." *My dear Mother* and *Dear John,* are common. In a personal letter to a close friend some people use a salutation that sounds exactly as if they were meeting. They write "*Hi Tom*" or "*Hello Mary.*"

Hints for Better Letters:

(c) As you write the BODY of the letter, imagine that you are talking to the person to whom you are writing.

(i) Avoid unnatural beginnings such as these: *How are you? I am fine* (or) *I now take my pen in hand to write this note.*

(ii) Begin a new paragraph, indented from the margin, whenever you start writing about a new topic.

(iii) Answer the questions contained in the letter to which you are replying. Ask questions in your letter. They help the reader to hear you talking.

(iv) Include comments on the activities you describe. A few sentences like "What I'll do the next time I sit down before a bowl of steaming corn on the cob, I don't know!" make your letter more like conversation.

(v) Avoid ending the message with groups of words that are not sentences: *Hoping that this finds you as it leaves me, I am— Thanking you for your last letter, I remain,—Trusting you are well,*

Follow the suggestion that the first word in the last sentence should never end in "ing."

(d) The COMPLIMENTARY CLOSING, as the word *compliment* suggests, contains one or more kind words. Exaggerated closings, such as "Yours forever" should not be used. Choose a closing that is appropriate. *Yours truly, Yours sincerely, With love, Your loving daughter, Your son,* are among those that are acceptable. Begin the closing directly in line with the left side of the heading. Capitalize ONLY the first word. (See page 119 for the origin of the word "sincerely.")

(e) Your SIGNATURE is written on a line below the complimentary closing. It follows the form, slant or block, that was used in the heading. NO PUNCTUATION MARK follows the signature.

In writing a letter for a class or a group never sign the letter "*The pupils of Room Six*" or "*The Members of the Beaver Club.*" State in the message part of the letter for whom you are writing and sign your name.

4. Proofread every letter carefully. Check for the correct use of capital letters and punctuation, and for correct spelling.

5. Fold the letter properly in order that it will fit the envelope, *and* in order that it may be unfolded easily by its receiver.

Complete and Legible Address-ing Speeds the Delivery of your Mail

A CORRECTLY ADDRESSED ENVELOPE

W. JACKSON
324 GRANVILLE ST.
VANCOUVER 2, B.C.

Mr. ROBERT BARRY
186 PRINCESS AVENUE
BRANDON
MANITOBA

1. Always address to street and number, Post Office box or rural route number, where applicable.
2. Province.
3. Return address in upper left hand corner.
4. Stamp in upper right hand corner.

5. Use standard size envelopes, say, not larger than 4⅛ in. by 9½ in. nor smaller than 2¾ in. by 4 in.
6. When writing to places outside Canada always add name of Country in full.

Give your Mail the Attention
You Expect it to Receive

11

This illustration is reproduced from a booklet entitled POSTAL INFORMATION that is published by the Canada Post Office whose motto is "Servire Populo". Those last two words, when translated from the Latin, read "To Serve the People".

People must co-operate with the Post Office, however, to obtain the service they desire. They can do this by observing correct mailing procedures. When preparing letters for the mail, observe the pointers given above.

Writing Real Letters

1. *Letters* should be written *to sick classmates* who may be in hospital or confined to their homes with a communicable disease. Before writing, jot down brief notes on the happenings at school that will be of interest.

2. Write *letters to invite parents and friends* to school concerts, to Open House, or to Home and School or Parent-Teacher meetings. These letters must contain all the information that your parents or friends will need. See Exercise 3 on page 6.

Here is a recurring opportunity to write real letters. Give reasons why an invitation of this type is better than one run off on the school duplicating machine and given to you to take home.

3. *Letters* may often be used *to express appreciation*. When favours are received, courtesy tells us not to forget to say "Thank you." After we have enjoyed a visit with friends or relatives, we should send them what many people call a "bread and butter letter" to thank them for their hospitality.

You and your classmates might write real letters of appreciation to:

(a) your school custodian, after the Christmas or Easter vacations, to express thanks to him and his staff for making the classroom spick and span again.

(b) the Home and School or Parent-Teacher Association for its work on behalf of the pupils in providing the school with the prizes for some contest or for some other contribution to the welfare of the school.

(c) the secretary of your school board, asking him to express to the members of the board the appreciation of the class for some equipment or books that have recently been provided.

(d) the local clergyman for conducting the lessons in religious education.

4. Your inspector dislikes planning a visit to your school or to your class and finding no one present when he arrives. When your class plans to go on an excursion, or to have its annual picnic, you have an opportunity to write *a real letter to advise your inspector* of the dates.

Your teacher may decide to have the first letter of any type that you write composed co-operatively on the chalkboard.

In some cases your teacher may decide that only one letter, or perhaps three or four, should be selected by the class and sent to the person to whom each pupil has written.

Model Letters

This letter was written by a pupil to a friend in the same grade who was having some difficulties with school work. The purpose of the letter was to give, in a kindly way, some suggestions which might help that friend to improve.

Read the letter carefully. Then proceed with the exercises on the next page.

25 Parkhill Road,
Peterborough, Ontario,
September 15, 19 ...

Dear Susan,

When I was visiting you last summer, we looked through some of your tests. I remember that I noticed that you were not doing well with some of your school work. I have decided to write to you to give you some ideas on how to improve your work habits and have a better time at school.

I saw that you had lost a great number of marks due to poor spelling. I would like to suggest that you learn to spell all the hard words in your different subjects.

If you want to be successful, you had better not study in front of television. You can also improve by setting a special time aside. Study every night at that time in a room by yourself, with no radio going. You told me you sometimes study in bed. That never works, because you usually fall asleep. Study before going to bed. Susan, I believe it is better to do homework at night than at eight forty-five in the morning. I also find that if I'm eating while studying I just skim over my work.

When you are to have a test, I advise you to study a few nights before it. If you try to do all your studying in one night, you will put too much knowledge in your head at once. Upon receiving your results, your marks will not be as good as they could be.

Always keep your work books tidy, and always try to do your best writing in all of them. If you are absent, you should borrow someone's record books and bring your own notes up to date. If you have assignments to do, you should get them done soon after they are assigned to you.

➡ 163

Model Letters:

Reading will also help you in your study habits. Do a little reading each night. It will help you to learn more about your school subjects.

Sometimes, when studying for a test, it often helps if you write down a few questions. Ask one of your parents to ask you these questions, if they are not too busy. If one of them gives you some advice, take it! Parents are usually right.

I hope that these few suggestions will help you in your studies, and that you can improve your average. I usually follow them, and I still have time for recreation.

Your friend,

Sally Sutton

EXERCISE 1: There are eight paragraphs in Sally's letter. The first paragraph clearly states the purpose of the letter. The last paragraph describes the results that the writer expects.

(a) Write a word or phrase which states the topic of each of the paragraphs from number two to number seven.

(b) What does the writer do in the third paragraph to make the reader feel that she is listening to a conversation?

EXERCISE 2: Write a letter to a friend whom you know very well. *Either* give the suggestions you think will help that person to improve his or her school work *or* tell that person why you think they are making good progress in school.

Use a separate paragraph for each topic. Assume that your letter is being written from your home address.

If your letter suggests help and if it is kindly worded, your friend will be pleased to receive it.

EXERCISE 3: Imaginary letter writing may sometimes make it possible to write social studies notes in a more interesting way.

Study the model letter on the next page. Use the imaginary letter when the opportunity arises during the preparation of your written records in social studies work.

164

Model Letters:

This imaginary letter came from a Grade VIII class in a rural school. After listening to a school radio broadcast in a series on pioneer life in Upper Canada, the pupils pretended they were the early settlers, and that they were writing to relatives in the mother country to tell them about the construction of their new home.

York County, Canada,
July 6, 1815.

Dear Grandmother,

We certainly have had a busy time in the last few days! On our second day in the woods, Dad and Peter decided to start clearing the land. They worked for some time cutting down a very large tree. When it finally fell, it landed on the kettle which contained our dinner! Next one of the axes broke, and the other became too dull to cut with.

A few minutes later our nearest neighbour, Jake Hull, arrived. He lives only eight miles away. Were we ever glad to see him! That night he took mother and me home with him so we could have a rest. Dad and Peter stayed at our camp.

The next day Mr. Hull and his son, Eli, went to our place to help Dad and Peter finish the clearing for our cabin. By the following day they were ready for what the people here call a "bee." That is a gathering of all the men and women who are neighbours. They work together to get a particular job done.

What a rush there was at our "bee"! The men cut trees and split them in halves to make the logs to build our home which is twenty-four feet by eighteen. Raising the framework was the hardest and most dangerous part of all because the heavy beams or rafters might fall on anyone. Basswood trees were used to make the floor. Cedar shingles were put on the roof. White paper dipped in oil was used in place of glass.

While the cabin was being built, the women were preparing meals for the hungry hard-working men. By supper time our home was almost completed. Two men decided to stay over to finish shingling the roof. That night we slept in the cabin even though it was not finished. As I lay awake watching the stars winking at me through the trees, I was thinking how lucky we were to have such wonderful neighbours.

Your loving granddaughter,

Nancy

Abbreviations

ABBREVIATIONS are the shortened forms of words. They ALWAYS REQUIRE PERIODS. They are used when the space available will not take the written word in full. Abbreviations are most commonly used in the headings and addresses of letters.

EXERCISE 1: In writing to school superintendents, inspectors, and teachers, the abbreviations for university degrees are often used.

On a page in your language book copy these names of degrees in alphabetical order in a column: Master of Arts, Bachelor of Arts, Bachelor of Pedagogy, Bachelor of Education, Master of Education, Doctor of Philosophy, Bachelor of Science, Doctor of Pedagogy, Associate of the Royal Conservatory of Toronto, Bachelor of Library Science, Bachelor of Music.

Copy these abbreviations beside the name for which each stands: B.Paed., A.R.C.T., B.L.S., D.Paed., B.A., B.Ed., M.A., B.Sc., Ph.D., Mus.Bac., M.Ed.

EXERCISE 2: Abbreviations are frequently used when writing dates. For example, Hallowe'en may be written *Oct. 31, 1957* or *31 Oct., 1957* or *31/10/57*. Note that in the last method the order is day, month, and year. Never mix these methods of abbreviating dates by using *Oct. 31/57*.

Write this year's date for each of the following occasions using either the first or second method, and the third: your birthday, April Fool's Day, Groundhog Day, Canada's Birthday, Queen Victoria's Birthday, the spring equinox, the autumn equinox, St. John de Baptiste Day, United Nations Day, St. Valentine's Day, St. Patrick's Day.

EXERCISE 3: On a page in your language notebook write the heading *Abbreviations I Have Met*. When you encounter new abbreviations in the newspapers, on signs, in advertisements, or in captions beneath pictures, write them, in a column, on this page. Consult a dictionary for the words for which each abbreviation stands.

REMEMBER:

1. The use of abbreviations is seldom permitted within a sentence.

2. The greatest use for abbreviations is in the headings and the addresses of letters.

3. Abbreviations for place names when used on envelopes may cause confusion. Write all place names in full.

4. When in doubt whether to use an abbreviation, always write the word in full.

---

19 Linden Street,
Carleton Place, Ontario,
May 5, 19 . .

Mr. George M. Smiler, Owner,
Smiler's Super Service Station,
Seaview, Ontario.

Dear Mr. Smiler,

When Dad came back from his fishing trip, he told me that this year your son, David, will be working in a chemical plant near the university. I have been wondering if you might be looking for a young fellow to pump gas and do the odd jobs around your service station during the holidays. As I would like to make a little money while we are at our cottage this summer, I am writing to say that I would like to work for you.

As you know, I have always been interested in cars. Therefore a job where I can be near some of the biggest and the newest of them appeals to me. As I am big for my age and fairly strong I think I can be of some help to you. I would do my best.

We shall be going to the lake over the holiday week end this month. I shall come in to see you as soon as we arrive. I do hope that this is the first application that you have received.

Yours truly,

Paul Maynard

Note the following points that pertain to a business letter:

1. Use white paper of a standard size, 8½ by 11 inches. Write on one side only.

2. The inside address must be the same as that which appears on the envelope.

3. The signature must be complete.

A girl's signature should appear: (Miss) Helen Harper

A married woman's signature appears: Jane Smithers
          (Mrs. F. B. Smithers)

Business Letters:

These exercises provide all the material, in the proper order, for sample business letters of the type which Grade VIII pupils write most frequently. Read the contents of each letter carefully. Decide how much goes in each of the six parts of the business letter. Write each letter in its proper form using capitals and punctuation as required. Two paragraphs are required in the body of each letter.

EXERCISE 1: A LETTER OF APPRECIATION.

mountain view school west vancouver british columbia february 24 19 .. mrs j c anderson 2573 spencer ave west vancouver british columbia dear mrs anderson the pupils of grades seven and eight of this school are still talking about the know canada geography contest that your association planned for the schools of this district by taking part in the preliminary contests to select our school representatives all of us have learned much more about our great country we know that you and the other members of the executive of your association worked hard to make this contest a success we send all of you our thanks for making one part of our school work much more exciting and interesting yours sincerely margot french

EXERCISE 2: A LETTER OF INVITATION.

queen elizabeth school royal drive maytown ontario march 5 19 .. mr i c weller elementary school inspector 15 valley road maytown ontario dear mr weller after christmas the pupils of room 14 started planning for education week we decided to make a display of something of which we might be proud after dividing into two groups we worked our hardest to develop something of real interest one project is called transportation through the ages the other is entitled sport and entertainment through the ages we have enjoyed the work we hope all who see the display will find their visit both pleasant and profitable on behalf of the class i wish to invite you to visit and inspect our work you may drop in any time between 3.00 and 4.30 on either march 6 or 7 the projects will be displayed in the school cafeteria we shall look forward to receiving your comments on our work yours sincerely susan blair

EXERCISE 3: A LETTER TO ACCOMPANY A REMITTANCE.

maple school r r 2 endover ontario november 17 19 .. excello sporting goods ltd 29 playfield road hamilton ontario gentlemen the pupils of this school wish to thank you for filling our order for the classroom activities kit so promptly and for sending it on approval after giving a demonstration for our parents we had no trouble in raising the money we needed a post office money order for the full amount of your bill is enclosed yours truly brian stork

168

Business Letters:

The following addresses and suggestions are included here to indicate the type of business letter that the pupils of Grade VIII might write. All pupils, of course, would share in the planning and writing of the letters, but only one letter would be sent to each address. *If one of the pupils' letters were to be sent it should be countersigned by the teacher.*

1. The Canadian Audubon Society, 46 St. Clair Ave. E. Toronto 5, Ontario.

This letter would be to request the free information which is available to tell Canadian boys and girls about the *Audubon Junior Club*. The society promises that participation in the activities of this club will open up a new and exciting world of adventure.

2. The Canadian Red Cross Society, 95 Wellesley Street East, Toronto 5, Ontario.

If the address of the Provincial Division Headquarters of the Canadian Red Cross Society is not known, send a letter to this address requesting the information. Then letters could be written to inquire about subscription rates to the Canadian Red Cross Junior Magazine and about the procedure for forming a Junior Red Cross Club in your school or classroom.

3. The United Nations Association in Canada, 237 Queen Street, Ottawa, Ontario.

To obtain material to be used in preparing for the observance of UN DAY, October 24, or in studying about Canada's part in the work of this organization a letter of request might be sent. A letter might also be written to inquire about the service the association provides to encourage young Canadians to correspond with students in other parts of the world.

4. The Superintendent of Publications, The Queen's Printer, Ottawa, Ontario.

Canadian Government Publications include low-priced books that are reliable, informative, timely, and interesting. Descriptive pamphlets and order forms might be requested.

5. The Canadian Library Association, 46 Elgin Street, Ottawa, Ontario, Canada.

A letter might be sent early in October to ask for order forms for book lists, posters, and other materials that would be useful in celebrating Book Week which comes in November.

XI ▲ RECORDS AND REPORTS

School Newspapers

The illustrations on this page and on page 173 show both the classroom paper and the school year book type of publication. Production of papers of this kind is an interesting project for a Grade VIII class.

Read the descriptions of these papers presented on the next two pages. With your teacher's help, organize a staff to produce the paper. Perhaps your room will wish to make arrangements to co-operate with other Grade VIII classes. In this activity every pupil has the opportunity to participate by contributing material for the various sections of the paper.

School Newspapers:

What kind of newspaper or year book will be produced? These descriptions of the school and classroom productions shown in the illustration on page 170 may help you to decide.

1. The KING ALBERT SCHOOL YEAR BOOK is typical of the kind of school year book that can be published when the senior class or classes in the school assume responsibility for its preparation. The enterprising or fortunate staff for this particular year book was able to obtain the co-operation of an engraver and a printer to supply five pages of photographs of school activities. Twenty pages of copy material were stencilled on 8½″ by 11″ paper.

2. The EASTSIDE TIMES is a class newspaper of twenty-six pages printed on 8½″ by 14″ paper. The copy was typed on stencils for duplicating. Printing appears on only one side of each sheet. On page one the following heading appears:

> THE EASTSIDE TIMES
> Queen Elizabeth School
>
> Vol. One — Established 1954 — Number 6
> A Grade Eight Publication.

Beneath the heading the titles of the editorial staff and of the sections of the paper are listed. Included are the following: Editor, Assistant Editors, Production Advisor (the teacher), Class News, Current Events, Classified Ads, Social Studies, English, Science, Health, Mathematics, Sports, Music, Illustrations and Designs, School News. Opposite each of these the names of the responsible pupils are given.

A feature of this paper is a section entitled "Tips for Teens" which includes well-written items on "Spare Time Jobs," "Baby Sitting Hints," and "Courtesy in Your Teens."

3. The STUDENT VOICE is another school paper for the production of which the students of Grade VIII were responsible. This paper has a stiff yellow cover which makes it very attractive. The Editor's Message from this paper will be of help to other Grade VIII pupils as they plan their own papers. The editor wrote as follows:

> As our newspapers and magazines reflect the life of our country, our school paper should reflect the life and activities of our school. Your editorial staff has kept this in mind in bringing to you this issue of the STUDENT VOICE.
>
> Our special thanks go to the representatives from Grades

171

School Newspapers:

> 7 and 8, Vicky Weir and Bill Turner, for the very fine work that they have done. Our thanks also go to the representatives of the other grades whose efforts made it possible to produce our paper. We are grateful to all who have articles in this paper, and to all generally who certainly helped us immensely with their co-operation.
>
> We express a special "Thank you" to Miss Hart and Mr. Dawson, our councillors, and to Miss Grey, our chief printer.
>
> We do hope all our readers will enjoy this paper.
>
> —Sue McK., Grade 8

4. The CENTRAL STAR is a paper of more modest proportions. It consists of only four pages. It was duplicated on a hectograph. It contains sections for school sports, poems and stories, interesting school news, and a prominent announcement which reads: THE PROCEEDS FROM THE SALE OF THIS PAPER WILL BE GIVEN TO THE SCHOOL SPORTS FUND.

5. The GROVE SCHOOL REVIEW is a fourteen page paper. It contains stories, poems, and accounts of interesting happenings. Pupils in all grades contributed. Small pieces of ribbon in the school colours were stapled to the cover of this annual publication. They can be seen in the illustration.

6. The Q.E. YEARBOOK was duplicated by using stencils. The cover pages of this paper were attractively coloured by pupils who used pencil crayons. Features of this paper include: "Biographies of the Teachers" (written by pupils following interviews); a "Just for Fun" section; "The Music Corner"; "The Drama Corner"; "The Poets' Corner"; "Overheard Here and There"; "Who's Who" (This section presents a five to eight line report on every pupil in the class. These reports are exceptionally well-written, and every comment is in the best of taste); "Looking Back-Items of Interest" (This section includes short reports on the highlights of the year, including one of the inspector's visits).

How often should a school or class paper be published? Many of the larger schools produce an annual YEAR BOOK, usually in the spring term. Many classrooms and rural schools turn out a newspaper at Christmas, at Easter, and again before the summer vacation.

How is a class organized to produce a newspaper or magazine? A committee will be named to carry out the work. The chairman will be the editor-in-chief who will have assistant editors in charge of the various sections: news, literary, humour, sports, music, and art. These people will encourage all members of the class to make contributions. They must select the material that will be used and prepare it for publication. Under the editor will be other helpers to do the printing, duplicating, stapling, and distributing.

172

School Newspapers:

The production of school newspapers provides more than purposeful practice in writing stories, poems, records, and reports. If pupils keep their own copies in a carefully selected spot at home, they will be able to turn to them in the years to come and to read them again and again with pleasure. If copies of each issue are kept in the school library, they will become items of interest to visitors and to all the new pupils as they come along through the grades.

SOME SUGGESTIONS:

1. The editorial staff for the school paper must be carefully chosen. Their messages, or editorials, will be the most important items in the paper. The quality of its contents will also depend on their editorial work. They must be able to edit or revise the material that is contributed by other pupils.

Before naming the editor-in-chief and the assistant editors, the class should first do the exercises on page 174. The staff should then be selected from that group of pupils who complete both the oral and written work most effectively.

2. Interesting story writing contests can be conducted by using one of the exercises on pages 50, 51, and 52, or on pages 54 and 55 of this text. All pupils would be eligible to compete. The editorial staff might be the judges. Some Grade VIII classes, that produce bi-monthly papers, carry serial stories developed from these opening paragraphs. Autobiographies and puzzle-pen-portraits are other good contest themes. Consult the index for the page numbers.

3. Contests for the writing of poetry will also stimulate interest in the class or school paper. Use the material in Chapter XII to obtain help in verse making.

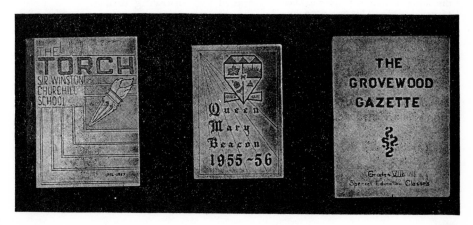

Writing Editorials

A school newspaper, like a daily newspaper, should contain both news stories and editorials. News stories give information about events. An editorial expresses the editor's opinion on some topic. It may also contain a plea for action.

Read the editorial reprinted on this page. Note the theme or topic of each paragraph: (i) Newspaper Boy Day; (ii) The Young Merchant's Work; (iii) One Way to Express Appreciation.

Examine the punctuation used by the writer. Read aloud a sentence that uses a dash, one that uses a semicolon in place of a coordinate conjunction, one that uses a coordinate conjunction to emphasize a conjunction, and one that uses a colon.

He Serves You

Today is Newspaper Boy Day across this country, and across this continent. Although it honors him, it is not a holiday, for he is a young merchant in business for himself—a business that calls for him to work each weekday of the year. But it is a special day for all that, a time to express esteem for the young army of 2,000 who turn out every morning to deliver The Globe and Mail—often before their customers are up.

We are with good reason proud of this army of—as we called them—young merchants. For each carrier boy buys his papers at wholesale and sells them at retail, and he makes his entire profits out of sales and collections. He is also a public servant, a part, just as the rest of us are part, of a vast and complex apparatus. He is the front man; he brings the world to your door and is your direct and intimate contact with that world. He is trained in business methods, and very, very often he rises to eminence in his mature years.

Your carrier boy is worth knowing. He is also worth encouraging; but he doesn't ask for help. What he does ask, and what we ask for him, is that finest of all inspiration: prompt payment when he comes to collect. He wants no finer stimulant than that; and he could encounter no greater discouragement than to have to make repeated trips—at his own expense—for his money. So that is the simple but really great contribution which each of us can make to Newspaper Boy Day—and to the grand lads themselves whom it honors.

Exercise 1: Cut from discarded newspapers two editorials that are written on topics of which you have some understanding.

Prepare to read each editorial aloud to the class, and to explain the editor's purpose in writing it.

Exercise 2: Write an editorial of at least two paragraphs on one of the following topics:

(1) Spelling Bees or Public Speaking Contests—Are contests of this type worthwhile school activities?

(2) Should schools participate in contests sponsored by companies for advertising purposes where prizes such as television sets are awarded?

(3) School Uniforms for Both Boys and Girls.

(4) More Courtesy in Crowded Corridors.

(5) Spectators Should Display More Sportsmanship.

Book Reviews

The writing of book reviews provides a real *Target for Today*. (See page 19.) When you do this kind of writing, your purpose or aim is to interest your readers in a particular book and to help them decide whether to read it.

Several types of book reviews or book reports are presented in this section of DEVELOPING LANGUAGE SKILLS—GRADE VIII. Read each of these reviews. Select the one that best creates interest in the book it describes. Be prepared to give reasons for your choice.

1. This type of review is sometimes called A DUST JACKET REPORT as it resembles the outline of the story that sometimes appears on the protective paper cover that is provided with a new book. It is written in paragraph form. It introduces the characters and presents a brief but incomplete summary of the story.

FROZEN FIRE

From the moment Peter Warner agreed to take young Bud Chandler on his expedition in search of medicinal herbs in the Amazon jungles, trouble began to hit his party.

The trouble centred around half an ancient Incan treasure map which Bud owned and which he was determined to follow. Dom Pedro Solino, a sinister little Brazilian, wanted that map. Thomas Brown, a ruthless and unsavory character, was the only foreman that Warner could obtain for the expedition.

What happened on that search for a fabulous treasure is the thrilling story of Armstrong Sperry's FROZEN FIRE. It is a book filled with adventures ranging from encounters with headhunters to those with deadly snakes. The reader is left feeling that he has spent a very harrowing month in the dark and mysterious Brazilian jungles. If you like excitement, don't miss FROZEN FIRE.

Note that this report arouses the reader's interest by providing the answers to these questions:

1. Who was the leader of the expedition?

2. What was Bud Chandler's main ambition?

3. Who coveted Bud's possession of the map?

4. Why is the foreman expected to contribute to the excitement?

Book Reviews:

2. A form of book report which many girls and boys like to write is illustrated in this review which was written by a Grade VIII pupil. It is a letter written to the teacher. In it, as in any friendly letter, the pupil seems to be talking on paper. Perhaps that is why this type of report seems easier to write and why it is preferred by many.

466 King George Street,
Peterborough, Ontario,
April 30, 19 —.

Dear Mr. Crown,

The book which I read this month and which I shall tell you about in this letter is entitled New Zealand. It gives the reader a very vivid description of this picturesque country as it is today. It also tells much about the history of this southern land.

The section which I enjoyed most told about the land's first inhabitants. The Maoris, who are the natives of New Zealand, came over the sea to this country centuries ago. They called the land "Aotearroa" or "Land of the Long White Cloud". At first they resented the arrival of the white men. Many cruel battles were fought, but it is now over eighty years since the last shot was fired. The Maoris signed a solemn treaty by which they now live in peace with the white men.

I enjoyed this book very much. I am sure that anyone who reads it will be as fascinated by it as I was.

Yours truly,

Gary Grierson

Book Reviews:

3. This type of book report is made by using a very simple outline. In the classrooms in which these reports were used the pupils wrote on unlined 8½ by 11 inch paper and used only one side of the sheet. The reports were kept in folders on a library shelf in order that all the pupils might read them.

(a)   BOOK REPORT No. 1

1. *Name of Book*—The Swiss Family Robinson

2. *Author*—Johann R. Wyss

3. *Summary*—

The family in this story had set out from England when a fierce storm came upon their ship. The island on which their wrecked vessel was cast appeared deserted. The wreck itself proved to be a treasure trove that supplied the Robinsons with everything they needed until they could explore the amazing island upon which they had been marooned, and until they could build their ingenious tree house in which they lived for some time.

As the years passed and the memories of their faraway European home faded, the Robinsons fell in love with the land which they had named New Switzerland. One day when a ship anchored off shore and they were offered passage back to civilization, they found that they couldn't bear to leave their island home.

This is a very good book which I recommend to either boys or girls.

—Karen Ann W.

(b)   BOOK REPORT No. 2

1. *Name of Book*—The Mystery of the Cave

2. *Author*—Betty Anderson

3. *Summary*—

This book tells a story about two boys who went to a training school. They had certain rules to follow, and if they didn't obey they were punished.

One day they were out in a boat fishing. As they were not catching anything they decided to explore. They looked carefully to see whether there was anyone on shore and then started towards Black Mike's Cave. When they got inside the thieves came, and—

Oh, I must not tell you what happened. Read the book for yourself. Don't forget the title—"The Mystery of the Cave."

—Donna F.

Outlines for Book Reports

The headings for two other types of book reviews are given below.

(a) This outline is usually duplicated on sheets of 8½″ by 11″ paper. If more space is needed to complete any item, the reverse side of the sheet is used.

Book Report

Student's Name: *Date:*

Title of Book:

Author: *Publisher:*

Number of Pages: *Date Begun:*   *Date Finished:*

Type of Book: Bracket the best word to describe it—Adventure, Animal Story, History, Biography, Science, Travel, Drama, Children of Other Lands, or _____

A Short Outline of the Story:

The Character or Characters I Remember Best and Why I Remember Them:

Why I Liked This Book or What I Liked Most About This Book:

Words Which I Learned from This
Book and Which I Can Now Use: *Their Meaning:*

Books by the same author which I would like to read, or other remarks:

(b) The report that is made by using the following headings is usually written on foolscap. The headings are written in the left hand margin.

1. *The Title:*
2. *Time of the Story:*
3. *The Characters:*
4. *The Story:*
5. *Why I Liked or Disliked This Book:*

(NOTE: For completed models of the above reports see Developing Language Skills—Grade VII, page 169.)

The illustration above shows six booklets which were prepared by Grade VIII pupils in carrying out an exercise entitled "Romantic Names." The covers, as you can see, have been suitably decorated and lettered.

Beneath the covers are the pages which were cut to have the same shape. On these pages, after consulting reference books, the pupils wrote an account of the place named on the cover. Their purpose was to tell some interesting facts about the place and to indicate why the romantic name had been given to it. Two of these accounts follow.

Alaska—Uncle Sam's Ice Box

Uncle Sam's Ice Box was purchased by the United States from Russia in 1867, which is also the year of Canada's birthday. It includes the Aleutian Islands which stretch for thousands of miles out into the Pacific Ocean. Its winters are cold and dark but the short summers have very long days.

Romantic Names:

Alaska, which is larger than the province of Ontario, has many mountains, the highest peak being Mt. McKinley. At one time this country contained only Indians and Eskimos. Now, since the Alaska Highway was built north from Edmonton up through the Yukon, many Americans, including soldiers and airmen, live there. Those people who coined its nickname because they believed it to be frozen worthless wasteland would now be surprised to see its main cities, Juneau, the capital, Skagway and Fairbanks.

I would like to see Uncle Sam's Ice Box some time, in the summer.

—R. St. D.

The Roof of the World

"Himalayas" is a Sanskrit word meaning "Abode of Snow" and is the name of the world's highest mountain system, which separates the peninsula of India from the elevated tableland of Tibet. This great rampart of mountains stretches from the Indus River on the west to the Brahmaputra on the east.

The Himalayas consist of several parallel mountain ranges. They contain the loftiest peaks in the world of which the highest, Mt. Everest, rises to a height of 29,141 feet. A New Zealander, Sir Edmund Hilary, and Tenzing Norgay were the first to conquer it.

Vegetation and animal life are varied at the lower levels. These mountains are particularly famous for their wealth of rhododendrons. Tigers, leopards, elephants and monkeys are numerous. The home of the yak is also in this region.

—C. M.

EXERCISE 1: Select one or more of the topics from the list given below. Using encyclopedias, geographies, and other books find the facts that will be useful in writing an interesting account on each of the topics. Using ONLY words or short phrases jot down these facts on a page in your exercise book. (Do NOT copy whole sentences from the reference books.) Use these jottings as a source of ideas during the writing of your account in a class period.

Prepare a suitably illustrated cover for the page or pages on which the transcribed copy of your corrected account is written. This cover should also contain the romantic name in carefully made letters. See the illustration on page 179.

Romantic Names:

1. Mexico —Land of Golden Empires
2. Atlantic Ocean —The Sea of Darkness
3. Australia —The Island Continent (or)
   The Land of the Golden Fleece
4. Belgium —Land of the Carillons
5. Bermuda —Coral Island of the Atlantic
6. Bolivia —Tin Roof of the Andes
7. Canada —The Land of Waterways
8. Cape of Good Hope —The Cape of Storms
9. Chile —The Shoestring Republic
10. Copenhagen —Merchant's Harbour or Haven
11. Cuba —The Sugar Mill of the Antilles
12. English Channel —The Narrow Seas
13. Mount Everest —Goddess, Mother of the World
14. Egypt —The Gift of the Nile
15. Florida —The Empire of the Sun
16. Fuji Yama —Sacred Mountain
17. Gibraltar —The Pillars of Hercules
18. Thames River —Liquid History
19. Norway —Land of the Midnight Sun
20. Winnipeg —Gateway of the West
21. The Taj Mahal —The Crown of Palaces
22. Panama —The Bridge of the World

EXERCISE 2: Make a class collection of Romantic Names to add to the list presented in Exercise 1 above. Be ready to explain orally where you obtained the "Romantic Name" which you bring to class. Some may be found by reading magazines like the *National Geographic*. Others may be learned by talking with adults.

An Assignment for Adventuresome Reporters

These topics are for those pupils who plan to be newspaper reporters of the type that are called foreign correspondents who travel to remote parts of the world for their stories.

To write one of these stories you will have to show that you possess many of the qualities of a real adventuresome reporter who has perseverance, initiative, imagination, courage, and the ability to write to make your readers feel that they have been with you on your journeys.

Select one of these topics. By using encyclopedias, geographies, and other reference books find interesting facts about that topic. After completing your research weave these facts into a story which tells about your imaginary experiences on an adventure which you hope may some day come true. Illustrate your story with your own sketches.

1. My Visit to Pitcairn Island: Here you live and talk with the descendants of the men who staged the mutiny on the *Bounty*.

2. Climbing to the Rim of Mount Izalco: This volcano in El Salvador has been erupting every fifteen minutes for one hundred and seventy-five years.

3. A Non-stop Pole-to-Pole Flight: This story will tell about your experiences as you travel over zone after zone in the aircraft of your choice on a route chosen for its interest.

4. I Walked the Bottom of the Sea of Galilee: This account reveals what you saw and did as you explored beneath the surface of this sea located in the Holy Land.

5. Through the Northwest Passage: Follow the route which many early explorers sought and which the R.C.M.P. vessel *St. Roch* followed. Take your trip on any craft you choose.

6. To the Top of Kilimanjaro: This mountain in Africa causes many adventurers to dream of ascending to its peak.

7. In the Heart of the Afghanistan Jungle: Here you will tell about your adventures in what is the least-known and most inaccessible jungle in the world.

8. By Gypsy Caravan in Spain: You join a band of real gypsies, one of the few that still roam through Europe. You live as they live and report your experiences. Perhaps you can quote from some poems about gypsies as if your adventures help you recall the lines you read in school.

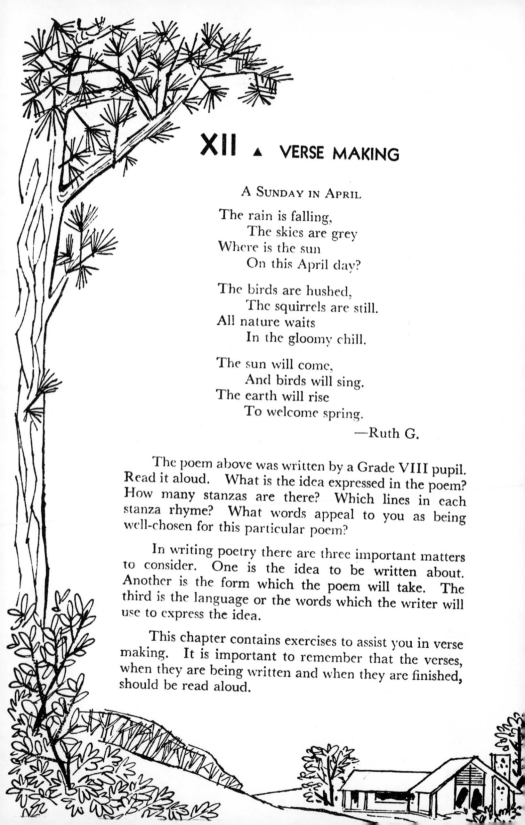

XII ▲ VERSE MAKING

A Sunday in April

The rain is falling,
 The skies are grey
Where is the sun
 On this April day?

The birds are hushed,
 The squirrels are still.
All nature waits
 In the gloomy chill.

The sun will come,
 And birds will sing.
The earth will rise
 To welcome spring.

—Ruth G.

The poem above was written by a Grade VIII pupil.
Read it aloud. What is the idea expressed in the poem?
How many stanzas are there? Which lines in each
stanza rhyme? What words appeal to you as being
well-chosen for this particular poem?

In writing poetry there are three important matters
to consider. One is the idea to be written about.
Another is the form which the poem will take. The
third is the language or the words which the writer will
use to express the idea.

This chapter contains exercises to assist you in verse
making. It is important to remember that the verses,
when they are being written and when they are finished,
should be read aloud.

Verse Making:

One of the enjoyable qualities which many people find in music is the rhythm. Some of us respond by keeping time with our feet, our hands, or our head. It is this same quality to which we respond when poetry is read aloud. Read the following two-line stanza aloud:

> I saw a bird upon the wing,
> A happy song he had to sing.

Read it aloud again, beating the time with one hand. You should find four beats in each line. Repeat the rhythm by saying aloud:

> And ONE and TWO and THREE and FOUR,
> And ONE and TWO and THREE and FOUR.

Each beat is known as a *foot*. There are four beats, or four feet, in each of these two lines of verse. Read the following aloud:

> I saw | a bird | upon | the wing,
> A hap | py song | he had | to sing.

Each foot contains two syllables. The second syallable is stressed and is called the *accented* syllable. The first syllable is not stressed and is called the *unaccented* syllable. This pattern of verse may be illustrated as follows:

> Ĭ sáw | ă bírd | ŭpón | thĕ wíng,
> Ă háp | pў sóng | hĕ hád | tŏ síng.

This rhythm pattern may be written as follows:

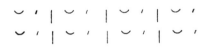

EXERCISE 1: Write a second line of verse to rhyme with each of the following first lines. Note that the rhythm pattern is the same as shown above:

1. I went along the road today,

    .   .   .   .   .

2. The sky is bright, the day is long,

    .   .   .   .

3. It must be fun to own a goat,

    .   .   .   .   .   .

Verse Making:

In another rhythm pattern the first beat may be on the first syllable.

Read the following stanza aloud:

> Once I found a dollar bill,
> That, to me, was quite a thrill.

Repeat the rhythm by saying aloud:

> ONE and TWO and THREE and FOUR.
> ONE and TWO and THREE and FOUR.

Note that the first foot in each line has only one syllable and it is accented. Each of the other feet has the regular pattern of an unaccented syllable and an accented syllable as follows:

$$\prime \ \mid \ \smile \ \prime \ \mid \ \smile \ \prime \ \mid \ \smile \ \prime$$
$$\prime \ \mid \ \smile \ \prime \ \mid \ \smile \ \prime \ \mid \ \smile \ \prime$$

Examine the following lines which have the same pattern:

> Then I heard the queerest sound,
> What do you suppose I found?

EXERCISE 2: For each of the following, write a second rhyming line of verse to maintain the rhythm pattern which is the same as that shown above:

1. How he came I do not know,

    .   .   .   .

2. Once upon a time, I'm told,

    .   .   .   .

3. Never more he'll sail the sea,

    .   .   .   .

EXERCISE 3: Read the first line of each of the following to determine the rhythm pattern. Compose a second line to match the rhythm pattern of the first line.

1. The fluffy clouds sail on up high,

    .   .   .   .   .   .

2. Down the road to London town,

    .   .   .   .

3. Once I had a happy thought,

    .   .   .   .   .   .

4. The lesson's over, my work is done,

    .   .   .   .

Verse Making:

INDIAN SUMMER

Along the line of smoky hills
    The crimson forest stands.
And all the day the blue-jay calls
    Throughout the autumn lands.

Now by the brook the maple leans
    With all his glory spread,
And all the sumachs on the hills
    Have turned their green to red

Now by great marshes wrapt in mist,
    Or past some river's mouth,
Throughout the long, still autumn day
    Wild birds are flying south.

          —William Wilfred Campbell

Another quality which is found in poetry is rhyme. Examine each stanza of the above poem to find which lines rhyme. Then examine the rhythm pattern for each stanza.

The four-line stanza with the second and fourth lines rhyming and with a rhythm pattern of four feet, three feet, four feet, three feet, is a common one.

EXERCISE 4: Complete a four-line stanza for each of the following using the rhyme and rhythm pattern above:

1. Across the valley ran a road,
    And climbed to yonder hill.
    So near the trees but by the stream,
    ·   ·   ·   ·   ·   ·

2. This morning I got up so gay;
    The day it was so bright.
    ·   ·   ·   ·   ·   ·   ·
    ·   ·   ·   ·   ·   ·

3. I heard the rain upon the roof,
    ·   ·   ·   ·   ·   ·   ·
    ·   ·   ·   ·   ·   ·   ·
    ·   ·   ·   ·   ·   ·   ·

4. But when in doubt, take care, I'm told,
    ·   ·   ·   ·   ·   ·   ·
    ·   ·   ·   ·   ·   ·   ·
    ·   ·   ·   ·   ·   ·   ·

Verse Making:

1.
> From far away
> I've come to say
> That this bright day
> Was meant for play.

2.
> From over there
> I've come to say
> That this bright morn
> Was meant for play.

3.
> From far away
> I've come to say
> That if you would
> To play we should.

4.
> From far away I've come to say
> That, if you would, to play we should.
> The day is bright, my heart is light,
> I hope that you feel happy too.

The four stanzas above illustrate four different rhyming schemes. The first one may sound monotonous with too much rhyme unless the writer is trying to get a special effect. The second example with the second and fourth lines rhyming is a common one. The third example has each pair of lines rhyming and this scheme is useful when writing more than four-line verses. The fourth example gets its rhyme within each line. These four rhyme schemes may be written as follows:

1	2	3	4
a	a	a	a
a	b	a	b
a	c	b	c
a	b	b	d

EXERCISE 5: Write the rhyme scheme for the first stanza of the poem on page 183.

EXERCISE 6: Complete each of the following stanzas using a suitable rhyming scheme.

1. I have a little feathered friend,
   He sings so merrily,
   .   .   .   .   .   .
   .   .   .   .   .   .

2. There is a day I like the best,
   It's better far than all the rest.
   .   .   .   .   .   .
   .   .   .   .   .   .

187

Verse Making:

TREES

They're often found along the glen
    Or on a hilly mountain side,
Where winds sweep down with magic **blow**
    And fill them full with pride.

Their loving arms stretch out in space
    As if they're going to pray
Some day to move from spot to spot
    Wherein their trunks might sway.

—Karen W.

Read the above poem. What gives it a poetic quality? In writing verse it is usually necessary to replace words, to change the order of words, to add or subtract words, or to completely rearrange the line, in order to obtain a smooth rhythm, a suitable rhyme, and a true poetic sound. *Reading aloud* is the best method to determine if all these qualities have been provided.

Examine the following:

In this strange land across the sea
There are queer sights to see.

Work on the revising of the second line could produce these alternative ideas which might be more suitable.

There are queer sights for one to see.   (or)
Queer sights there are for one to see.   (or)
Many the sights there are to see.   (or)
Queer the sights there are to see.

Which of the four do you prefer? Why?

Nowhere in English is the need for revision greater than in verse making.

EXERCISE 7: Compose at least two stanzas for one of the following first lines:
1. When I am all alone at night,
2. The moon came out, the stars were bright,
3. At dawn the lake is very calm,
4. At noon I hurry home from school,
5. After the rain, the rainbow,
6. Because my manners I'd forgot,

Verse Making:

THE DAY IS DONE

The day is done, and the darkness
Falls from the wings of Night,
As a feather is wafted downward
From an eagle in his flight.

. . . . .

And the night shall be filled with music,
And the cares that infest the day
Shall fold their tents, like the Arabs,
And as silently steal away.

—Henry Wadsworth Longfellow

There is a musical quality in words which rhyme.   There is also word music when words begin with, or contain, the same sound, such as the *d* in the line above:

The day is done and the darkness. . . .

This word music is known as *alliteration*.   Notice the *f*'s in the first stanza above.   Find an example of alliteration in the last stanza.

When revising or polishing a piece of verse it is often possible to work in a moderate amount of alliteration which gives a very pleasing effect when the verse is read aloud.

Here are some examples of alliteration:

1. The soft winds sigh through the sand

2. A wild winter wind set the waves awash

3. A gentle gleam glowed in the mist

4. In the merry month of May

5. A big bad boy chased a little limping lad

EXERCISE 8: Using one of the five examples above as a first line, or creating one of your own, write two stanzas that contain some examples of alliteration.   Be careful not to overdo it.

Look for examples of alliteration in the poems you are studying this year.   Make use of this word music in the verses you will be writing.

Verse Making:

THE HIGHWAYMAN

The wind was a torrent of darkness among the gusty trees,
The moon was a ghostly galleon tossed upon cloudy seas,
The road was a ribbon of moonlight over the purple moor,
And the highwayman came riding—
    Riding—riding—
The highwayman came riding, up to the old inn door.

    .   .   .   .   .

And dark in the old innyard a stable-wicket creaked
Where Tim the ostler listened; his face was white and peaked;
His eyes were hollows of madness, his hair like mouldy hay,
But he loved the landlord's daughter,
    The landlord's red-lipped daughter,
Dumb as a dog he listened, and he heard the robber say:

—Alfred Noyes

When a writer wishes to make something very clear and striking to the reader, he may compare some person or thing to another object of a different class. For example, most of us have heard expressions like the following:

    He was as cunning as a fox.
    She was as clumsy as an elephant.
    The earth wore a show-white blanket.
    Her eyes shone like diamonds.

These examples of picturesque speech are often referred to as figurative language, or figures of speech.

1. When one thing is compared to an object of a different class, such as "his hair like mouldy hay" in the above poem, the comparison is called a SIMILE. The word *like* or *as* always appears in a simile. Find another simile in the poem.

2. When one thing is compared to an object of another class by calling it that object, such as "The moon was a ghostly galleon," the comparison is called a METAPHOR. Find another metaphor in the poem.

Look for similes and metaphors in the poetry and in the prose you will be reading this year. Use these devices in your writing but particularly in your verse making.

Verse Making:

WINTER'S END

The snow is gently falling
    Upon the ground today,
And even though the sun is here
    It does not melt away.

But as the days do linger on
    And Spring is drawing near,
We shall not see the snow again
    Until another year.

               —Carter S.

SIGNS OF SPRING

The tulips and the daffodils
    Are coming through the ground,
And in another week or two
    Bright flowers will be found.

The snowdrops and narcissus
    Are also pushing through,
Oh, how glorious it will be
    To know that winter's through!

               —Terry W.

EXERCISE 9: The two poems above illustrate how two pupils expressed
themselves about one season.
Write at least two stanzas about each of the following seasons. Give
each poem a title.

     1. Summer   2. Autumn   3. Winter

EXERCISE 10: Complete the following using the rhyme scheme: a,a,
b,b, c,c, d,d, etc.

    A is for apple that grows on a tree,
    B is for baker, I'm sure you'll agree.
    C . . . .
    D . . . .
    E . . . .
    F . . . . . .
    etc.

Verse Making:

THE MISER OF NOBLEND

Beside the fire he sits alone,
    His dog his only friend,
His friends are none or are not known,
    The miser of Noblend.

Uncared for in his humble shack,
    Though richer than a king,
Though anything he need not lack,
    He has not anything.

Beside the fire he sits alone,
    This man without a friend,
To all the world he is not known,
    The miser of Noblend.

                —Nancy I.

EXERCISE 11:

1. Using the method illustrated on page 184 write the rhythm pattern of any stanza in the above poem.

2. Write the rhyme scheme of any stanza.

3. Using the same pattern of rhythm and rhyme write a poem of two or more four-line stanzas about one of the following:
    (a) A famous explorer
    (b) A fairy tale
    (c) A lonely tramp
    (d) A story-book character
    (e) Yourself

EXERCISE 12: Write a stanza of six lines or more about one of the
             following:
    1. Night
    2. Snow
    3. Storm
    4. Fog
    5. Stars

Verse Making:

SEPTEMBER

The goldenrod is yellow;
    The corn is turning brown;
The trees in apple orchards
    With fruit are bending down.

The gentian's bluest fringes
    Are curling in the sun;
In dusky pods the milkweed
    Its hidden silk has spun.

The sedges flaunt their harvest
    In every meadow nook,
And asters by the brookside
    Make asters in the brook.

From dewy lanes at morning
    The grape's sweet odours rise;
At noon the roads all flutter
    With golden butterflies.

By all these lovely tokens
    September days are here,
With summer's best of weather
    And autumn's best of cheer.

—Helen Hunt Jackson

EXERCISE 13:

1. Write the rhythm and rhyme pattern for the above poem.

2. List five ideas which the poet has used to suggest the characteristics of the month of September.

3. Make a class collection of poems about the other months of the year.

4. During each month compose a poem of several stanzas about that particular month.

5. Make a class booklet, suitably illustrated, for the poems about a particular month.

Verse Making:

> Somebody said that it couldn't be done
> But he with a chuckle replied
> That "Maybe it couldn't," but he would be one
> Who wouldn't say so till he'd tried.[1]

—Edgar Guest

EXERCISE 14: Following is a list of first lines to provide the start for further verse making activities:

1. If the sky were always blue

2. I brush my teeth each morning

3. Look up and down before you cross

4. The days are getting shorter

5. I do not know if I like snow

6. I heard the whistle of a jet

7. The bluebird sings a merry song again

8. What is so long as the night before Christmas

9. On Monday we start off the week with school

10. To be healthy and strong is a very good thing

11. When I was just a little girl (or boy)

12. Early one morning, sparkling with dew

13. The frost makes pretty pictures

14. The cowboy sat in his saddle straight

15. The rapids faced him just ahead

16. The lightning flashed, the thunder rolled

17. Once upon a time, many years ago

18. I took a spin upon my bike

19. With white sails billowing against the ocean blue

20. After the day is over, after the day is done

---

[1]From "It Couldn't Be Done" in Collected Verse of Edgar A. Guest, copyright 1934. By permission of Reilly and Lee Co., Chicago.

Verse Making:

In your reader and in books of poetry, you will find samples of rhythm patterns other than those examined thus far. You may wish to attempt some more complicated rhythm patterns in your own verse making.

HOW THEY BROUGHT THE GOOD NEWS

I sprang to the stirrup, and Joris, and he;
I galloped, Dirk galloped, we galloped all three;
"Good speed!" cried the watch, as the gate-bolts undrew;
"Speed!" echoed the wall to us galloping through;
Behind shut the postern, the lights sank to rest,
And into the midnight we galloped abreast.

—Robert Browning

Read the verse aloud. Read it again and beat out the galloping rhythm on your desk.

Repeat the procedure for these swashbuckling lines from "A Ballad of John Silver" by John Masefield.

We were schooner-rigged and rakish, with a long and lissome hull,
And we flew the pretty colours of the crossbones and the skull;
We'd a big black Jolly Roger flapping grimly at the fore,
And we sailed the Spanish Water in the happy days of yore.

Now examine these lines from "Our Island Home" by William Shakespeare who was a master of this form of writing known as *blank verse* because the lines do not rhyme.

This royal throne of kings, this sceptred isle,
This earth of majesty, this seat of Mars,
This other Eden, demi-paradise,
This fortress, built by nature for herself
Against infection and the hand of war,
This happy breed of men, this little world,
This precious stone set in the silver sea,
Which serves it in the office of a wall,
Or a moat defensive to a house,
Against the envy of less happier lands,
This blessèd plot, this earth, this realm, this England,
This land of such dear souls, this dear, dear land.

When you are studying poems this year, read them aloud to enjoy the rhythm and rhyme which the poet intended that you should hear.

. . . . . .

"Poetry was made to make its impact upon the ear."

PREFACE TO PART II

The work in Part II of DEVELOPING LANGUAGE SKILLS is the presentation of a course in grammar to meet the needs of Grade VIII pupils. It has been organized under the following headings:

    1. The sentence and its parts.
    2. The parts of speech.

Two major objectives have been kept in mind as the explanations and the exercises have been composed and arranged:

    1. To provide a working knowledge of sentence structure and word function in the sequence which will make that knowledge easily understood.

    2. To provide exercises in which practice is given using each newly-acquired grammatical term or construction so that the ability will be developed to use that knowledge in checking, and in explaining, the accuracy of written and spoken language.

It is hoped that in working toward these objectives, the means have been provided whereby mastery of some of the basic principles of English grammar may be attained.

To make the work in grammar more interesting and profitable, an effort has been made to compose exercises in which the content of the sentences presents worth-while information.

In using the material of Part II of DEVELOPING LANGUAGE SKILLS the exercises should be performed *in the order in which they appear.* It is suggested that many exercises might be done *orally.*

—The Authors

XIII ▲ THE SENTENCE AND ITS PARTS

Sentence Sense

Ideas are expressed in words. Words are grouped into sentences. *A sentence is a group of related words expressing a complete thought.* Every sentence must begin with a capital letter and end with a period, a question mark, or an exclamation mark.

It is important, in the revision step of any written work, to check carefully for any incomplete sentences in your own writing. You will do this most efficiently by reading, aloud but softly, what you have written before you leave it.

EXERCISE 1: Read each of the following groups of words to determine whether or not it is a sentence. Make a sentence out of any group of words that does not express a complete thought. Write each sentence correctly using the proper punctuation.

1. during the Middle Ages long camel caravans travelling from China to seaports on the Mediterranean Sea

2. on the backs of the plodding camels, bales of spices, ginger, tea, sugar, dyes, silks, cottons, and drugs

3. merchants who met the dusty caravans and bargained for their precious loads

4. the rich cargoes stored away on sailing vessels and transported to the seaports of Western Europe

5. after the Holy Land was captured by the Mohammedans, expeditions, known as the Crusades, were sent from Europe to free the land

6. while in the Holy Land, the Crusaders had the opportunity of seeing the amazing things brought from the Far East

7. when they went home carrying samples of these goods, all of Europe realizing the wealth of the Orient

8. in the fifteenth century the Turks moving westward and capturing the important trading seaport of Constantinople

9. the conquerors of Constantinople had no love for the peoples of Western Europe and the flow of eastern goods was almost stopped

10. the European countries forced into making a choice between fighting the Turks and finding new trade routes to India and China

11. was it surprising, then, that some Europeans began to think that a sea route might lie beyond the explored waters of the African continent

---

Test by sound. Read aloud.

Sentence Sense:

One of the most common faults in writing is the use of a *sentence fragment*. A sentence fragment is a group of related words written in the form of a sentence but which does not express a complete thought. It should either be joined to the sentence with which it belongs, or expanded into a complete thought by itself.

INCORRECT: *Having read the story of the Phoenicians.* They were connected with the early history of Britain.

CORRECT: I have read the story of the Phoenicians who were connected with the early history of Britain.

CORRECT: I have read the story of the Phoenicians. They were connected with the early history of Britain.

EXERCISE 2: This exercise contains a number of sentence fragments. Correct them in one of the ways shown in the examples above.

1. The story of early Britain not in any written records.

2. How people lived in what we now call prehistoric times.

3. Before the last ice age, Britain was joined to the mainland of Europe.

4. Leaving Britain as an island. Any newcomers had to come by sea.

5. The earliest invaders usually referred to as Iberians.

6. Short in stature, with dark hair, skin and eyes.

7. Living in villages surrounded by earthwork defences which protected them from attack.

8. Homes usually pit dwellings. These consisted of circular holes dug in the ground with earth thrown up to form the walls.

9. Homes covered with thatched roofs.

10. Although the Iberians lived in villages. They pastured their herds in open upland areas.

11. Weapons and implements made from polished flints.

12. In Britain today descendants of these early Iberians.

When revising written work, make sure that it has no sentence fragments.

Sentence Sense:

Another common fault is the use of the *run-on* sentence. As the name implies, this type of sentence runs on and on instead of being made into two or three sentences.

INCORRECT: Norway is a country in north-west Europe and is part of the Scandinavian Peninsula when I am older I would like to visit this land.

CORRECT: Norway is a country in north-west Europe. It is part of the Scandinavian Peninsula. When I am older, I would like to visit this land.

CORRECT: Norway, a country in north-west Europe, is part of the Scandinavian Peninsula. When I am older, I would like to visit this land.

EXERCISE 3: This exercise contains a number of run-on sentences. Rewrite them to improve their sentence structure.

1. Part of Norway lies above the Arctic Circle and in the summer the sun never slips below the horizon the country is often referred to as the Land of the Midnight Sun.

2. Spain and Switzerland are mountainous countries of Europe but Norway has many mountains too their slope to the sea is short and steep and the rivers are not very useful for navigation.

3. Norway's cataracts plunging down steep gorges cut between the mountain ranges supply the water-power needed to produce electricity and this is very beneficial to the country because of the lack of coal.

4. The coast-line is very irregular and dotted with many islands and inlets, known as fiords, cut between steep mountains and sometimes reach inland a distance of fifty to one hundred miles.

5. Norwegians have always loved the sea many years before Columbus made his first journey to the West Indies, Viking ships had crossed the Atlantic Ocean to reach America.

6. The spirit of the Vikings lingered on in Norway in 1911 Roald Amundsen became the first man to set foot on the South Pole and in Tromso today is a statue to this great explorer.

7. The cities of Norway are mainly along the coast the capital is Oslo and it is situated on a fiord about fifty miles from the open water of the Skagerrak.

Avoid the use of run-on sentences
in written English.

Sentence Sense:

Pupils in primary grades learn to write short simple sentences. When sentences of this kind are the only type used by older pupils they are sometimes called *infantile sentences*. Pupils in senior grades need to combine some thoughts, to add descriptive groups of words, or to rearrange the order of words for better effect. The use of a series of *infantile sentences* should be avoided.

Examine the following examples:

1. In olden days there were minstrels. The minstrels wandered from castle to castle. They sang before kings and nobles. This was before the days of printing.

2. They made up songs. The songs told of the brave deeds of heroes. The songs were not written down. Few people knew how to write.

Each of these series of infantile sentences can be combined into one good sentence as follows:

1. In olden days before the invention of printing, minstrels wandered from castle to castle to sing before kings and nobles.

2. Their songs, which told of the brave deeds of heroes, were not written down because few people knew how to write.

EXERCISE 4: Combine each series of infantile sentences into one good sentence. Write the sentence which you have composed.

1. Asbestos is a rock. It is found in the province of Quebec.

2. This rock was known in ancient times. Asbestos means unburnable. The Greeks named it.

3. Asbestos is an unusual rock. It peels off in fibres. The fibres are much like cotton. The French sometimes call this queer mineral "stone of cotton."

4. Some fibres can be woven into cloth. Neither fire nor water can damage the cloth. It has many uses.

5. The tough, coarser fibres cannot be woven. They are too stiff. They can be made into fireproof paper and felt. This can be used for insulation.

6. These fibres can also be used in shingles. They are known as asbestos shingles. These shingles give protection against fire. They are put on the roofs or walls of buildings.

7. Asbestos is an important mineral. Canada produces more than any country in the world. All Canadian asbestos is found in the Eastern Townships of Quebec.

Avoid a series of infantile sentences
in written English.

201

Kinds of Sentences

In speaking or in writing, sentences are used in the following four ways:

1. ASSERTIVE — to make a statement
2. INTERROGATIVE — to ask a question
3. IMPERATIVE — to give a command
4. EXCLAMATORY — to express strong feeling

When it is written, each sentence must be terminated by some mark of punctuation. What kinds of sentences require a period? Which kind of sentence requires a question mark? Which kind requires an exclamation mark?

When it is read aloud, an interrogative sentence or an exclamatory sentence must be read in such a way that the listener will know it is that particular kind of sentence.

EXERCISE 1: Read silently each of the following sentences to determine what kind it is. Read each sentence aloud in such a way that a person listening will know what kind of sentence it is. Then write the sentence, using the correct punctuation, and tell its kind.

1. Have you read stories of pirates

2. Many exciting tales have been told of bold buccaneers lying in wait for Spanish treasure ships

3. Look for adventure in the accounts of wild sea fights on the Spanish Main

4. The Spanish Main of yesterday is known as the Caribbean Sea today

5. What a thrill it must be to holiday in its bright blue waters

6. When wintry storms cover Canada with a blanket of snow, wouldn't you like to bask in the brilliant sunshine and warmth of the islands of the West Indies

7. How entrancing these islands are

8. Although you may find people of many nationalities there, would you be surprised to find that Spanish is the language of many islanders

9. We may never see the beauties of the West Indies in our travels

10. However, a study of the islands and their people can be as exciting as a tale of buried treasure off the Spanish Main

Variety in the Sentence

One way to get *sentence variety* is to use different kinds of sentences in your writing.

EXERCISE 1: Rewrite the following paragraph and supply the necessary capital letters and punctuation marks to divide it into sentences. Note the variety of sentences in the paragraph.

Look at Canada to find a country rich in natural resources the early pioneers thought of Canada as a land of plenty they saw no need to conserve her forests or to think of saving her soil or water but what has been happening during the last three hundred years trees have been cut down for lumber or to clear the land for crops the prairies have been ploughed to raise wheat today cities are spreading out across the landscape the scarcity of forests and grass is causing rivers to stop flowing in summer and springs and wells to go dry running water washes away the top layer of fertile soil and produces devastating floods farm land is being dominated by sprawling factories what a wonderful country Canada was three hundred years from now will people say just that

EXERCISE 2: Write the numbers from one to twelve in a column. Beside each number write the name of the kind of sentence that corresponds with the sentence of that number in the paragraph above.

EXERCISE 3: Select one of the following topics and write a story. Revise the story so that it contains at least three different kinds of sentences.
1. We Need Forests
2. We Need Water
3. We Need our Topsoil
4. We Need Electricity from Water-Power
5. Man's Greatest Menace
6. Conserve to Preserve

EXERCISE 4: Compose a three-sentence paragraph for one of the topics indicated below, following the pattern shown to give sentence variety.
1. (About a baseball game)
   Exclamatory—Assertive—Interrogative
2. (About fishing)
   Interrogative—exclamatory—Assertive
3. (About Mexico)
   Imperative—Assertive—Exclamatory

203

Subject and Predicate

Every sentence consists of two main parts, the *subject* and the *predicate*. Examine the following sentences:

SUBJECT	PREDICATE
1. The rabbit	hopped.
2. The white rabbit	hopped down the path.
3. The little white rabbit	hopped down the path to the garden.
4. The little white rabbit with pink ears	hopped merrily down the path to the garden.

The part of the sentence that tells what you are talking about is called the SUBJECT.	The part of the sentence that says something about its subject is called the PREDICATE.

Sentence fragments will not occur in written work if the writer makes certain that each group of related words, intended to express a complete thought, has a subject and a predicate.

EXERCISE 1: Write the following, expanding any sentence fragment into a sentence. Draw a vertical line in each sentence to separate the subject and the predicate. Add punctuation.

1. Rome the most powerful nation in the ancient world
2. Roman legions having conquered land in Gaul
3. Britain was invaded by a Roman army led by Julius Caesar in 55 B.C.
4. Not advancing far into the island
5. The land of the Britons was invaded again the following year
6. Britain a Roman province about a hundred years later
7. Caractacus and Boadicea resisting the rule of the Romans
8. Law and order was established throughout the country
9. Augustine bringing Christianity to the Romans
10. Roman influence is seen in parts of Britain to this day

> A knowledge of subject and predicate should help a writer to avoid the use of sentence fragments in written work.

Subject and Predicate:

Every complete sentence must have a subject and a predicate. Examine each of the following groups of words to determine why it cannot be considered a sentence.

1. A very exciting story.
2. One of the largest lakes in the world.
3. Having eaten my lunch.
4. Going to the store on the corner.

The first two groups of words have only a subject. A predicate must be added before either can be called a sentence.

1. A very exciting story | was read to the class.
2. One of the largest lakes in the world | is Lake Superior.

The third and fourth examples above have no subject or predicate. They might be made into sentences such as:

3. I | had eaten my lunch before the game.   or
3. Having eaten my lunch I | headed for the game.
4. Tom | was going to the store on the corner.   or
4. Going to the store on the corner Tom | found the letter.

EXERCISE 2: Using your knowledge of subject and predicate make a sentence out of each group of words which does not contain a subject and a predicate. Write each of the sentences and draw a vertical line between the subject and the predicate.

1. Joan of Arc was born in 1412 in Domremy, France.
2. Having learned about this French girl.
3. The king of England had overrun France with his army.
4. This unusual girl heard angel voices.
5. Telling her to go to the French Dauphin.
6. Allowed her to lead the French army into battle on a white charger.
7. The Dauphin was crowned King of France at Rheims after many of her victories.
8. Joan's fortunes changing after several defeats.
9. Having fallen into the hands of the English who burned her at the stake as a heretic.
10. The name of St. Joan is revered today for her purity and her love of France.

```
Avoid sentence fragments in your
written English.
```

Subject and Predicate:

Note the position of the subject in each of the following sentences:

1. Is *Paris* the capital of France?
2. Does *the province of Ontario* have its own hydro system?
3. There is *Niagara Falls!*
4. What an inspiring sight *that cataract* makes!

To locate the subject and the predicate more easily in an interrogative sentence or in an exclamatory sentence, write the sentence in natural order with the subject at the beginning, thus:

1. Paris | is the capital of France?
2. The province of Ontario | does have its own hydro system?
3. Niagara Falls | is there!
4. That cataract | makes what an inspiring sight!

What is the subject in each of the following sentences?

5. Walk on the left side of the highway.
6. See your dentist twice a year.

In most imperative sentences the subject *you* does not appear and therefore it is said to be "understood." These sentences may be written:

5. [You] | walk on the left side of the highway.
6. [You] | see your dentist twice a year.

EXERCISE 3: Write all of the following sentences in natural order. Draw a vertical line between the subject and the predicate.

1. Turn to a map of South America.
2. Brazil is the largest country of this continent.
3. Would you believe this statement about its size?
4. This vast country is the fourth largest in the world.
5. What a tremendous river the Amazon is!
6. This hot, rainy, forest-covered area is inhabited by few people.
7. Do many people of Brazil speak Portuguese?
8. Locate the cotton and coffee areas of the country.
9. What imaginary line cuts across the northern part of Brazil?
10. The city of Rio de Janeiro is the capital.

> To find the subject and the predicate more easily, first rearrange the sentence so that it is written in natural order.

Variety in the Sentence

Examine the following sentences:

1. *A rosy glow* could be seen in the light of early morn.
2. In the light of early morn could be seen *a rosy glow.*
3. In the light of early morn, *a rosy glow* could be seen.

A sentence is written in NATURAL order when the subject comes at the beginning of the sentence.

A sentence is written in INVERTED order when the subject comes at the end of the sentence.

A sentence is written in SPLIT order when the predicate is split with the subject coming between the two parts.

Most sentences are written in the natural order. Sometimes a better effect can be obtained by putting a sentence in the inverted order or in the split order. When written work is being revised, variety in sentences may be obtained by using inverted and split order in some sentences.

EXERCISE 1: Write each of the following sentences in natural, inverted, or split order, whichever seems to you to give the best effect. Indicate which order you have used.

1. Man has invented the airplane recently.
2. The imaginations of men have been at work on the miracle of flight for hundreds of years.
3. Predictions of flying can be found in the poetry of many ages.
4. Man's aspiration to fly can be found in the story of Daedalus.
5. This Grecian workman was refused permission to leave the island of Crete to return home.
6. He constructed immense wings with feathers and wax for himself and his son Icarus.
7. They soared like birds from Crete's rocky shores far above the Aegean Sea.
8. Icarus was unmindful of his father's warning in flying too close to the sun.
9. A sorrowful father was left to continue the journey alone.
10. Man's attempt to conquer space goes relentlessly onward.

EXERCISE 2: Write a paragraph using one of the following topic sentences. Revise the paragraph so that it contains sentences written in natural, inverted, and split order.

1. With a sickening sensation I heard the ball crash through the window.
2. From that little shack in the clearing came a thin spiral of smoke.
3. The dreaded moment had arrived!

Variety in the Sentence:

The use of a series of short infantile sentences should be avoided in most written English. On the other hand, the continuous use of long involved sentences may cause the reader to lose interest. Variation in the length of sentences in any story will usually produce the best effect.

EXERCISE 3: Combine each of the following pairs of sentences to make one sentence. Avoid the frequent use of "and" or "but."

1. Costa Rica was given its name by early Spanish explorers. They explored its eastern coast.

2. They called the land "Costa Rica." This means "rich coast."

3. Most of the people live on a fertile plateau in the central part of the country. It is more valuable than the eastern coast.

4. There is plenty of rain here but no extreme heat or frost. Nearly all the rain falls in the summer.

5. The rich volcanic soil is suitable for growing coffee. The climate is also suitable for coffee growing.

6. The dry sunny winter is used for harvesting and drying the coffee. Drying coffee would be difficult in the open if there were frequent rains.

7. Some banana plantations are found in the hot rainy lowlands. Coffee remains the most valuable crop of the country.

8. The Pacific lowlands of Costa Rica are less rainy. This coast is better for raising cattle.

9. The Costa Ricans need the cattle for beef and leather. Few of the animals are exported.

10. The capital of Costa Rica is San José. This city is located in the central highlands.

VARIETY IN SENTENCES IS OBTAINED BY
(a) Using different kinds of sentences.
(b) Using inverted and split order in sentences.
(c) Varying the length of sentences.

CHECK SENTENCES TO AVOID
(a) Sentence fragments.
(b) Run-on sentences.
(c) Infantile sentences.

Bare Subject and Bare Predicate

1. Some prospectors | discovered gold.
2. One of the rich areas | can be found in Northern Ontario.
3. Gold ore | is mined at Timmins.

The main word in the subject is called the BARE SUBJECT. The main word in the predicate is called the BARE PREDICATE. The bare predicate can consist of one or more words.

EXERCISE 1: Write each of the following sentences in natural order. Draw a vertical line between the subject and the predicate. Underline the bare subject with a wavy line and the bare predicate with a straight line as shown in the examples above.

1. Molten rock hardened into igneous rock.
2. Granite is an igneous rock.
3. The white glassy particles are called quartz.
4. In red granite the softer pink rock is called feldspar.
5. Find thin, black, shiny sheets of rock in the granite.
6. Have you heard the name mica before?
7. Name three minerals in granite.
8. The hardness of granite resists weathering.
9. Slabs of granite can be cut from a quarry.
10. In the manufacture of tombstones granite is often used.

EXERCISE 2: If more practice is needed, do this exercise. Follow the instructions given in the exercise above.

1. Minerals have been used from the earliest times.
2. For thousands of years man worked with stone.
3. Then he discovered the use of copper and bronze.
4. The Iron Age became another era in man's development.
5. Minerals have determined the history of nations.
6. In ancient times the knowledge of copper made Egypt into a strong country.
7. Spain reached the height of her power with the silver and gold of Mexico and Peru.
8. The Industrial Revolution in England was aided by her resources of iron and coal.
9. The development of Northern Ontario responded to the discovery of gold, silver, and nickel.
10. During the last few years Alberta has developed its resources of natural gas and petroleum.

Modifiers of Bare Subject and Bare Predicate

1. (Some) birds fly [south] [early].
2. (The) migration (of birds) has been charted [for many years].
3. One (of the bird sanctuaries) was developed [by Jack Miner of Kingsville].

Words that are used to describe the bare subject are called MODIFIERS OF THE BARE SUBJECT. Round brackets may be drawn around them in graphic analysis.

Words that tell *how, when, where,* or *why* about the bare predicate are called MODIFIERS OF THE BARE PREDICATE. Square brackets may be drawn around the modifiers of the bare predicate.

EXERCISE 1: Analyse the following sentences in a manner similar to that shown in the examples below. This is called graphic analysis. Write each sentence in natural order before doing the analysis.

Example: (Many) birds migrate [to the southern States].

Many (of the birds) migrate [to the southern States].

1. Most birds are preparing for their southern trip.
2. Each kind of bird flies along the migration route of its ancestors.
3. The main routes have been charted along the Atlantic Coast and down the Mississippi Valley.
4. Definite information about the travels of birds is obtained by banding.
5. Many people co-operate with governments in banding birds.
6. In order to do this birds are caught in harmless traps.
7. A numbered band is placed on one leg of each bird.
8. Later the same bird may be caught again hundreds of miles away.
9. Then reports are forwarded to wild life authorities.
10. From all these reports information about bird migration is gathered.

EXERCISE 2: Add a modifier of the bare subject or a modifier of the bare predicate to each sentence below to make a more interesting sentence. Analyse your sentence graphically.

1. Trees come out in full leaf.
2. Leaves are formed from buds.
3. Carbon dioxide is taken into the leaves.
4. Oxygen escapes from the leaves.
5. Chlorophyll combines with sunshine.

Misplaced Modifiers

Examine the following sentences:

1. Tom found a wallet going down the street.
2. We saw a circus parade sitting in the window.
3. Mary bought a scarf from the clerk that was blue.
4. With a roar we heard the motorcycle start.
5. Across the river we played ball in the field.

One of the causes of lack of clearness in a sentence is the *misplaced modifier*. Modifiers should be placed near the word which they modify so that no doubt is left in the mind of the reader. The above sentences should have been written as follows:

1. Going down the street, Tom found a wallet.
2. Sitting in the window, we saw a circus parade.
3. Mary bought a blue scarf from the clerk.
4. We heard the motorcycle start with a roar.
5. We played ball in the field across the river.

EXERCISE 1: Rewrite each of the following sentences and place the modifier where the meaning, which the writer intended, is made clear to the reader. Make any other changes that you find necessary to improve your sentence.

1. I saw a jet plane walking to school.
2. There were chocolate cookies in the box which we ate.
3. My cousin only stayed for two days.
4. Did you see the boat on the river that was painted green?
5. We saw a flock of crows going to the cottage.
6. I bought a hat for this boy that is too small.
7. Tom noticed the time coming in for supper.
8. She saw a horse that was lame at the corner.
9. We climbed a mountain that was steep last summer.
10. The boys nearly ate the whole cake.

EXERCISE 2: Rewrite these sentences and make any necessary changes to make their meaning clear.

Example: (a) Helping Mother, the cup fell to the floor.
(b) When I was helping Mother, the cup fell to the floor.

1. While crossing the street the light turned red.
2. Going to school the birds were singing.
3. After reaching the cabin the rain stopped.
4. Reading the ghost story the door blew shut with a crash.

---

1. A modifier must have something to modify.
2. Keep modifiers close to the words they modify.

Completing Parts in the Sentence

Notice that these bare predicates have no completing part:

1. Mackenzie <u>explored</u>.
2. His men <u>paddled</u> to its mouth.
3. They <u>had suffered</u>.

By this we mean that the sentence does not say:

1. Mackenzie explored *anything*.   or that
2. His men paddled *anything*.   or that
3. They had suffered *anything*.

Now the sentences might have said:

4. Mackenzie explored a great <u>river</u>.
5. His men paddled their <u>canoes</u> to its mouth.
6. They had suffered many <u>hardships</u>.

In sentences 4, 5 and 6 the bare predicates have completing parts: *river, canoes, hardships.*

To discover if there is a completing part in a sentence, read the bare subject with the bare predicate and add the word *something* as a question.

These bare predicates can be called *action words.* The bare subjects are the *doers of the action.* The completing parts are the *receivers of the action.*

(doer)	(action)	(receiver)
4. Mackenzie	explored	river
5. men	paddled	canoes
6. They	had suffered	hardships

> In a sentence where the bare predicate is an action word and where the completing part is the receiver of the action expressed by the bare predicate, the completing part is called an
>
> OBJECT.

7. They explored for many miles.

Does the sentence say that they explored something? No, it does not. We know, therefore, that there is no completing part.

8. They explored the river for many miles.

This sentence does say that they explored something. They explored the *river.* The bare predicate is an action word, the completing part is the receiver of the action, and *river* must be the *object.*

212

Completing Parts in the Sentence:

EXERCISE 1: Arrange the following sentences in natural order and analyse them graphically, checking to find out whether there is a completing part which is an object. Underline each object with two straight lines. Objects may have modifiers around which you put round brackets.

> *Example:* (a) (The) sun reaches (its) (most southerly) point [in December].
>
> (b) This marks (the) beginning (of winter).

1. A new season comes in September.
2. At the equinox we have twelve hours of daylight.
3. The sun is crossing the equator at this time of year.
4. The shortest day of the year comes in December.
5. Have you ever seen the northern lights?
6. Point to the North Star.
7. On a dark night the Big Dipper can be seen.
8. The moon reflects the light of the sun.
9. How fast does light travel?
10. The absence of sunlight causes winter darkness at the North Pole.

EXERCISE 2: Analyse each of these sentences graphically.

1. During the summer a tree takes water from the soil through its roots.
2. In the autumn the tree forms a thin layer of cork between the stem of each leaf and the twig.
3. No sap can now reach the leaf.
4. The green colour in the leaf changes into many other colours.
5. Deciduous trees lose their leaves during the first weeks of fall.
6. Evergreen trees form the tiny layers at any time during the year.
7. They continually lose their needles throughout the year.
8. Take a walk in the woods in autumn.
9. The leaves make a very good carpet.
10. How do the leaves make good soil?

EXERCISE 3: Analyse each of these sentences graphically.

1. Have you studied the largest island in the West Indies?
2. Cuba exports much of the world's sugar.
3. Sugar is refined from the juice of the sugar cane.
4. Sugar cane needs a long growing season.
5. One cane planting may last for five or ten years.
6. On certain kinds of soil in western and central Cuba tobacco grows well.
7. The country people raise most of their own food.
8. In the mountains miners have discovered valuable deposits of copper, chromium and iron.
9. Locate the capital city on a wall map.
10. Many tourists visit Havana in the winter season.

Completing Parts in the Sentence:

Test to see if there is a completing part:
1. Sugar is sweet.
2. Lemons are sour.

Does the first sentence say that sugar is *something?* Yes, it does. Does the second sentence say that lemons are *something?* Yes, it does. Then we know that these sentences have completing parts. But the bare predicates are not action words, and the completing parts cannot be receivers of the action. Therefore, the completing parts cannot be objects.

Study these examples, noting the bare predicate and the completing part:
3. The train was *late.*
4. We were *tired.*
5. Mother became *excited.*
6. Father seems *angry.*

Note that the completing part in each sentence describes the subject.

Now study the following examples to determine what the completing part does:
7. Ottawa is the *capital.*
8. Drake was a famous *sailor.*
9. These boys are *brothers.*
10. He is the *captain.*

In sentences 7, 8, 9 and 10 the completing part is a noun which means the same person, place or thing that is named by the subject.

---

1. Note that the bare predicates—is, are, was, were, became, seems—are NOT action words.
2. Note that the completing part after these bare predicates either
   (a) describes the subject   or
   (b) means the same as the subject.

A completing part that follows a non-action bare predicate and which either (a) describes the subject or (b) means the same as the subject is called a
SUBJECTIVE COMPLETION.

The knowledge concerning objects and subjective completions which you have gained will be useful when you are ready to study pronouns and must decide whether to use the subject or object form of the pronoun. The knowledge will also be useful when making the correct choice of an adjective or an adverb in sentences with non-action bare predicates.

214

Completing Parts in the Sentence:

EXERCISE 4: Analyse the following sentences graphically, underlining any subjective completions with a straight line and a wavy line. Put round brackets around any modifiers of the subjective completion.

Example: Paris is (the) capital (of France).

1. Ocean water is salty.
2. The Pacific is the world's largest ocean.
3. Three Canadian provinces are prairie provinces.
4. The Jersey is one of the dairy breeds.
5. Jersey milk tastes creamy.
6. Macdonald became the first prime minister of Canada.
7. He was one of the Fathers of Confederation.

> To find the main parts of a sentence follow these steps:
> 1. Write the sentence in natural order.
> 2. Read the bare subject and the bare predicate together and test to find out if there is a completing part.
> 3. Examine the bare predicate to see if it is made up of action or non-action words.
> 4. If there is a completing part, make the decision whether it is an OBJECT or a SUBJECTIVE COMPLETION.

EXERCISE 5: This exercise will contain both objects and subjective completions. Analyse graphically.

1. The African jungle grows in a hot moist climate.
2. The Ontario farmer grows winter wheat on southern slopes.
3. A child grows discouraged after several failures.
4. After the lesson the girls tasted the cake.
5. After the candy the apple tasted bitter.
6. Little acorns became huge oak trees.
7. What is the name of a large desert in Africa?

EXERCISE 6: Analyse graphically.

1. Buenos Aires is the capital of Argentina.
2. It is the largest city south of the equator.
3. Ocean ships unload freight from other lands at her great docks.
4. The Pampa in Argentina is a vast fertile treeless plain.
5. Without the wheat, corn, and cattle of the Pampa, Buenos Aires would be a much smaller city.
6. Many times in the past great swarms of locusts have destroyed almost every growing plant.
7. The supply of minerals in Argentina is very small.
8. The Argentine people celebrate Christmas in mid-summer.

Completing Parts in the Sentence:

Find the completing part in each of the following sentences:

1. Tom gave me the apple.
2. His mother bought the girls some grapes.

Does the first sentence say that Tom gave something? Does the second sentence say that his mother bought something? We have learned that *apple* and *grapes* are called *objects*.

In the first sentence the word *me* tells *to whom* the apple was given. In the second sentence the word *girls* tells *for whom* the action was performed. If the sentences had contained the words "to me" and "for the girls," these phrases would have been modifiers of the bare predicate. But when the first part of the phrase has been omitted, the word which tells *to whom* or *for whom* an action was performed is known as the *indirect object*.

EXERCISE 7: Analyse the following sentences graphically. Underline each of the indirect objects with three straight lines.

1. Mary read us the letter.
2. Indians gave the early settlers trouble.
3. Tell me the answer of the question.
4. The speaker gave the audience a vivid picture of his native land.
5. Have you shown your father that new sweater?
6. Forgive us our trespasses.
7. Pick each of us an apple from this tree.
8. For each game last winter he loaned me a pair of skates.
9. We send each other presents at Christmas.
10. His uncle left him several hundred dollars.

EXERCISE 8: Write each of the following sentences in natural order and analyse it graphically.

1. In 1454 in Germany Gutenberg discovered a method of printing books.
2. Soon an Englishman brought a printing press to England.
3. His name was William Caxton.
4. Up until this time the copying of a single book by hand required many months' work.
5. After the discovery of printing books became much cheaper.
6. One of the first books printed was the Bible.
7. An important result of printing was its effect upon the English language.
8. People spoke differently in various parts of England.
9. After the introduction of printing everyone in England could read the same printed word.
10. Soon they were speaking the same language.

Review I

EXERCISE 1: Write a correct English sentence for each of the following:

1. Many methods of communicating with one another.
2. One method is by speaking. We speak words aloud. We call this oral language.
3. By speaking words, ideas are communicated.
4. Writing words is another way of talking we call this method written language.
5. A third means of communication by means of signs.
6. Animals make sounds. Man can imitate. Perhaps man learned to speak this way.
7. No written record of its first beginnings.
8. By carving signs and pictures in stone, walls have given us some knowledge of early peoples.
9. Modern means of communication including telegraph, telephone, radio, and television.
10. Would a common language for all the nations help us to understand one another better?

EXERCISE 2: Analyse graphically.

1. The octopus is one of nature's strange animals.
2. It received its name from its eight arms.
3. These tentacles are fastened together by a web surrounding the mouth.
4. The octopus lives on other animals of the sea.
5. On the underside of each of the eight tentacles are two rows of powerful suckers.
6. The octopus has a very useful funnel beneath its head.
7. Through the funnel it can discharge a black liquid to cloud the water.
8. This gives the octopus a hiding place from its enemies.
9. The octopus is a very savage looking animal.
10. Have you ever seen one?

EXERCISE 3:

1. Rearrange the following sentences so that each is in split order:
(a) You could travel all over the world today without finding a single living dinosaur.
(b) The last dinosaur died thousands of years ago.
(c) Dinosaurs probably became extinct because of changes in climate.

2. Rearrange the following sentences so that each is in inverted order:
(a) The harbour of Saint John is situated across the Bay of Fundy in New Brunswick.
(b) The famous Reversing Falls can be observed here every day.

Compound Subjects and Predicates

1. *Cherries*   grow in Ontario.
2. *Many grapes*   are grown in the Niagara district.
3. *Cherries* and *grapes*   are grown in Ontario.
4. Red *cherries* and blue *grapes* are grown in Ontario.

> When the subject contains one main word it is called a
> SIMPLE SUBJECT.
>
> When the subject contains two or more main words it is called a
> COMPOUND SUBJECT.

1. We *watched*.
2. We *were listening*.
3. We *watched* and *listened* carefully.
4. We *had been watching* intently and *were listening* carefully.

> When the predicate contains one main word it is called a
> SIMPLE PREDICATE.
>
> When the predicate contains two or more main words it is called a
> COMPOUND PREDICATE.

Note that a simple predicate may consist of only one word, or it may have one main word with a helper, e.g. *were listening*.

In the graphic analysis of sentences which contain compound subjects or compound predicates, an oval is drawn around the joining word.

EXERCISE 1: Analyse the following sentences graphically. Be on the lookout for compound subjects and predicates.

1. Halifax and Vancouver are ocean ports.

2. Ocean freighters load and unload cargoes on their docks.

3. With the completion of the St. Lawrence Seaway many inland ports will need larger docks.

4. Toronto and Hamilton should see ships from many lands.

5. Many other lake ports should grow and thrive with this great development.

The Simple Sentence

1. Maple trees	grow in Canada.
2. The maple leaf	is a Canadian emblem.
3. Maple syrup	is manufactured in the spring.
4. Many types of furniture	are made from maple wood.
5. Maples	have colourful leaves in the fall.

In each of the above sentences there is one subject and one predicate. Examine the sentences below to determine how many subjects and predicates there are in each sentence.

6. Pine and spruce	are Canadian trees.
7. They	grow and thrive in our climate.
8. Douglas fir and red cedar	are important west coast types.
9. Mild climate and heavy rainfall	provide good growing conditions.
10. Newsprint and lumber	are important products of our forests.

Note that a compound subject is still only one subject. Similarly, a compound predicate is one predicate.

> A sentence which contains one subject and one predicate is called a
> SIMPLE SENTENCE.

EXERCISE 1: At certain times the use of simple sentences can be very effective. At other times it is better to combine two or three short, simple sentences into one longer sentence.

Read each of the following groups of sentences aloud. Discuss whether the groups are more effective if left as they are or whether they should be combined into one sentence. Combine the latter groups.

1. I stepped across the threshold. The room was dark and still. I crouched against the wall. Then it happened.

2. After school I went to the game. My brother plays for the school team. It was a soccer game.

3. The evening sun was low in the sky. It cast long shadows across the valley.

4. One lone beaver dashed toward the water. The water was very calm.

5. Last Saturday I decided to help Dad. He was raking leaves from the back lawn. The lawn was a yellow and orange carpet.

6. Yesterday I awoke early. The sun was shining. It sparkled on a blanket of new snow.

7. The day dawned. Birds were singing. The forest animals stirred. The world yawned and was awake.

The Compound Sentence

Why is each of the following a simple sentence?

1. The nights turned cold.
2. Frost covered the ground.

These two simple sentences may be joined by a conjunction such as *and* to form a *compound sentence*. When this is done each simple sentence becomes what is called a *clause*. *A clause is a group of words containing a subject and a predicate.*

3. The nights turned cold and frost covered the ground.

Each clause in a compound sentence expresses a complete thought by itself. It does not depend on the other clause in the sentence. Therefore it is called an *independent clause* or a *principal clause.*

Examine the following compound sentences:

4. The days were getting shorter but Indian summer had not arrived.
5. Farmers were ploughing meadows or they were harvesting corn.
6. The days were cold but the cattle still grazed in the pasture and the sheep wandered across the hill.

Select the principal clauses in sentences 4, 5 and 6. Name the conjunctions. What punctuation mark might be used in the last sentence if the conjunction *but* were removed?

Sometimes compound sentences may be improved, or variety obtained, by removing the conjunction and substituting a semi-colon.

7. The days were getting shorter; Indian summer had not arrived.
8. Farmers were ploughing meadows; they were harvesting corn.
9. The days were cold; the cattle still grazed in the pasture; the sheep wandered across the hill.

A sentence which contains two or more principal clauses is a
COMPOUND SENTENCE.

EXERCISE 1: Join the following simple sentences with a conjunction or a semi-colon to make a compound sentence.

1. Outside was the sound of footsteps. Rover barked furiously.
2. Promises make friends. Performance keeps them.
3. Jim's baseball bat was broken. He mended it with tape.
4. Cold Arctic water meets the Gulf Stream. The meeting produces dense fogs.
5. During the night a storm blew up. The wind rose in intensity. Several fishing craft took shelter in the cove.

220

The Compound Sentence:

In a compound sentence the clauses are of equal value but the clauses must have some relationship to each other. Compare the two sentences below:

1. Quebec is an old city and we visited it last summer.
2. Quebec is an old city and the walls of the fortress can still be seen.

In the first sentence the two clauses refer to Quebec but the main ideas of the two clauses are not related. Therefore it is not a good compound sentence.

In the second sentence, each clause refers to the ancient appearance of the city and accordingly the two ideas are related. This is a good type of compound sentence.

Examine the following compound sentences:

3. The road to the cottage is in poor condition *and* it must be repaired this summer.
4. The road to the cottage is not in good condition *but* it is much better than last year.
5. We can drive to the cottage by road *or* we can take a boat from the landing.

The italicized conjunctions in the three sentences above join two principal clauses and are called *co-ordinate conjunctions*. In order to express the correct relationship between two or more clauses in a compound sentence, the correct co-ordinate conjunction must be used. The conjunction *and* is used to add one idea to another. *But* shows a contrast between two ideas. *Or* expresses an alternative idea or a choice of ideas.

EXERCISE 2: Write two compound sentences for each of the co-ordinate conjunctions *and*, *but*, and *or*.

EXERCISE 3: Write a compound sentence about each of the following:
1. the appearance of an old house
2. the contrast between two pets
3. the choice between two favourite sports
4. two places you would like to visit
5. your last holiday

Subordinate Clauses

A clause is a group of words containing a subject and a predicate. Examine the clauses in the following sentences:

1. *Ottawa is a city.*
2. *Ottawa is a city* which is the capital of Canada.
3. *Ottawa,* which is the capital of Canada, *is a city in Ontario.*

The clause in italics in each sentence above would make a simple sentence because it expresses a complete thought by itself. It is a *principal clause.*

The group of words *which is the capital of Canada* is a clause because it contains a subject and a predicate. This clause would not make a complete thought by itself. It is called a *subordinate clause.*

Look for (a) the principal clause, (b) the subordinate clause in each of these sentences:

1. After we cross the Detroit River we arrive in the United States.
2. Washington, which is the capital of the United States, is in the District of Columbia.
3. It has a mild winter because it is closer to the equator.
4. Because it is a warm current of water, the Gulf Stream, which flows along the eastern coast, moderates the climate.

Did you find two subordinate clauses in the last sentence? Note that a subordinate clause may be found at the beginning of a sentence, at the end of a sentence, or in the middle of a sentence.

EXERCISE 1: Select the principal clause and the subordinate clause or clauses from each of the following:

Example: They arrived after the bell had rung.
"They arrived"—principal clause
"after the bell had rung"—subordinate clause

1. Mother bought some salmon which was caught in British Columbia.
2. The fish are frozen before they are shipped to inland markets.
3. When we were in Sudbury we visited the nickel mine.
4. We also heard about the gold mines that are located in Timmins and Kirkland Lake.
5. Wheat which is grown on the prairies is shipped by rail to ports on the Great Lakes.
6. Many lake freighters that carry wheat dock at Port Arthur and Fort William.
7. After we had spent our holiday in Algonquin Park, we had many pleasant memories.
8. We visited the Habitation at Port Royal when we were in Nova Scotia.
9. If you travel across the continent by C.N.R. you will see Jasper.
10. The mountains which tower above the clouds are very impressive.

Subordinate Clauses:

Examine the italicized words in the following sentences.

1. (a) *Mountain* roads can be dangerous.
   (b) Roads *through the mountains* can be dangerous.
   (c) Roads *that wind through the mountains* can be dangerous.
2. (a) The *British* flag is the Union Jack.
   (b) The flag *of Britain* is the Union Jack.
   (c) The flag *which Britain flies* is the Union Jack.
3. (a) The ancient king was a *wealthy* man.
   (b) The ancient king was a man *of great wealth*.
   (c) The ancient king was a man *who was very wealthy*.

Note that the italicized word in each example (a) above is an adjective, and that each italicized group of words in (b) is an adjective phrase. They have the value of adjectives because they modify nouns.

In each of the (c) examples the italicized group of words contains a subject and a predicate. Therefore each group of words is a clause. The clause is not a complete thought by itself and accordingly it must be a subordinate clause. Each clause describes a noun and therefore it is called a *subordinate adjective clause*.

In the examples above, note the variety that may be obtained by using an adjective on some occasions, an adjective phrase sometimes, or a subordinate adjective clause at other times.

EXERCISE 2: Select the subordinate adjective clauses from the following sentences and give the relation of each.

Example: Penn, who founded Pennsylvania, was a Quaker.
   "who founded Pennsylvania"—is a subordinate adjective clause modifying the noun "Penn".

1. William Penn, who was the son of an English admiral, became a Quaker.
2. There came to him the idea that he might found a Quaker colony in the New World.
3. The monarch, who was King Charles II, granted him a large tract of land in America.
4. This land, which stretched westward from the Delaware River, was called Pennsylvania.
5. On the Delaware River was built a settlement which grew into the city of Philadelphia.
6. In four years it was larger than New York which had been founded fifty years earlier.
7. The Quakers, who did not believe in war, made peace with the Indians.
8. Both sides agreed to a treaty which was kept faithfully during the lifetime of the Quaker leader.

Subordinate Clauses:

EXERCISE 3: Expand the italicized word or group of words into a subordinate adjective clause. Write the sentence.

1. *Honest* people are happier people.
2. Irish linen may be purchased at the *corner* store.
3. *East* winds usually bring a storm.
4. Florence Nightingale was a woman *of great courage.*
5. Rudyard Kipling was a *famous* author.
6. The Welland Canal *joining the two lakes* is in Ontario.
7. Much of the sugar *used* is obtained from sugar cane.

EXERCISE 4: Write the subordinate adjective clauses from the following sentences. Underline the bare subject with a wavy line and the bare predicate with a straight line to prove that the group of words is a clause.

1. The caribou is a deer which lives in the far north.
2. An animal that is native to Australia is the kangaroo.
3. That bear that we saw hibernates in the winter.
4. The llama is a beast of burden which can work in the Andes mountains.
5. A native bird that is used on the New Zealand emblem is the kiwi.
6. The centipede is an animal that has one pair of legs for each part of its body.
7. The ladybug is one of the best friends that the farmer has.

EXERCISE 5: Write the principal clause from each sentence. Select each of the subordinate adjective clauses and give its relation.

1. A Nor'Wester who helped to blaze the way to the Western Sea was David Thompson.
2. He had an interesting career which began in the service of the Hudson's Bay Company.
3. The early years were spent at posts that were situated on the shores of Hudson Bay.
4. Inland posts that increased the fur trade gave him further experience.
5. Thompson was placed under the care of a company surveyor who gave him a thorough training.
6. Discontent caused him to change to a rival company that was known as the North West Company.
7. In their service he was the first white man who descended the Columbia River.
8. This explorer who kept careful records of his travels through the fur country drew the first map of the Canadian West.
9. His map which formed the foundation for all future maps of that area was very important.
10. The boy who had come to Hudson Bay as a lonely orphan had made a great name for himself.

224

Subordinate Clauses:

>   1. Lima is the capital of Peru.
>
>   2. In many ways it looks like an old Spanish city.

These two simple sentences may be joined with a conjunction to form a compound sentence if the writer wishes each thought to be of equal importance.

>   3. Lima is the capital of Peru *and* in many ways it looks like an old Spanish city.

However, if the writer wishes one thought to have more importance than the other, he can make the more important thought into a principal clause and the other into a subordinate adjective clause.

>   4. Lima, *which in many ways looks like an old Spanish city*, is the capital of Peru.
>
>   5. Lima, *which is the capital of Peru*, looks in many ways like an old Spanish city.

EXERCISE 6: Read each of the following pairs of sentences and decide which thought is the more important. Combine them into one sentence by making the less important thought into a subordinate adjective clause.

>   1. Latitude is the distance north and south of the equator. It is measured in degrees.
>
>   2. Astronomy is the study of stars and planets. It is the oldest of all the sciences.
>
>   3. Alaska belongs to the United States. It was purchased from Russia in 1867.
>
>   4. The Grand Canyon of the Colorado River is the world's most famous canyon. In places it is over a mile deep.
>
>   5. The koala bear eats only the leaves of the eucalyptus tree. This animal is native to Australia.
>
>   6. Montezuma was the emperor of the Aztecs. He was subdued by Cortez.
>
>   7. Another Spanish adventurer was Balboa. He discovered the Pacific Ocean.
>
>   8. The banana plant grows to a height of twenty feet. Only one stem of bananas is grown at a time.

USING PRINCIPAL AND SUBORDINATE CLAUSES:

1. Combine two or more related thoughts of equal importance with co-ordinate conjunctions such as, <u>and</u>, <u>but</u>, <u>or</u>.

2. Combine two or more related thoughts which are not of equal importance by making the less important thoughts into subordinate clauses.

Subordinate Clauses:

Examine the italicized words in the following sentences.

1. (a) Jet planes travel *quickly.*
   (b) Jet planes travel *with great speed.*
   (c) The air force uses jet planes *because they travel so quickly.*
2. (a) We shall visit the Museum *today.*
   (b) We shall visit the Museum *after lunch.*
   (c) We shall visit the Museum *when we are in Toronto.*
3. (a) *Here* stood an Indian village.
   (b) *At this place* was built the city of Quebec.
   (c) *Where two great rivers meet* the city of Montreal was built.

These italicized words or groups of words tell *how, when, where* **or** *why* about the bare predicate. They all have the value of adverbs. The single italicized word in each example (a) above is an adverb, **and** each italicized group of words in (b) is an adverb phrase.

In each of the (c) examples, the italicized group of words contains **a** subject and a predicate. Therefore each group of words is a clause. The clause is not a complete thought by itself and accordingly it must **be** a subordinate clause. Each clause has the value of an adverb and therefore it is called a *subordinate adverb clause.*

In the examples above note the variety that may be obtained **in** written English by varying the three forms, the adverb, the **adverb** phrase, or the subordinate adverb clause.

EXERCISE 7: (a) Select the subordinate adverb clauses from the following sentences and give the relation of each.

Example: When you cross the St. Croix River you have reached New Brunswick.

"When you cross the St. Croix River" is a subordinate adverb clause modifying the verb "have reached."

1. When sugar cane is fully grown it towers above a man's head.
2. The climate becomes warmer as we approach the equator.
3. Because it is salty, the ocean does not freeze.
4. If you lived in Australia, Christmas would be in the summer.
5. Canada became British after the Seven Years' War ended.
6. Because the earth turns from west to east, the sun rises in the east.
7. Unless the earth travelled in its orbit around the sun, seasons would remain the same all year.
8. We were in the province of Quebec when the train reached Montreal.
9. Since Halifax is an ocean port vessels can dock there in winter.
10. Although Victoria is on an island, it can be reached quickly by air.

(b) Make a list of the words which were used to introduce the subordinate adverb clauses in the exercise above.

Subordinate Clauses:

When two thoughts are related and nearly equal in importance, they may be combined by using a compound sentence. When one thought is less important than the other, it may be written as a subordinate clause.

EXERCISE 8: Combine each of the following pairs of sentences into one sentence by making the less important thought into a subordinate adverb clause.

1. We travelled north towards Newfoundland. The weather became colder.

2. The warm water of the Gulf Stream meets cold Arctic water. Dense fogs often result.

3. The temperature reached the freezing point. Then the water began to freeze in the large glass container.

4. The glass in the container cracked. Water must expand when freezing.

5. Clouds can be carried many miles away by the wind. The moisture in them may fall as rain.

6. Often there is a change in the weather. Before this there usually is a change in air pressure.

7. A change in air pressure affects the reading on a barometer. Therefore the barometer helps us to forecast weather.

8. Weather stations are located throughout Canada. Changes in the weather can be predicted many hours in advance.

EXERCISE 9: Rewrite each of the following compound sentences, making one of the principal clauses into either a subordinate adjective clause or a subordinate adverb clause. Be ready to tell which it is.

1. Julius Caesar was a Roman general and he wrote a book about his wars.

2. Caesar was an able writer and he told us much about the people of Britain.

3. This book was written in Latin but it has been translated to tell us much about the ancient Britons.

4. The ancient Britons were tall and strong and they had blue eyes and long fair hair.

5. They spent their time in hunting and fishing but they were fond of war.

6. The people were divided into tribes and each tribe had its own chief.

7. Besides the warriors the ancient Britons had priests and these men were called Druids.

8. Other men were the bards and they composed songs in honour of the noble men of their tribe.

Subordinate Clauses:

Examine the italicized words in the following sentences:
1. (a) I read the *report*.
   (b) I read *what he had written*.
2. (a) The prospector discovered the *cave*.
   (b) The prospector discovered *that the opening led into the cave*.
3. (a) Then we learned the *reason*.
   (b) Then we learned *why the prospector wanted the map*.
4. (a) A stranger expected his *arrival*.
   (b) A stranger knew *when he would arrive*.

Each of the italicized words in the (a) examples is a noun, object of the verb in the sentence. Each italicized group of words in the (b) examples is a clause acting as a completing part because it answers the question:

1. (b) I read something?	—what he had written
2. (b) The prospector discovered something?	—that the opening led into the cave
3. (b) We learned something?	—why the prospector wanted the map
4. (b) A stranger knew something?	—when he would arrive

Each of these clauses has the value of a noun which is the object of a verb. Each clause is, therefore, a *subordinate noun clause*.

EXERCISE 10: Select the subordinate noun clauses from the following sentences and give the relation of each.

Example: He discovered that the West Indies were north of the equator.

"that the West Indies were north of the equator" is a subordinate noun clause, object of the verb "discovered."

1. We learned that the largest island in the West Indies is Cuba.
2. I know Cuba is famous for sugar.
3. The teacher told us that Cuba exports more sugar than any other country.
4. In this picture can you see what the men on the plantation are doing?
5. This geography book states when the tobacco crop is harvested.
6. It also reports some Cubans work in mines in the mountains.
7. From the map I discovered that Havana is the capital of Cuba.
8. I believe it is the largest city of the island.
9. This poster says winter is the tourist season in Havana.
10. We know why Havana is a popular resort for tourists.

Subordinate Clauses:

A subordinate noun clause may also be used in the following ways:

1. Subject of a verb

   (a) *What we learn in science* is interesting.

   (b) *How the telephone works* is explained in this book.

2. Subjective completion of a verb

   (a) That is *what we should do.*

   (b) The reason was *that it was too cold.*

3. Object of a preposition

   (a) They filled the barrels with *what they had picked.*

   (b) He was praised for *what he had done*

Although a subordinate noun clause is most frequently used in a sentence as object of the verb, it may be used in any one of the other three ways noted above.

> A subordinate clause which has the value of a noun is called a subordinate noun clause. It may be used as
> (a) object of a verb.
> (b) subject of a verb.
> (c) subjective completion of a verb.
> (d) object of a preposition.

EXERCISE 11: Select the subordinate noun clauses from the following sentences and state the relation of each.

1. I know that the earth turns from west to east.
2. That the earth turns on its axis is a well-known fact.
3. This turning is what gives us day and night.
4. We obtained this knowledge from what we had been taught.
5. We also learned that the earth travels in an orbit around the sun.
6. Do you know what is the distance to the sun?
7. How fast light travels can be determined.
8. The teacher explained that the moon reflected light from the sun.
9. Our science book indicates what causes the four seasons.
10. From time to time we observe what is called an eclipse of the sun.

The Complex Sentence

     1. Ottawa is the capital of Canada.

Because this sentence contains one subject and one predicate, it is called a *simple sentence*.

     2. Ottawa is the capital of Canada and it is situated on the Ottawa River.

Because this sentence contains two principal clauses, it is called a *compound sentence*.

     3. Ottawa which is the capital of Canada is situated on the Ottawa River.

     4. When we were in Ottawa, we visited the Parliament Buildings.

     5. We learned that Ottawa is the capital of Canada.

Each of the three sentences above contains a principal clause and a subordinate clause.   Select each subordinate clause and tell what kind it is.

> A sentence which contains a principal clause and one or more subordinate clauses is a COMPLEX SENTENCE.

     6. Ottawa which is the capital of Canada is a large city and it is situated on the Ottawa River.

Because this sentence contains two principal clauses it might be called a compound sentence.   Because it also contains a principal clause and a subordinate clause, it might be called a complex sentence.   However, since it has the requirements of both a compound sentence and a complex sentence, it is called a *compound-complex* sentence.

EXERCISE 1: Combine each of the following series of sentences into a complex sentence, by making the less important thought into a subordinate clause.

     1. Newfoundland was Britain's oldest colony.   It is now Canada's tenth province.

     2. The capital of Newfoundland is St. John's.   St. John's is an old city.

     3. It is built on a deep sheltered bay.   This gives it an excellent harbour.

     4. Newfoundlanders are not fond of living inland.   They love the sea.

     5. In the interior are great forests.   The chief products from these forests are pulp and paper.

     6. One of the pulp mills is at Grand Falls.   It is on the railway line. The railway crosses the interior.

     7. The railway is different from that in other parts of Canada.   The tracks are of a narrower gauge.

     8. Newfoundland is the part of Canada nearest to the British Isles. Trans-Atlantic planes stop to re-fuel at Gander airport.

The Complex Sentence:

EXERCISE 2: Combine each pair of sentences into a complex sentence. Write the principal clause and the subordinate clause telling its kind and relation as proof that the sentence is a complex sentence.

> *Example:* The Richelieu River drains Lake Champlain. It empties into the St. Lawrence River.
>
> The Richelieu River which drains Lake Champlain empties into the St. Lawrence River.
>
> "The Richelieu River empties into the St. Lawrence River" is the principal clause.
>
> "which drains Lake Champlain" is a subordinate adjective clause modifying the noun "Richelieu River."

1. The earth is the most familiar planet to us. We live on it.

2. The smallest planet is Mercury. It is nearest the sun.

3. One other planet is nearer the sun than the earth. It is Venus.

4. Mars has two small moons. They revolve about this planet.

5. Jupiter is the largest planet in the sun's family. Twelve moons revolve about it.

6. Many small moons move quite rapidly about Saturn. They seem to make solid rings around the planet.

7. Plants or animals could not live on Jupiter, Saturn, Uranus, or Neptune. Each of these planets has poisonous gases in its atmosphere.

8. No one knows about the atmosphere of Pluto. It is too far away.

9. The five planets out beyond Mars are very cold. They are far away from the sun.

10. The planets are considered members of the sun's family. They revolve about the sun.

EXERCISE 3: Combine each of the following series of sentences into a compound-complex sentence with two or more principal clauses and one or more subordinate clauses.

1. Fur seals spend much of the year in the warmer waters of the Pacific Ocean. As warmer weather comes, they migrate north.

2. Sequoia trees are very large plants. These huge trees are found in California. Sequoia trees are among the largest plants ever known in the history of the world.

3. Rice is a flowering plant. It belongs to the grass family. Rice is the principal food of nearly half the people in the world.

The Complex Sentence:

Complex sentences can be used to avoid making statements such as the following which do not say what the writer intended to say. Read each carefully and state orally why the meaning is not clear.

    1. (a) Sitting in the car, a large brown bear crossed the road.
       (b) I saw a jet plane walking to school.
       (c) Tom noticed the time coming in for supper.

Note how the following complex sentences clarify what the writer intended to say:

    2. (a) While we were sitting in the car, a large brown bear crossed the road.
       (b) I saw a jet plane when I was walking to school.
       (c) As he was coming in for supper, Tom noticed the time.

Examine the following sentences:

    3. (a) We saw a boat on the river that was painted green.
       (b) There were chocolate cookies in the box which we ate.

Modifiers should be placed near the words which they modify. Note the following complex sentences:

    4. (a) On the river we saw a boat that was painted green.
       (b) In the box there were chocolate cookies which we ate.

A complex sentence is made up of:
(a) a principal clause and a subordinate adjective clause, or
(b) a principal clause and a subordinate adverb clause, or
(c) a principal clause and a subordinate noun clause, or
(d) a principal clause and one or more subordinate clauses.

EXERCISE 4: Rewrite each of the following using a complex sentence to make the meaning clear to the reader.

  1. Crossing the tracks the train hit the cow.
  2. We saw an overturned motor boat crossing the bridge.
  3. Tom heard the clock strike nine coming from the movie.
  4. We went to the game and we were late and we didn't get a seat.
  5. There was the robin. It was collecting food. The food was for the young robins in the nest.
  6. While crossing the street the light turned red.
  7. Bill saw a totem pole visiting the museum.
  8. The tree shaded the entrance. It was dark. I could not see the gate.
  9. There were only five of us and we needed an extra player to commence the game.
  10. After reaching the cottage the rain stopped.

The Complex Sentence:

Examine the following complex sentences. Select the word which introduces each subordinate clause.

1. We visited the Citadel *after we reached Halifax.*
2. This is the spot *where the main fortress was built.*
3. We learned *that it houses an interesting museum.*

Each of these words joins the clause to the word which the clause modifies. These joining words are known as *conjunctions*. Because each of these conjunctions begins a subordinate clause, it is called a *subordinate conjunction*.

In the following examples, note that a subordinate clause may be used to introduce a sentence. In sentences of this type the first word will be a subordinate conjunction.

4. Before we reached Nova Scotia, we crossed the Bay of Fundy.
5. Although the fog was heavy, the sun finally broke through.
6. Until the boat docked at Digby, we basked in the warm sunshine.

EXERCISE 5: Select the subordinate conjunctions from the following complex sentences:

1. When a metal is heated, it expands.
2. The barometer falls before the weather becomes unsettled.
3. Ice floats because it is lighter than water.
4. If you travel up a river, you may reach its source.
5. Although glass is hard, a diamond will scratch it.
6. Electricity is produced while water power turns the generator.
7. Unless the night is clear, you cannot see an eclipse of the moon.
8. I do not know whether Montreal will remain Canada's largest city.
9. Since Churchill is farther north, it has much colder winters.
10. Because salt water does not freeze, ocean ports can remain open all winter.

EXERCISE 6: (Oral) A knowledge of subordinate conjunctions enables a person to construct complex sentences much more readily.
Use each of the following words as a subordinate conjunction in a complex sentence.

when	unless	although	until
as	because	before	if
after	though	where	wherever
whenever	whether	while	since

Review II

1. State in a sentence answer the name of the kind of sentence which:
   (a) asks a question.
   (b) expresses strong feeling.
   (c) makes a statement.
   (d) gives a command.

2. Write the following sentence in (a) inverted order (b) split order:
   A wisp of smoke drifted upward from a little pile of wood dust.

3. Analyse graphically:
   (a) Alaska was purchased by the United States from Russia in 1867.
   (b) Now gold is one of Alaska's valuable exports.
   (c) Every summer its beautiful scenery brings many tourists to the territory.

EXERCISE 2:

1. Combine the following three sentences to form:
   (a) a simple sentence.
   (b) a compound sentence.
   (c) a complex sentence.

Near the bank of the river was a clearing. We saw an overturned boat. It was hidden under a pile of brush.

2. (a) Tell whether each of the following sentences is simple, compound or complex.
   (b) Select the principal clauses.
   (c) Select the subordinate clauses and tell their kind and relation.

During the sixteenth century European sailors were searching for a sea route to China. Some believed that they could find it north of Canada. Because many of them added some new island or sea to our knowledge, the map of northern Canada is filled with the names of these explorers. It was Amundsen who first sailed from the Atlantic to the Pacific. The first vessel which sailed the route in both directions was the R.C.M.P. boat *St. Roch*. Northern Canada is still not completely explored and there is much to be learned today beyond the Arctic Circle.

3. From the above paragraph select:
   (a) a co-ordinate conjunction joining two nouns.
   (b) a co-ordinate conjunction joining two principal clauses.
   (c) a subordinate conjunction introducing a subordinate adverb clause.

XIV ▲ THE PARTS OF SPEECH

Language exercises that deal with developing sentence sense, with the kinds of sentences according to function and according to construction, and with the parts of the sentence, have been presented. Putting sentences together in natural, split, and inverted order, using assertive, imperative, interrogative, and exclamatory sentences, combining ideas into simple, compound, and complex sentences are all means by which written English may be improved. Continued use of these means, from day to day, in all forms of written work, will surely and steadily develop language skills.

Now that a knowledge of the parts of the sentence has been mastered, a study of the different kinds of words which are found in sentences will begin. The classifications or names of words are called PARTS OF SPEECH. A knowledge of the parts of speech should help a person to speak and to write correctly. This knowledge will provide the skill necessary in revising written work, to determine if what has been written is correct.

Here is a list of the names of the eight main parts of speech:

noun	verb	adjective	preposition	interjection
pronoun		adverb	conjunction	

In addition to the parts of speech, sentences include the following:

the definite article—*the*
the indefinite article—*a, an*

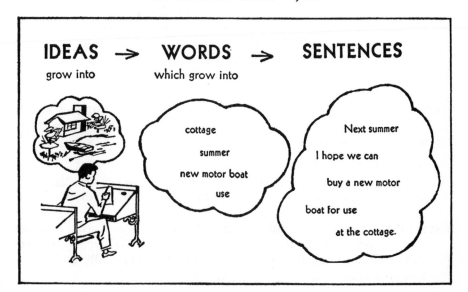

IDEAS → WORDS → SENTENCES
grow into   which grow into

cottage

summer

new motor boat

use

Next summer

I hope we can

buy a new motor

boat for use

at the cottage.

Nouns

1. Nouns name persons or places:
   (a) *Mackenzie* reached the *Pacific Ocean*.
   (b) *Winnipeg* is the *capital* of *Manitoba*.

2. Nouns name things:
   (a) A *bicycle* has two *wheels*.
   (b) A *quadruped* is an *animal* with four *feet*.

3. Nouns name unseen things or qualities:
   (a) He has a good *sense* of *humour*.
   (b) Its *thickness* will increase its *strength*.

> A word that names a person, a place, a thing, or an unseen thing or quality is called a
> ## NOUN.

EXERCISE 1: As an oral exercise, give a list of nouns that name:

1. Five boys	11. Five minerals
2. Five girls	12. Five trees
3. Five famous people	13. Five automobiles
4. Five world capitals	14. Five fish
5. Five European rivers	15. Five wild animals
6. Five oceans	16. Five games
7. Five islands	17. Five holidays
8. Five African countries	18. Five mountains
9. Five states of the United States	19. Five unseen things
10. Five counties	20. Five qualities

EXERCISE 2: A word that names a group of persons or things is known as a *collective noun*. Write the collective noun which might be used for a group of:

Example: cattle—herd

ducks	bees	singers	birds	pupils	spectators
soldiers	players	scouts	fish	sailors	directors

EXERCISE 3: From your reader select ten nouns which you consider desirable to add to your vocabulary. Write each of them in a sentence and look for opportunities to use them orally to help fix them in your mind.

Nouns:

Examine these two lists of nouns:

1. girl   boy   province   strait   sea   apple
2. Mary   John   Alberta   Cabot   Black   Delicious

The first list names any person, place, or thing and these words are called COMMON nouns.

The second list names a particular person, place, or thing. These are called PROPER nouns. Note that *all proper nouns must begin with capital letters.*

Common nouns do not require capital letters. But if they are used with a proper noun as the name of a particular place, they will then become proper nouns. Examine the following sentences:

1. We crossed the lake last summer.
2. We crossed Lake Superior last summer.
3. The first explorers crossed the ocean.
4. The first explorers crossed the Atlantic Ocean.

EXERCISE 4: Select a proper noun for each of the following and use that proper noun in a sentence:

1. a town
2. a park in your province
3. a city in England
4. a university
5. the Prime Minister of Canada
6. an island in the West Indies
7. a country in Central America
8. a famous Canadian poet
9. the largest ocean in the world
10. an important international body
11. an Asiatic country
12. the capital of Spain
13. a very large river
14. a planet
15. the shortest month
16. the title of a book
17. a famous street
18. the largest province
19. a race of people
20. a reigning sovereign

EXERCISE 5: As an oral exercise state as many common nouns as you can that correspond with each of the following proper nouns:

Ottawa	Washington	Lisbon	Vancouver
Nelson	Suez	April	Radisson
Ohio	Mexico	Ungava	Plymouth
Superior	Laurier	Europe	Robson
Simcoe	Halifax	Calgary	Hudson

Number in Nouns

Examine these two lists of nouns:

1. boy valley city loaf brush tomato
2. boys valleys cities loaves brushes tomatoes

When a noun names only one of its kind, as in the first list, it is said to be in the SINGULAR number. When a noun names two or more things it is said to be in the PLURAL number.

Letters and figures add an apostrophe and *s* to make them plural as shown in the following examples:

3. two a's; three b's; four 5's; five 9's

EXERCISE 1: Write the plural form of each of the following by following the directions given:

1. girl—by adding *s* to the singular
2. goose—by changing the vowel sound
3. calf—by changing *f* to *v* and adding *es*
4. hero—by adding *es*
5. child—by adding a suffix
6. lady—by changing *y* to *i* and adding *es*
7. father-in-law—by making the most important part plural
8. man-servant—by making both parts plural
9. deer—by using the same word
10. radius—by changing the *us* to *i*
11. larva—by adding an *e*
12. memorandum—by changing *um* to *a*
13. crisis—by changing *is* to *es*
14. phenomenon—by changing *on* to *a*
15. 8—by adding an apostrophe and *s*

EXERCISE 2: Write each of the following singular nouns. Beside each write its plural form.

toy	cargo	woman	oasis	knife
mouse	solo	ox	terminus	brother-in-law
half	belief	tooth	spoonful	ditch

EXERCISE 3: On the chalkboard, where they may be left for several days, make lists of those nouns which form their plurals in the same way. See Exercise 1 for the headings.

EXERCISE 4: Make lists of the following:

1. Nouns which have no plural—e.g. steel
2. Nouns which have the same plural form as the singular—e.g. sheep
3. Nouns which are used only in the plural—e.g. scissors
4. Nouns plural in form but singular in meaning—e.g. news

Nouns

Examine the following sentences:

1. George, please bring me the dictionary.
2. You, Jean, are to find the meaning of the word.
3. I think, my young friend, that you are correct.

A noun, such as "George," "Jean," or "friend," used to name a person addressed is said to be the *nominative of address*. It is important, in this case, to make sure that the word of address is separated from the rest of the sentence by a comma.

Examine these sentences:

1. Mozart, the musician, has become very famous.
2. Have you met Shirley, the new pupil?
3. Mr. Jones, our neighbour, is her father.

A noun, such as "musician," "pupil," or "neighbour," added as an explanatory word but denoting the same person it is explaining, is said to be a *noun in apposition*. It is important, in this case too, to make sure that the noun in apposition is separated from the rest of the sentence by a comma.

Examine the following sentences:

1. An *intelligent* person could not believe that.
2. A person of such *intelligence* could not believe that.

A sentence may be varied by replacing a word such as "intelligent" with a phrase containing the noun form of the word, "intelligence."

EXERCISE 1: Replace the italicized word with a phrase that contains the noun form of the word. Use this alternate form orally in a sentence.

1. such an *important* discovery
2. the *unmerciful* ruler
3. a *happy* state
4. a *distinguished* friend
5. an *exciting* event
6. an *able* leader
7. a *courageous* soldier
8. an *interesting* story
9. a *mathematical* text
10. a *violent* storm

Possessive Form of Nouns

Study the form of each underlined noun in the following sentences:

1. The man's hat blew across the street.

2. The lady's gloves were left on the chair.

3. Ross's sister is in Europe.

Notice that each of these underlined nouns shows possession. **Each of these nouns is singular.**

A singular noun shows possession by adding an apostrophe and s.

Study the form of each underlined noun in the following sentences:

1. The women's group meets on Tuesday.

2. The children's library is upstairs.

3. The lumbermen's boots are spiked.

Notice that each of these underlined nouns which show possession is plural. Each of these plural nouns does not end in s.

A plural noun not ending in s shows possession by adding an apostrophe and s.

EXERCISE 1: Write sentences for each of the following nouns, using

(a) the possessive singular form of the noun.

(b) the possessive plural form of the noun.

Example: (a) The man's coat was on the floor.

(b) The men's coats were on the floor.

1. man	5. ox	9. policeman
2. woman	6. foreman	10. mouse
3. child	7. salmon	11. Englishman
4. deer	8. sheep	12. fireman

Possessive Form of Nouns:

Study the form of each underlined noun in the following sentences:

1. (a) The boy's cap is on the shelf.
   (b) The <u>boys'</u> caps are on the shelf.

2. (a) Each boy has a boy's stick.
   (b) The boys play on the <u>boys'</u> rink.

3. (a) If the boy has a club it is the boy's club.
   (b) If the boys have a club it is the <u>boys'</u> club.

> A plural noun ending in s shows pos-
> session by adding an apostrophe only.

Much of the difficulty in writing the correct possessive form of nouns will disappear if you

(a) *write the noun that is to show ownership;*
(b) *decide how to make that noun show possession.*

Examples: 1. A girl has a bracelet.
   (a) girl; (b) girl's
   Now you know the correct form: the girl's bracelet.

2. The girls have skates.
   (a) girls; (b) girls'
   Now you know the correct form: the girls' skates.

EXERCISE 2: Write each of the following in the possessive form in a sentence. Note that the plural nouns do end in *s*.

Example: The horses of the cowboys.
   The cowboys' horses thundered across the bridge.

1. shoes for ladies
2. the cabin for hunters
3. the trail of foxes
4. equipment for soldiers
5. the claws of eagles
6. the home of my aunts
7. the uniforms of scouts
8. the meeting for mothers
9. the attendance of several pupils
10. the library for girls and boys

Possessive Form of Nouns:

> Follow these steps in writing the possessive form:
> 1. Write the noun that is to show ownership.
> 2. Decide how to make that noun show possession.

EXERCISE 3: Write each sentence, using the correct possessive form:

1. A man buys a ————————————— hat.
2. The men have organized a ————————————— club.
3. A child should use a ——————————— toothbrush.
4. Children may borrow books from the ——————————— library.
5. If a girl has a bracelet we say it is a ——————————— bracelet.
6. The girls spent July at a ——————————— camp.
7. If John buys a tie it is ——————————— tie.
8. The boys come into the school through the ——————————— entrance.
9. We should buy a ——————————— watch for the lady.
10. The ladies went to the store for a sale of ——————————— coats.

EXERCISE 4: Write each of the following sentences, inserting the apostrophe to show the correct possessive form of the nouns.

1. That boys writing is excellent.
2. Several boys maps are on the table.
3. Mens and boys overshoes are on sale.
4. Doctors offices are on the second floor.
5. This pupils work is complete.
6. This is a ladys shoe; those are girls.
7. The principal examined pupils writing in three classes.
8. A nurses residence has just been built beside the hospital.
9. The firemens helmets were covered with ice.
10. Mother joined a ladies group at the church.

EXERCISE 5: Read and complete the following sentences orally:

Example: The boy's book belongs to __a boy__ .

1. The girl's belt belongs to ———————.
2. The girls' collection belongs to ———————.
3. The boys' game was played by the ———————.
4. My uncles' horses belong to my ———————.
5. My aunt's letter was written by my ———————.
6. The pupils' efforts refers to the efforts of the ———————.
7. The pupil's writing is the writing of ———————.
8. The ladies' bazaar was run by ———————.
9. The engineer's cap belongs to ———————.
10. The Scouts' uniform is worn by ———————.

Nouns Used in Sentences

Examine the use of the italicized noun in each sentence:

1. *Wheat* grows in Canada.
2. Canada exports *wheat*.
3. This grain is *wheat*.
4. Flour is made from *wheat*.

The noun *wheat* is used in the following ways:

(a) subject of a verb, "grows."
(b) object of a verb, "exports."
(c) subjective completion of a verb, "is."
(d) object of a preposition, "from," in the phrase "from wheat."

EXERCISE 1: State the relationship of each of the nouns in italics.

1. The *Thames* is a *river* in *England*.
2. Southampton has an excellent *harbour*.
3. Liverpool is an important *port* on the Mersey River.
4. Sheffield is noted for its *cutlery*.
5. *Shakespeare* was born at *Stratford* on the Avon River.
6. Oxford and Cambridge are two famous university *towns* in the *country*.

Nouns which name objects which actually exist are called *concrete nouns*.

For example: boy, horse, city, book

Nouns which name qualities, feelings or things that we cannot see are called *abstract nouns*.

For example: beauty, poverty, growth

Abstract nouns should be followed closely by a concrete noun so that the meaning may be clear and definite.

For example: The *wisdom* of *Solomon* is recorded in the Bible.

EXERCISE 2: Use each of the following abstract nouns in a sentence. Make sure that each abstract noun is closely followed by a concrete noun so that its meaning is well defined.

speed	honesty	strength	poverty
safety	beauty	accuracy	pleasure
endurance	danger	freedom	triumph
interest	wonder	courage	growth

Pronouns

To avoid repetition, other words may sometimes be used in place of nouns. They are called *pronouns*. The word for which the pronoun stands is called the *antecedent* of the pronoun.

1. (a) Mary has a radio. *She* brought *it* to school.

   (b) The pupils listen to two programs. *They* enjoy *them* very much.

> A word that takes the place of a noun is called a
> PRONOUN.

In the examples at the top of the page, the antecedent of the pronoun *she* is *Mary*. Select each of the other pronouns and give its antecedent.

A pronoun must agree with its antecedent. Examine the following:

2. The boys brought the dog with (him, them).

3. The boys shouted, "(I, we) shall help (myself, ourselves).

The following sentences are correct:

2. The boys brought the dog with them.

3. The boys shouted, "We shall help ourselves."

The pronoun *who* or *whom* is used when the antecedent names a person. *Which* is used only when the antecedent names an animal, place, or thing. *That* may refer to a person, place, or thing. Note the following examples:

4. The explorer *who* built the Habitation was Champlain.

5. The city *which* now stands on its site is Quebec.

6. A governor *that* became famous in New France was Frontenac.

EXERCISE 1: Select each pronoun from the following exercise and beside it write its antecedent.

1. Here was the explorer who rounded the Cape of Good Hope.

2. The man, about whom the class studied, was a famous sailor.

3. Tom said, "I have a picture of the ships and it shows they have many sails."

4. Bill asked Tom, "Would you lend me the picture?"

5. Tom replied, "We can find a picture of them in this book."

Kinds of Pronouns

Examine the following sentences and select the pronouns.
1. (a) I brought the books with me.
   (b) We brought the books with us.

2. (a) You brought the books with you.
   (b) You brought the books with you.

3. (a) He brought the books with him.
   (b) She brought the books with her.
   (c) They brought the books with them.

Pronouns which denote persons are called PERSONAL PRONOUNS.

In group 1 above, the pronouns refer to

	SINGULAR	PLURAL
the person speaking	I, me	we, us

In group 2 above, the pronouns refer to

the person spoken to	you	you

In group 3 above, the pronouns refer to

the person spoken about	he, him, she, her	they, them

Pronouns referring to the person speaking are called pronouns of the FIRST PERSON:

    I, me, myself, mine; we, us, ourselves, ours

Pronouns referring to the person spoken to are called pronouns of the SECOND PERSON:

    you, yourself, yours; you, yourselves, yours

Pronouns referring to the person or persons spoken about are called pronouns of the THIRD PERSON:

he, him, himself, his, she, her, herself, hers; they, them, themselves, theirs

---

Examine the following sentences:

	SINGULAR	PLURAL
First person	1. I run.	We run
Second person	2. You run.	You run
Third person	3. He runs. She runs.	They run

When the pronoun, used as a subject, is the third person singular, **note** that *s* must be added to the verb.

Kinds of Pronouns:

1. *Who* discovered it?
2. *Which* is the larger river?
3. *What* is the date of its origin?
4. *Whom* did the settlers fear?
5. *Whose* is this?

> Pronouns which are used in asking questions are called
> INTERROGATIVE PRONOUNS.
> who, which, what, whom, whose

6. Here is a sample of each pupil's writing. *This* is the best.
7. *That* was written by the new pupil.
8. *These* are the work of the pupils in the first row.
9. *Those* were put up yesterday.

> Pronouns used to point out some particular person or thing are
> DEMONSTRATIVE PRONOUNS.
> this, that, these, those

10. Some girls brought umbrellas; *some* brought rain capes.
11. *Some* of the girls got wet.
12. *Several* of the boys waited in the old barn.
13. *All* were glad when the storm was over.

Note that the words in italics are pronouns. However, the first word in sentence 10 is an adjective, and not a pronoun. Why? The italicized words in the following are used as:

ADJECTIVES	PRONOUNS
Some boys shouted.	*Some* of the boys shouted.
Several girls ran.	*Several* of the girls ran.
Mary saw *one* robin.	Mary saw *one* of the robins.
Few children noticed it.	*Few* of the children noticed it.

> Pronouns which refer to some indefinite person or thing are
> INDEFINITE PRONOUNS.
> some, several, few, one, other, any, none, many, either, neither, each, somebody, something, everybody, anything, all, both, enough

Kinds of Pronouns:

EXERCISE 1: Select each of the pronouns from the following sentences and state whether it is a personal, interrogative, demonstrative, or indefinite pronoun.

1. Who has read about the original inhabitants of Nova Scotia, the Micmac Indians?

2. The records of early explorers describe them as friendly and intelligent.

3. Some of the warriors hunted bears in winter by detecting vapours rising from their dens.

4. Then they killed the sleepy animals with spears.

5. Caribou were hunted with bow and arrow, and these provided the skins for summer clothing.

6. Micmac garments were alike for men and women, but those for women reached a foot lower than those worn by men.

7. What did the Micmacs worship?

8. They turned toward the east when asking favours for themselves.

9. Only after he had become the best hunter or warrior might a brave be selected as a chief.

10. Few of this race now inhabit Nova Scotia.

EXERCISE 2: A pronoun should have its antecedent definitely and clearly expressed. It should also agree with its antecedent in number. Rewrite the following sentences, making any necessary changes to make the meaning clear. Note that in some sentences only the order needs to be rearranged.

1. I found a purse on the road which had a long leather strap.

2. Ted had to carry the dog belonging to his brother because he had a sore paw.

3. The team won all of its games which was a credit to the school.

4. Jim carried the basket and the pail although it was too heavy for him.

5. Either girl may go if they wish.

6. Each of the boys may bring theirs.

7. Mother said I must wash the cups for my aunts although they weren't dirty.

8. We tied the score at half time which made it very exciting.

9. A dog is an intelligent animal and they are easy to train.

10. I saw a midget in the building that was only three feet high.

Kinds of Pronouns:

Examine the italicized pronoun in each of the following sentences:

1. Balboa was the man *who* reached the Pacific.
2. The land *that* he crossed is now known as the Isthmus of Panama.
3. The standard *which* Balboa carried was the flag of Spain.

Note that:

(a) Each italicized word is a pronoun which takes the place of its antecedent.

(b) Each italicized word acts as a subordinate conjunction because it introduces a subordinate clause.

> A pronoun which introduces a subordinate clause is called a conjunctive pronoun or a
> ### RELATIVE PRONOUN.

Remember:

who, whom are used when the antecedent names a person.

which, what are used when the antecedent names a place or thing.

that may be used when the antecedent refers to a person, place, or thing.

EXERCISE 3: Write the following sentences, supplying a suitable relative pronoun.

1. The Frenchman ————— explored the Mississippi was LaSalle.

2. The Mississippi is a river ————— flows into the Gulf of Mexico.

3. An American city ————— is located at its mouth is New Orleans.

4. It was Spanish priests ————— built missions in California.

5. A great discovery ————— led many people to rush to California was made in 1848.

6. These men ————— reached California in 1849 were called Forty-niners.

7. ————— California now considers as liquid gold is the water from her mountain streams.

8. It was Ponce de Leon ————— claimed Florida for Spain.

9. He gave it this name perhaps for the flowers ————— he saw everywhere.

10. Ponce de Leon is famous as the man ————— searched for the Fountain of Youth.

Case in Pronouns

Some pronouns have both a subject and an object form.

Subject Form	Object Form
I	me
we	us
he	him
she	her
they	them
who	whom

Examine the pronouns in the following sentences:

1. *He* did it.   It was *he*.
2. *They* are here.   It is *they*.
3. Father carried *him*.
4. Give the letter to *him*.

The subject form of the pronoun is used as: (a) the subject of a verb, (b) the subjective completion of a verb.   Pronouns which are used as subjects or as subjective completions are said to be in the subjective case or the NOMINATIVE CASE.

The object form of the pronoun is used as: (a) the object of a verb, (b) the object of a preposition in a phrase.   Pronouns which are used as objects are said to be in the OBJECTIVE CASE.

EXERCISE 1: Five examples showing the difficulties commonly encountered in using pronouns are given below.   Following each correct example as a pattern, compose five other sentences, using a different pronoun each time if possible, and read them orally.   (One of these difficulties per day might be treated over a period of a week, and the process repeated several times throughout the year.)

1. Object form of the pronoun separated from the verb or preposition by another noun or pronoun:
   (a) Mother chose Tom and *me*.
   (b) Divide the candy between you and *me*.
2. Who and whom difficulty:
   (a) I know *who* is there.   (b) I know *whom* you saw.
3. Subjective completion difficulty:
   (a) It is *he* who was there.   (b) It was *she* whom you met.
   (c) Was it *they* who ran?   (d) Is it *we* whom you see?
   (e) It was Tom and *I* who went.
4. Pronoun used as an adjective:
   (a) *We* boys are going.   (b) Give it to *us* boys.
5. Subject form when the predicate is understood:
   (a) Mary is taller than *I* (am).
   (b) The girls are not as fast as *we* (are).

Review III

EXERCISE 1: Write each of these common nouns, and beside it write a proper noun which corresponds with it.

river	street	author	explorer	bay
city	holiday	country	capital	boy

EXERCISE 2: Write the plural form of each of the following:

woman	solo	calf	radius	m
valley	hero	goose	deer	mouse

EXERCISE 3: Write the plural form of each italicized noun and then make it possessive.

man coats   *lady* meeting
girl dresses   *foreman* office
child library   *guide* equipment
ox yoke   *hunter* cabin
soldier helmets   *pupil* entrance

EXERCISE 4: State the relationship of each of the italicized nouns.

1. The *capital* of Alberta is *Edmonton*.
2. It has one of the largest *airports* in *Canada*.
3. The city is situated on the *bank* of the North Saskatchewan River.
4. The C.N.R. links *Edmonton* with the other *provinces* of Canada.
5. This thriving *metropolis* is the *gateway* to the *North*.

EXERCISE 5: Write the following sentences, changing any pronoun used incorrectly.

1. It was Karen which was late.
2. Tom and me were first.
3. The boys soon found Tom and me.
4. It was Tom and me.
5. Ken is younger than me.
6. I know who you saw.
7. Please send us girls for the globe.
8. Was it us whom you saw?
9. I'll divide the apples between you and I.
10. The oranges were given to Mary, Jean, and I.

Review:

EXERCISE 6: Analyse graphically.

1. The longest river in the world is the Amazon.
2. Does the province of Newfoundland have any fogs?
3. With pen and ink write the names of the five zones.
4. What a magnificent view of the falls you get here!
5. The Klondike region was once the scene of a gold rush.
6. In the Okanagan Valley of British Columbia many orchards are found.
7. Mexico needs many more railroads and highways.

EXERCISE 7: Write each of the following sentences in (a) inverted order, (b) split order. Put a star beside the sentence which you prefer in each group.

1. Uranium has been found in many widely separated parts of Canada.

2. The names of many famous Canadians are found throughout the pages of our history.

3. A great quantity of exports is carried from our eastern cities to the markets of the world.

EXERCISE 8: Combine each of the following pairs of sentences to form a compound sentence or a complex sentence. Select the kind of sentence which makes the better expression. Indicate what kind of sentence you have constructed.

1. Martin Frobisher was a brave seaman. He lived at the time of Queen Elizabeth I.

2. Magellan was his hero. The story of this renowned sailor inspired him to undertake a similar trip around the world.

3. Magellan had travelled a southern route. He hoped to reach the Pacific by a route around the north coast of North America.

4. In 1576 Frobisher sailed north-west from England. He sighted the glaciers and mountains of Greenland.

5. He travelled further westward to a large island. Later this land was called Baffin Island.

6. The ships were anchored in a bay. Today this water is known as Frobisher Bay.

7. Frobisher mistook some Eskimos for Chinese. They had round faces, flat noses, and slanty eyes.

8. This explorer returned to England with little except a piece of shiny black stone. He had picked it up on the shore of the bay.

9. A second expedition returned to England with a great quantity of this black ore. It was considered of no value.

10. No one thought of looking for minerals in this land of ice and snow. Today the great iron beds of Labrador and Quebec are of immense importance in the future development of Canada.

Adjectives

Examine the italicized words in the following sentences:

1. The men in the *scarlet* uniforms were *British* soldiers.
2. After *their long* march they camped beside a *rippling* stream.
3. They were *courageous* in battle.

Each of these words describes or modifies a noun or a pronoun.

A word that describes or modifies a noun or a pronoun is an

ADJECTIVE.

EXERCISE 1: Select the adjectives from the following sentences and, after each one, write the noun or pronoun that it modifies.

1. A noble eagle began a sweeping spiral movement up into the blue sky.
2. It is the golden season of the year that takes us by the painted woods and along the amber-coloured streams.
3. A silken cloth concealed a huge, iron-bound, oaken chest.
4. The lion is a meat-eating animal but the cow is herbivorous.
5. Growing on the rocks were many kinds of sweet flowers, green moss with pink flowers, blue soft-belled gentians, and transparent white lilies.
6. The birds are hushed, the squirrels are still;
   All nature waits in the gloomy chill.

EXERCISE 2: Select the adjectives which this writer has used to give the reader a better word picture of Treasure Valley.

In a secluded and mountainous part of Styria, there was, in old time, a valley of the most surprising and luxuriant fertility. It was surrounded on all sides by steep and rocky mountains, rising into peaks which were always covered with snow and from which a number of torrents descended in constant cataracts. One of these fell westward over the face of a crag so high that, when the sun had set to everything else and all below was darkness, its beams still shone full upon this waterfall so that it looked like a shower of gold. It was, therefore, called by the people of the neighbourhood, the Golden River. It was strange that none of these streams fell into the valley itself. They all descended on the other side of the mountains and wound away through broad plains and by populous cities. But the clouds were drawn so constantly to the snowy hills and rested so softly in the circular hollow that in time of drought and heat, when all the country round was burnt up, there was still rain in the little valley; and its crops were so heavy and its hay so high and its apples so red and its grapes so blue and its wine so rich and its honey so sweet that it was a marvel to every one who beheld it, and was commonly called the Treasure Valley.

—*The King of the Golden River*, by John Ruskin

Proper Adjectives

Examine each pair of sentences below. Note that the first sentence in each case contains a proper noun. In the second sentence in each pair, a form of the proper noun is used to describe another noun.

1 *Ireland* is noted for its linen. *Irish* linen is world famous.

2. *Switzerland* produces cheese. *Swiss* cheese is imported into Canada.

Because the words "Irish" and "Swiss" describe nouns, we must call them adjectives. Because these adjectives were formed from proper nouns, we call them PROPER ADJECTIVES. Note that each proper adjective requires a capital letter.

EXERCISE 1: Make a proper adjective from each of these proper nouns and use it orally in a sentence.

Europe	Canada	England
Asia	Mexico	Scotland
Africa	Brazil	Wales
America	Peru	France
Australia	Chile	Denmark
India	Argentina	Spain
Russia	Cuba	Italy
China	Vienna	Holland
Japan	Hungary	Norway
Egypt	Siam	Greece

EXERCISE 2: The use of antonyms can be an effective method of showing contrast in your writing. Use each of these adjectives together with its antonym in a sentence.

Example: proper—improper

This is the proper way to make it; that is the improper way.

shallow	scarce	distinct	generous
honest	convenient	wise	skilled
satisfactory	obedient	accurate	honest
responsible	agreeable	effective	patient
necessary	pleasant	perfect	movable

Adjectives make word pictures brighter.

253

Pronominal and Descriptive Adjectives

Examine the italicized words in the following sentences:

1. *I* have a book. It is *my* book.
2. *You* have a book. It is *your* book.
3. *She* has a book. It is *her* book.

The words "I," "You," and "She" are pronouns. The words "my," "your," and "her" look like pronouns but are used to describe nouns. Because they describe nouns they are adjectives. Because these adjectives were formed from pronouns, they are called PRONOMINAL ADJECTIVES.

Examine the italicized adjectives in the following sentences:

4. *Great* torrents of *muddy* water gushed through the *inundated* valley.
5. In the *grey* mist of *early* dawn we could see the chimneys of *submerged* houses.

Each of these adjectives describes the noun which it modifies and gives us a clearer picture of the scene. Adjectives such as these are called DESCRIPTIVE ADJECTIVES.

The words *a, an,* and *the* are called ARTICLES.

6. Bring *a* pear and *an* orange.
7. Bring *the* cookies from *the* table.

Because *a* pear or *an* orange could mean any pear or any orange, the words *a* and *an* are called INDEFINITE ARTICLES.

Because *the* cookies and *the* table refer to definite things, the word *the* is called the DEFINITE ARTICLE.

The indefinite article *an* is used before a word commencing with a vowel, or a vowel sound. Examples: an atlas, an honest man.

EXERCISE 1: State whether the word in italics is the definite or the indefinite article, a proper adjective, a descriptive adjective, or a pronominal adjective.

1. *A Danish* ship docked at Halifax.
2. An *appetizing* aroma arose from *the steaming* pot.
3. The *coal-burning* locomotive is being replaced by the *diesel* engine.
4. *Your* friend is a very *graceful* skater.
5. In the *fading* light a *lone* goose could be seen.
6. That is known as a *Norwegian* fiord.
7. He was a *mischievous* urchin, bent on a *destructive* mission.
8. *His cautious* temperament would not let him make the attempt.
9. He was *an extraordinary* figure in a tall *pointed* hat and a red jacket.
10. *The African* continent is referred to as the Dark Continent.

254

Predicate Adjectives

Examine the italicized words in the following sentences:

1. The sun was *bright*.
2. The sky is *blue*.
3. All nature seems *serene*.

Each of the italicized words is an adjective used in the sentence as a subjective completion. Each completes an incomplete bare predicate. Each modifies the subject. Adjectives used in this way are known as PREDICATE ADJECTIVES.

EXERCISE 1: Select the predicate adjectives from the following sentences.

1. The weather was stormy.
2. The heat was intense yesterday.
3. Unknown was his destination.
4. Is he scientific in his method?
5. Be careful!
6. The water in the ocean is salty.
7. The amount of daylight is greater in the summer.
8. Unrelenting was the look upon his face.
9. Because the day had been pleasant, we were content.
10. The placid river flows silently on its way.

EXERCISE 2:

1. Make a noun from each of these adjectives:
   fragrant, angry, clean, distant, severe
2. Make an adjective from each of these nouns:
   appetite, twinkle, history, satisfaction, security
3. Write five adjectives using the prefix *un*.
4. Write five adjectives using the prefix *in*.
5. Write five adjectives using the prefix *dis*.
6. Write five adjectives using the suffix *able*.
7. Write five adjectives using the suffix *ful*.
8. Write five adjectives using the suffix *ible*.
9. Write five adjectives using the suffix *less*.
10. Write five adjectives using the suffix *ous*.

Overworked Adjectives

Although one may know the meaning of many words, they are not part of one's vocabulary until they are used in speech and in written work. A person whose vocabulary is small tends to overwork the words he knows and, as a result, what he has to say is often monotonous and inaccurate.

Discuss each of the following sentences and list on the chalkboard replacement words for each of the misused adjectives that are printed in italics.

1. It was a *cute* story. *Example:* quaint, touching, interesting.
2. Wasn't that a *good* programme?
3. We had a *swell* time at the game.
4. She's a *nice* woman.
5. It was a *grand* day.

EXERCISE 1: In each of the following sentences there is an overworked adjective. Rewrite the sentences, using more appropriate words.

1. I was in an awful hurry.
2. That was a marvellous cake.
3. It was terribly important.
4. That was a funny thing for him to say.
5. The pie was awfully good.
6. It was a nice book.
7. Isn't that a cute dress?
8. That was a gorgeous dinner!
9. I had an awful lot to finish.
10. She just bought a darling hat.

EXERCISE 2: Use each of the following words correctly in a sentence. The exact meaning can be found in your dictionary.

awful	terrific	pretty	swell	nice
cute	darling	gorgeous	funny	marvellous
lovely	grand	terrible	sweet	good

EXERCISE 3: Write the words from the above exercise in a column. Beside each write a list of possible substitutes to use in its place.

From a large vocabulary one can always select an appropriate adjective.

Comparison of Adjectives

Examine the italicized adjectives.

1. Jean is *young*. Jean is *younger* than Mary. Jean is the *youngest* girl in the class.
2. This writing is *good*. It is *better* than mine. That sample is *best*.
3. This story is *exciting*. It is *more exciting* than that one. I think it is the *most exciting* story in our library.

Adjectives are used to describe nouns, to compare one noun with another, or to compare one noun with two or more other nouns. Note the change in the form of the adjective in the above sentences. This is called the COMPARISON OF ADJECTIVES.

There are three degrees of comparison. The *positive* degree describes one noun. The *comparative* degree must be used when making a comparison between two nouns. The *superlative* degree is used when three or more things are being compared.

Adjectives are compared in three different ways:

	POSITIVE	COMPARATIVE	SUPERLATIVE
1. REGULAR COMPARISON	young tall	younger taller	youngest tallest
2. IRREGULAR COMPARISON	good many	better more	best most
3. PHRASAL COMPARISON	exciting reliable	more exciting less reliable	most exciting least reliable

Some adjectives cannot be compared. Discuss why each of the following words have no comparative and no superlative degree of comparison.

straight, perfect, complete, empty, parallel, true, round

EXERCISE 1: Rule three columns and label them: *Positive Degree*, *Comparative Degree*, and *Superlative Degree*. Under the appropriate heading, write the three degrees of comparison of the following adjectives.

cold	anxious	bad	noisy
much	sweet	important	high
courageous	little	near	far
warm	severe	successful	angry

257

Comparison of Adjectives:

EXERCISE 2: In the following sentences the correct degree of comparison for each adjective appears in italics. Read each of the sentences aloud and explain why the italicized word or words are correctly used.

1. Jane is *younger* than I.
2. She is an *industrious* student.
3. That was the *most delicious* apple in the basket.
4. Gerald is *taller* than his brother.
5. This is the *better* pen.
6. The Pacific is the *largest* ocean.
7. The price of this tie is *less* than that one.
8. This is the *hotter* side of the street.
9. Here is the *least valuable* coin I have.
10. Tom is *older*.

EXERCISE 3: Use the comparative form of each of the following adjectives, orally, in a sentence.

good	interesting	bright
few	little	beautiful
important	bad	cool
happy	effective	many
much	careful	neat

EXERCISE 4: Read each of the sentences in this exercise aloud. Repeat the sentence but replace the italicized adjective with the correct form of another adjective.

1. He is *taller* than I.
2. Today is *sunnier* than yesterday.
3. She is *more cautious* than he.
4. Of the two girls, Anne is the *more polite*.
5. The patient is *worse* today.
6. Jim wanted the *smaller* rabbit of the pair.
7. This is the *higher* of the two buildings.
8. This is the *highest* building in the city.
9. Of the two stories this is the *more interesting*.
10. The apple on the table is *larger*.

Adjective Phrases

Examine the groups of italicized words in the following sentences:

1. The building *across the street* is the Royal Ontario Museum.
2. A visit *to a museum* is a memorable event.
3. The view *from Mount Royal* extends across the city of Montreal.
4. Montreal is a city *of many churches*.
5. The residence *at Rideau Hall* is the Ottawa home *of the governor-general*.
6. State visitors *from other countries* have a formal meeting *with him*.

Note that each group of words contains:

    (a) a preposition and a noun   or
    (b) a preposition and a pronoun

A group of words that contains a preposition and a noun, or a preposition and a pronoun, is called a *phrase*. In the examples above, each phrase describes a noun. Therefore it is an *adjective phrase*. A phrase may also contain an adjective, such as in sentence 4.

EXERCISE 1: (Oral) For each of the following prepositions compose a sentence in which the preposition introduces an adjective phrase. Make sure that the phrase follows the noun which it modifies.

at	about	before	inside	through
in	above	beneath	outside	toward
of	after	behind	into	under
on	against	between	down	without
by	across	below	near	until
to	around	beside	off	with
up	along	beyond	over	except

EXERCISE 2: Select the adjective phrases from the following sentences and tell what each modifies.

Example: The trip during the storm was very hazardous.
"during the storm"—adjective phrase, modifying the noun "trip."

1. An island of the far north is Ellesmere Island.
2. A province near the Rockies is Alberta.
3. Name a district in the Northwest Territories.
4. What is an American territory beside the Yukon?
5. The state beyond the border of New Brunswick is the State of **Maine.**
6. List the names of the British islands in the Atlantic.
7. Ships on Lake Erie use the Welland Canal to reach Lake **Ontario.**
8. Name two Canadian outposts above the Arctic Circle.

Verbs

EXERCISE 1: Use each of the following words, orally, as a bare predicate in a sentence:

1. In an assertive sentence to make a statement:
   clang, creak, jostle, bustle, crackle

2. In an interrogative sentence to ask a question:
   scramble, swoop, thunder, resist, loiter

3. In an imperative sentence to give a command:
   deliver, accompany, disturb, dash, arrange

4. In an exclamatory sentence to make an exclamation:
   was, roar, glide, have, made

A word used as the bare predicate of a principal or a subordinate clause is a
VERB.

Examine the verbs in the following sentences:

1. Bill *runs*.
2. Bill *is running*.
3. Bill *has been running*.
4. Bill *might have been running*.

A verb that is made up of more than one word is a *verb phrase*. In a verb phrase the main word is called the PRINCIPAL VERB, and the helping verb or verbs are AUXILIARY VERBS.

EXERCISE 2: Select the verbs and the verb phrases from the following sentences. List them under the headings

AUXILIARY VERB   PRINCIPAL VERB

1. The wind whispered through the pine trees.
2. The paint was splattered across the kitchen floor.
3. Down the canyon could be seen a thin spiral of smoke.
4. An energetic squirrel had been scurrying across that rocky cove.
5. The ill-humoured crowd surged toward the front of the bus.
6. Long before now we should have been scampering home.
7. A suspicious looking character was sauntering down the aisle.
8. The course of the river could be traced under the ground until it emerged in the valley below.
9. The boy was dozing in the wigwam when a breath of cool air fanned his face.
10. Why did they shuffle toward the entrance?

Verb Phrases

Examine the italicized verb phrases in the following sentences:

1. We *have* never *seen* an eclipse of the moon.
2. A blanket of clouds *will* often *prevent* the formation of frost.
3. The earth *is* always *turning* from west to east.
4. The moon *does* not *have* any light of its own.

The verb phrases in the above sentences are separated by the words "never," "often," "always," and "not." These words are not verbs, and must not be considered part of the verb phrase. In the analysis of these sentences, words such as *never, often, always, not* would be modifiers of the bare predicate. They are adverbs modifying the verb phrase.

EXERCISE 3: Select the verbs and verb phrases from the following sentences.

1. Farmers often keep Holstein cattle for milk production.
2. The Holstein is usually designated as a dairy breed.
3. The pasteurization of milk has been required for a number of years.
4. The flavour of milk is not affected by pasteurization.
5. Milk from the Jersey breed has normally been considered very rich.
6. Timothy has often been grown as a hay crop.
7. Red clover and alfalfa are two other important hay crops.
8. You will recall that a bushel of wheat weighs sixty pounds.
9. Wheat is widely considered as important to the Canadian economy.
10. Good flour is frequently composed of a blend of hard and soft wheat.

EXERCISE 4: Analyse the following sentences graphically.

1. Man's first clothes were the skins of animals.
2. Cotton and wool are now widely used for this purpose.
3. Some of the synthetic fibres are becoming more important.
4. Cotton has a wide range of uses.
5. List ten different uses of cotton fabrics.
6. The finest cotton fabrics are often made from sea-island cotton.
7. The cotton-boll weevil has frequently caused great damage.
8. The most tedious part of the production of cotton is the picking.
9. The production of cotton was greatly increased after the invention of the spinning-wheel and the cotton gin.
10. Much of the cotton on this continent is grown on plantations in the southern United States.

Kinds of Verbs

Certain verbs such as *lay, raise, set,* are action verbs that require objects to complete the thought by naming receivers of the action. Examine the following verbs:

1. I *lay* my pencil down now.

2. I *laid* my pencil down.

3. I *have laid* my pencil down.

4. You *raise* the window.

5. She *has raised* the window.

6. He *set* the plant on the sill.

Select the verb from each of the above sentences. Explain why it is an action verb. State the receiver of the action in each case. What is the name of the part of the sentence that is the receiver of the action of the verb?

An action verb that requires an object to complete its thought is called a TRANSITIVE VERB. The word *transitive* means to *carry across.* With a transitive verb the action is carried across to its object.

Certain verbs such as *lie, rise, sit,* are action verbs that do not require objects to complete the thought by naming receivers of the action. Examine the following verbs:

7. I *lie* down. I *am lying* down.

8. I *lay* down yesterday.

9. I *have lain* down all evening.

10. You *rise* early.

11. We *rise* at seven.

12. They *sit* quietly.

Select the verb from each of the above sentences. Explain why it is an action verb. Is there a receiver of the action?

An action verb that does not require an object to complete its thought is called an INTRANSITIVE VERB. The word *intransitive* means *not carried across.* With an intransitive verb the action is not carried across to any completing part. Intransitive verbs do not have objects.

Kinds of Verbs:

Certain non-action verbs require subjective completions to complete the thought. They link or join the subjective completion to the subject in the sentence. Examine the following verbs:

13. It *is* I.
14. They *are* correct.
15. It *was* he.
16. The flowers *were* perennials.
17. He *became* a lawyer.
18. She *seems* studious.

Select the verb from each of the above sentences. Explain why it is a non-action verb. What is its completing part? What kind of completing part is it? Why is the completing part *subjective?*

A non-action verb that requires a subjective completion to complete its thought, and which joins the subjective completion to the subject, is called a COPULA VERB. The word *copula* means to *couple* or to *join.* The copula verb joins the subjective completion to the subject.

EXERCISE 1:

1. Use the transitive verbs *lay, raise, set,* orally in sentences with the subjects I, you, he, she, we, they, following the pattern of sentences 1, 2, and 3 on the previous page.

2. Use the intransitive verbs *lie, rise, sit,* orally in sentences with the subjects I, you, he, she, we, they, following the pattern of sentences 7, 8, and 9 on the previous page.

EXERCISE 2: Select the verbs from the following sentences and state the kind of each. After each transitive verb indicate the object. After each copula verb indicate the subjective completion.

1. Lay the parcel on the counter.
2. The injured animal lay on the lawn.
3. Will you raise the window, please?
4. We shall rise before daylight.
5. Jane and Jill sat in the balcony for the programme.
6. Would you set the plant in the water?
7. This apple tastes sour.
8. She could have been a nurse.
9. Lie down, Rover.
10. Erin was being stubborn about the book.

Agreement of Verb with the Subject

A verb has the same number and person as its subject. Examine the following sentences:

	SINGULAR	PLURAL
FIRST PERSON	I go.	We go.
SECOND PERSON	You go.	You go.
THIRD PERSON	He goes. She goes. It goes.	They go.

The form of the verb usually changes with a subject which is third person singular. *A verb must agree with its subject in person.*

Examine the verbs in the following sentences:

SINGULAR VERBS	PLURAL VERBS
Mary *was* there.	Mary and Joan *were* there.
The girl *is* here.	The girls *are* here.
She *has* a garden.	They *have* a garden.

A subject which is singular requires a singular verb. A subject which is plural requires a plural verb. *A verb must agree with its subject in number.*

> When two singular subjects are joined by the conjunction <u>or,</u> the conjunctions <u>either</u> . . . <u>or,</u> or the conjunctions <u>neither</u> . . . <u>nor,</u> they require a singular verb.

1. Jim or John *has* the cap.
2. Either Jane or Joan *was* here.
3. Neither Bob nor Bill *is* the culprit.

EXERCISE 1: (Oral) Compose five sentences for each of the sentence patterns above in which two singular subjects are joined by the conjunction *or,* the conjunctions *either* . . . *or,* or the conjunctions *neither* . . . *nor.* Make sure the verb is singular. Use a different verb each time.

> A singular subject, followed by an adjective phrase which contains a plural noun, requires a singular verb.

1. *Each* of the boys *is* here.
2. *One* of the girls *was* here.
3. *None* of the men *has* a hammer.
4. *Neither* of the churches *has* a tower.

EXERCISE 2: (Oral) Compose five sentences to follow the pattern of each of the above examples.

264

Agreement of Verb with the Subject:

1. A collective noun is usually considered as singular in number

   (a) The *team was* late in arriving.

   (b) The *crowd is* ready to leave.

However, a plural verb may be used when the writer is referring to the individual members of the group.

   (c) The *committee have decided* to adjourn.

2. Nouns such as *news, civics, mathematics, measles,* although plural in form but singular in meaning, require a singular verb.

   (a) The *news has been* very alarming.

   (b) *Mathematics is* an important subject.

3. *Anyone, everyone, no one, someone, anyone, anybody, everybody, nobody, somebody,* and subjects containing the words *each, every, either, neither, any, one, none,* which refer to persons or objects considered singular, require a singular verb.

   (a) *Everybody is* here.

   (b) *Someone has* the box.

   (c) *Either girl has* an equal chance.

   (d) *Each girl has* an equal chance.

4. A subject naming a sum of money is considered singular.

   (a) *Ten dollars is* the cost of the ticket.

   (b) There *is fifty cents.*

5. When a sentence is introduced by an adverb such as *there* or *here* and the subject follows the verb, the sentence should be rearranged (in the writer's mind) to ensure that the verb agrees with its subject.

   (a) There *goes your friend.*   (Your friend goes there.)

   (b) There *go your friends.*   (Your friends go there.)

   (c) Here (*is* or *are*) *your friends.*   (Your *friends are* here.)

Agreement of Verb with the Subject:

6. When one subject is joined to another by such expressions as *with, in addition to, as well as, together with,* the verb agrees with the first subject.

(a) *Charles,* with his parents, *was* at the station.

(b) A *dictionary,* in addition to an atlas, *is* needed.

(c) The *man,* as well as his sons, *has* an enviable record.

(d) The *girls,* together with their leader, *have* new uniforms.

7. Subjects joined by the conjunction *and* require a plural verb.

(a) *Tom and Jim are* ready.

(b) *Both Tom and Jim are* ready.

(c) *The fox and the hounds are* in sight.

8. The pronoun *you,* whether it refers to one person or to more than one person, requires a plural verb.

(a) (i) *You are* the winner.   (ii) *You are* the winners.

(b) (i) *You were* the champion.   (ii) *You were* the champions.

9. When a relative pronoun is used as the subject of a verb, the verb must agree in person and in number with the word for which the pronoun stands.

(a) George who *is* taller must stand.

(b) One of the boys who *has* a glove can be the catcher.

(c) You who *are* captain must give leadership.

10. The expression *the number* requires a singular verb; the expression *a number* requires a plural verb.

(a) *The number* of windows *is* six.

(b) *A number* of windows *were* broken.

11. When making a choice between using the verb *doesn't* and *don't,* only use *doesn't* when the subject is third person singular.

(a) *I don't* know the answer.

(b) *You don't* know the answer.

(c) *He doesn't* know the answer.

(d) *The boy doesn't* know the answer.

Agreement of Verb with the Subject:

Making use of the material on the three preceding pages, select the correct verb in each of the following sentences and be prepared to give the reason for your choice.

EXERCISE 3:
1. Eric and Ted (was, were) with him at the station.
2. Jane with her cousin (was, were) coming up the walk.
3. There (is, are) a set of books in the den.
4. The news of the two accidents (was, were) delayed for several hours.
5. Either Bob or Nancy (has, have) an eraser to lend you.
6. The herd of cattle (is, are) in the pasture near the orchard.
7. The rest of the wood (has, have) been chopped.
8. The rest of the bricks (has, have) been delivered.
9. Each of the dogs (is, are) doing a different trick.
10. There (is, are) fifty coppers in the purse.

EXERCISE 4:
1. I (lie, lay) down after the game.
2. I (lie, lay) the list on the bookshelf.
3. She has (laid, lain) down all afternoon.
4. Would you (set, sit) the cups on the counter?
5. There (is, are) a class of people who prefer this music.
6. There (is, are) people who attend regularly.
7. Five dollars (has, have) been donated to the fund.
8. None of the winners (has, have) received his award.
9. Ray as well as his sisters (is, are) taking a ticket.
10. A crate of oranges (has, have) arrived.

EXERCISE 5:
1. Each of the ladies (attend, attends) the evening meeting.
2. George or Michael (is, are) available.
3. Each of you (has, have) a duty.
4. Measles (has, have) caused a great deal of absence this month.
5. I (can, may) go after I wax the floor.
6. Half of the forest (was, were) destroyed.
7. Half of the trees (was, were) deciduous.
8. Both the girl and the boy (has, have) been chosen.
9. You who (is, am, are) the captain must make the decision.
10. She who (is, am, are) the oldest (think, thinks) it was wrong.

Tense

The PRESENT TENSE of a verb is the form used to indicate present time.

1. I *see* the pheasant.   (now)
2. I *do* my writing carefully.   (now)
3. I *go* to the library regularly.   (now)

The PAST TENSE of a verb is the form used to indicate that an action has taken place, or that something existed at some time in the past.

4. I *saw* the pheasant.   (some time in the past)
5. I *did* my writing carefully.   (some time in the past)
6. I *went* to the library regularly.   (some time in the past)

The FUTURE TENSE of a verb is the form used to indicate that an action will take place, or that something will exist at some time in the future.

7. I *shall see* the pheasant.   (some time in the future)
8. She *will do* her writing carefully.   (some time in the future)
9. He *will go* to the library regularly.   (some time in the future)

> When using <u>shall</u> and <u>will</u> as auxiliary verbs to make the simple future tense, use
> SHALL with I and WE; WILL with all other subjects.

EXERCISE 1:

1. State the tense of each verb or verb phrase in the following sentences:
   (a) Caroline came with her uncle.
   (b) We shall swim across the bay.
   (c) You are leading with the greatest number of points.
   (d) They will bring a paddle with them.
   (e) Jim was chosen captain.

2. Change the tense of each verb or verb phrase to the past tense.
   (a) The rivulet runs down to the stream.
   (b) Bananas are growing in a warmer climate.
   (c) You will see the Welland Canal on your trip.

3. Change the tense of each verb or verb phrase to future tense.
   (a) The dog hears the rustle of the leaves.
   (b) We are hurrying so that you are on time.

> When writing a paragraph, it is important to avoid shifting from one tense to another.

Tense:

Select the verb phrase from each of the following sentences:

1. The train has arrived.
2. I have bought my ticket.
3. The whistle has blown.

The verb phrase in each sentence indicates that the action is finished or completed. Verb phrases of this type are said to be in the PERFECT TENSE.

The auxiliary in each sentence is the present tense of the verb *have*. The principal verb in each sentence, *arrived, bought, blown*, is called the PERFECT PARTICIPLE.

A verb phrase made up of an auxiliary verb which is the PRESENT tense of the verb *have* and a PERFECT participle is said to be in the PRESENT PERFECT TENSE.

Examine the verb phrases in the following sentences:

4. The train had arrived.
5. I had bought my ticket.
6. The whistle had blown.

The verb phrase in each of these sentences also indicates that the action is completed and therefore is in the perfect tense.

Examine each auxiliary verb. Note that each one is the past tense of the verb *have*. The principal verb in each case is called the perfect participle.

A verb phrase made up of an auxiliary verb which is the PAST tense of the verb *have* and a PERFECT participle is said to be in the PAST PERFECT TENSE.

Examine the verb phrases in the following sentences:

7. The train will have arrived.
8. I shall have bought my ticket.
9. The whistle will have blown.

When does each of these verb phrases indicate that the action will be completed? What is the tense form of the auxiliary verbs *will have* and *shall have?*

A verb phrase made up of an auxiliary verb which is the FUTURE tense of the verb *have* and a PERFECT participle is said to be in the FUTURE PERFECT TENSE.

Tense:

EXERCISE 2: Select the verb or verb phrase from each of the following sentences and state its tense. Remember, when examining a verb phrase, to identify the tense of the auxiliary.

1. The plane lands at the airport.
2. It left Halifax this morning.
3. It will be over Montreal at noon.
4. The pilot had flown during the war.
5. He has received several decorations for bravery.
6. The record will have been broken on this flight.
7. The passengers have been very excited.
8. I see the plane overhead now.
9. When will it land?
10. The control tower has just given the signal.

Every verb has three forms which are called PRINCIPAL PARTS. They are as follows:

	EXAMPLES
1. PRESENT TENSE	see, go, ring
2 PAST TENSE	saw, went, rang
3. PERFECT PARTICIPLE	seen, gone, rung

The perfect participle is the principal verb in a verb phrase in the perfect tense which requires the auxiliary *has*, *have*, or *had*.

Here are the principal parts of some commonly used verbs.

PRESENT TENSE	PAST TENSE	PERFECT PARTICIPLE
see	saw	(*has*, *have*, or *had*) seen
am	was	been
come	came	come
do	did	done
go	went	gone
grow	grew	grown
lay (transitive)	laid	laid
lie (intransitive)	lay	lain
run	ran	run
swim	swam	swum

EXERCISE 3: Rule three columns similar to those above and write the principal parts of the following verbs:

is	bear	begin	bring	fly
eat	sing	have	break	know

EXERCISE 4: Use each of the principal parts of each verb in Exercise 3 orally in a sentence. Make sure that the auxiliary *has*, *have*, or *had* is used with the perfect participle.

270

Using Verbs Correctly

EXERCISE 1: Each of the following sentences contains an error in the use of the verb. Write the sentence correctly. Explain the reason for any change you have made.

1. We will arrive on the afternoon train.
2. Each of the players have a new sweater.
3. The boy come to the playground.
4. The game had began on time.
5. He didn't know he done it.
6. Has he came yet?
7. She is going to lay down now.
8. Have you wrote to your pen pal yet?
9. We run all the way to the show yesterday.
10. The level of the river is raising.

EXERCISE 2: Read each of the following sentences and explain why the italicized verb is correctly used.

1. I *grew* two inches last year.
2. None of the shrubs *has begun* to bud.
3. Some of them *will flower* in June.
4. *Have* you *done* your project yet?
5. George *lay* on the beach yesterday afternoon.
6. No one *had known* of the incident.
7. After I *learn* the code I shall *teach* it to you.
8. The dandelions *have sprung* up quickly.
9. *May* I come with you, please?
10. The regiment of soldiers *is* on the move.

EXERCISE 3: Copy each sentence and write the correct form of the verb or verbs in brackets.

(begin)	1. It has ————— to rain.
(do)	2. She ————— it last year all by herself.
(Shall, Will)	3. ————— he accept the position?
(lie, lay)	4. Mother had ————— the saucers on the counter.
(go)	5. Ted has ————— to visit his uncle.
(come)	6. Spring has ————— early this year.
(shall, will)	7. We ————— finish the biography this week.
(lay, laid)	8. Junior ————— the broken cup on the shelf.
(ride)	9. Have you ever ————— on a horse?
(wore, worn)	10. Should we not have ————— our uniforms?

Adverbs

Examine the italicized words.

1. Mary writes *carefully*.
2. She completed her chart *yesterday*.
3. *Where* did she put it?
4. *Why* has she hidden it?

Words that tell or ask *how, when, where, why,* or *how much* about the verb, are called adverbs.

Observe the relation of the adverbs in the following sentences:

5. The scout moved *silently*.
6. The moon could be seen *clearly*.
7. This book is *very* exciting.
8. It is a *most* unusual story.
9. The scout moved *very* silently.
10. The moon could be seen *quite* clearly.

> An adverb can modify (a) a verb
> (b) an adjective   (c) another adverb.

In the graphic analysis of a sentence, square brackets are placed around the modifiers of the bare predicate. Henceforth, square brackets should also be placed around adverbs which modify adjectives and other adverbs.   Examine the following:

11. (A) [very] (serious) accident happens [there] [quite] [frequently].

12. (That) [extremely] (sharp) curve is [quite] dangerous.

EXERCISE 1: Analyse the following sentences graphically.

1. Have you ever discovered the source of cork?
2. Cork is really the bark of the cork tree.
3. The cork tree is found in southern Europe and northern Africa.
4. It has a very thick bark on its trunk and larger limbs.
5. The life of the cork tree is quite long.
6. It sometimes lives for three hundred years.
7. Millions of corks are normally used every year in all types of bottles.
8. Another very important use is in the manufacture of cork flooring.
9. A completely new crop of cork is produced by the tree every nine years.
10. A very large amount of cork is used annually.

Using Adverbs Correctly

One of the difficulties which occurs in English is the use of the adjective when the adverb form of the word is required.

    1. He runs quickly.   NOT: He runs quick.

    2. She spoke harshly to me. NOT: She spoke harsh to me.

Another difficulty occurs with copula verbs such as *become, look, seem, appear, taste, feel, smell, sound,* which require a predicate adjective to complete them and not an adverb.

    3. The apple tastes sour. NOT: The apple tastes sourly.

    4. The board feels rough. NOT: The board feels roughly.

Good is an adjective. *Well* is an adverb, but sometimes it may also be used as an adjective.

    5. That answer was a *good* one. (adjective)

    6. Today George feels *well*. (predicate adjective)

    7. Alan plays *well*. (adverb)

Most is an adjective or an adverb; *almost* is an adverb. Do NOT use these expressions: most always, most every, most any.

    8. Most people enjoy music.

    9. Almost every one likes to sing.

Words such as *no, not, never, nobody, none,* and *nowhere* are called NEGATIVES. The adverbs *hardly* and *scarcely* are also called negatives. Two negatives must not be used together in a sentence. One negative will cancel the other.

10. He was hardly tall enough.   NOT: He wasn't hardly tall enough.

11. She was scarcely old enough. NOT: She wasn't scarcely old enough.

12. We never went anywhere.   NOT: We never went nowhere.

The adverb should normally come directly before the word it modifies. Adverbs which sometimes are misplaced are *only, often, never, ever, nearly*. Notice the three different meanings expressed in the following sentences:

    13. Only I saw the book. (No other person saw it.)

    14. I only saw the book. (I didn't touch or read it.)

    15. I saw only the book. (I saw nothing else.)

Comparison of Adverbs

Examine the three degrees of comparison of these adverbs.

1. I live *near* to the river.   (no comparison)
2. I live *nearer* to the river.   (comparing two)
3. I live *nearest* to the river.   (comparing more than two)
4. Tom works *quietly*.
5. Tom works *more quietly* than Bob.
6. Tom works *most quietly* of all the boys.
7. Bill writes *well*.
8. Jim writes *better* than Jane.
9. Joe writes *best* of all the pupils.

Like adjectives, adverbs have three degrees of comparison. Some have a regular comparison by adding *er* and *est*. Some have a phrasal comparison using the words *more* and *most* or *less* and *least*. A few adverbs are irregular in comparison.

	POSITIVE	COMPARATIVE	SUPERLATIVE
REGULAR	close early far soon	closer earlier farther sooner	closest earliest farthest soonest
PHRASAL	quickly neatly cheerfully noisily	more quickly more neatly more cheerfully more noisily	most quickly most neatly most cheerfully most noisily
IRREGULAR	well much badly little	better more worse less	best most worst least

EXERCISE 1: Use the comparative form of each of the following adverbs orally in a sentence.

rapidly	early	little
well	clearly	speedily
soon	badly	successfully

EXERCISE 2: Write the adverb which may be formed from each of the following adjectives and use the comparative form orally in a sentence.

speedy	sincere	faithful
loud	steady	merciful

Adverb Phrases

Examine the adverb phrases in the following sentences:

1 The plane flew *across the city.*
2. It was flying *at a great height.*
3 The child was friendly *with them.*
4. The day was full *of memories.*
5. We left early *in the morning.*
6. We returned late *in the evening.*

In the first two sentences each adverb phrase modifies a verb. In sentences 3 and 4 the adverb phrase modifies an adjective and in the last two sentences each adverb phrase modifies an adverb. Like a single adverb, *an adverb phrase can modify a verb, an adjective or an adverb.*

Like an adjective phrase, an adverb phrase is made up of a preposition and a noun, or a preposition and a pronoun. Adjective and adverb phrases are sometimes referred to as *prepositional phrases.* The position of a phrase in the sentence often determines whether it is an adjective or an adverb phrase Examine the following:

7. The store is located *at the corner.* (adverb phrase)
8 The store *at the corner* sells stamps. (adjective phrase)

Sometimes a phrase is found within another phrase. Examine the following sentence:

9. Dad planted a hedge along the side of the house.
"along the side of the house" is an adverb phrase modifying the verb "planted."
"of the house" is an adjective phrase modifying the noun "side."

EXERCISE 1: Select the adjective and adverb phrases from the following sentences and give their relation.

1. Coral is a type of sea animal with a hard skeleton.
2. Some varieties of corals absorb limestone from the water.
3. Over a long period of time a coral island may reach the surface of the ocean.
4. Island building coral are found only in clear warm sea water.
5. Coral islands are confined to the tropics and to shallow water.
6. The starfish is another one of the unusual sea animals.
7. It has five arms and at the tip of each arm is an eye.
8. Starfish have feet with suckers on the end of each.
9. These feet are pushed through holes on the lower surface of each arm.
10. With the suckers the feet are fastened to any object near them and the starfish is pulled forward.

Review IV

EXERCISE 1: State the relation of each italicized noun in the following sentences:

1. *Aluminum* is an important *metal*.
2. Because it is a good conductor of *heat*, it is used for cooking *utensils*.
3. It is also a good *conductor* of *electricity*.
4. Due to its *strength* and its light weight aluminum is used in the *manufacture* of airplanes.
5. As it does not tarnish or rust, it has many *uses* in the construction *industry*.

EXERCISE 2: Choose the correct pronoun from those in brackets.

1. Give the pictures to Joan and (I, me).
2. Don is taller than (he, him).
3. I did not see (who, whom) it was.
4. Was it Bob and (I, me) who were chosen?
5. That was the lady (who, which) lost the purse.
6. Divide the grapes between you and (I, me).
7. It was (they, them) who were there.
8. Mr. Jones saw my sister and (I, me) at the store.
9. Would you give it to (we, us) girls?
10. I know (who, whom) has the whistle.

EXERCISE 3: Select the subordinate clauses from the following sentences and tell their kind and relation.

1. (a) Swans are water birds which belong to the same family as geese.
   (b) Did you know that trumpeter swans are very rare now?
2. (a) Edison knew that an electric current could heat a wire until its glow could give light.
   (b) Because he persisted in his experiments, Edison made the first electric light bulb.
3. (a) The particular type of place where a plant or animal lives is called its habitat.
   (b) When the natural habitat of any wild animal is destroyed, the animal must migrate.
4. (a) Meteorologists are people who study the weather.
   (b) They know what causes weather to change and how we can foretell future changes.
5. (a) Milk ranks first in importance among foods because it supplies so many of our nutritional requirements.
   (b) Throughout our lives milk is the food that is most commonly used.

Review:

EXERCISE 4:

1. Use the adjective form of each of the following words in a sentence:

Spain   anger   disagree   mercy   **she**

2. Use the comparative form of each of the following adjectives in a sentence:

interesting   much   quick   good   capable

3. Use in a sentence the comparative degree of the adverb, which can be formed from each of the following words:

steady   skill   intelligence   anger   success

EXERCISE 5. Select the adjective and adverb phrases from the following sentences and give their relation.

1. Bermuda is a favourite tourist resort for Canadians.

2. Many go by ship; others go there by plane.

3. A trained pilot must guide ocean vessels through the difficult passage into Hamilton harbour.

4. This island of coral limestone is built on the summit of a sunken mountain.

5. Over the centuries tiny coral polyps have taken lime from the ocean water and this process has built the limestone rock which now forms the island.

EXERCISE 6: Copy each sentence and write the correct form of the verbs in brackets. Be ready to tell how you made your choice.

1. (shall, will)   I ———— finish the story in the morning.

2. (lie, lay)   Mother has ———— her parcels on the bench.

3. (see)   We ———— the exhibits yesterday.

4. (grow)   The plant had ———— over an inch.

5. (do)   If we'd ———— our work, we might have **gone.**

6. (is, are)   None of the boys ———— absent.

7. (was, were)   Neither Elaine nor Sarah ———— ready.

8. (has, have)   There ———— been a number of inquiries.

9. (is, are)   Frank, with his brothers, ———— at the game.

10. (begin)   Have you ———— your map yet?

277

Prepositions

Examine the italicized words in the following sentences:

1. A journey *across* Canada requires several days *by* train.
2. *On* it travellers may sleep *in* comfort.

> Each of the italicized words is a PREPOSITION.
>
> A preposition
>
> (a) introduces an adjective or an adverb phrase;
>
> (b) shows the relation between the noun or pronoun in the phrase and the word which the phrase modifies.

The noun or pronoun in a phrase is the object of the preposition. Therefore the object form of the pronoun is required when a pronoun is used in a phrase.   Note the following:

3. Come with me.
4. Come with Tom and me.
5. To whom did you give it?
6. (a) Whom did you come with? or (b) With whom did you come?
7. I reported to him.
8. I reported to Miss Brown and him.
9. It looks like her.
10. It looks like Mary and her.

Errors in the correct form of the pronoun following a preposition occur more frequently when the pronoun is separated from the preposition by another word or words as in sentences 4, 6 (a), 8 and 10.

EXERCISE 1: List alphabetically the prepositions given in Exercise 1 on page 259.

EXERCISE 2: The object forms of the most common personal pronouns are: *me, her, him, us, them.*

1. Use each of these pronouns orally in a sentence following each of these prepositions:

with, after, except, before, from, near, about

2. Repeat each of the oral sentences but separate the pronoun and the preposition with a person's name as in examples 4, 8, and 10 above.

3. Use each of the following pairs of pronouns orally in a sentence, after each preposition listed in 1 above:

her and me	them and me
him and me	her and them
her and us	him and them
him and us	us and them

Using Prepositions Correctly

Study the correct use of the following prepositions:

1. Things are divided *between* two and *among* three or more people.
   Divide the stamps *between* Tom and Mary.
   Divide the marbles *among* the five boys.

2. One differs *with* an opinion but one thing is different *from* another, not different than another.

   I differ *with* Charlie's idea about the boat.
   The colour of his jacket is different *from* yours.

3. One agrees *with* a person but agrees *to* or agrees *upon* a plan, a proposal, or a decision.

   I agree with Jane *about* the trip.
   We agreed *upon* this plan.

4. One can be angry *with* a person but angry *at* some thing.

   I am angry *with* Ted.
   He is angry *at* the puzzle.

5. Something may be taken *from* a person or *off* an object but never *off of* a person or an object.

   I took the pencil *from* John.
   She took the glass *off* the counter.

6 The preposition *in* means inside of. Movement from the outside to the inside requires the use of the preposition *into*.

   I walked around *in* the room.
   I walked *into* the room.

EXERCISE 1: Copy these sentences and supply a suitable preposition for each:

1. You may divide the piece of cake ———— Lynne and Larry.
2. We put the old map back ———— the trunk.
3. The lead in this pencil is different ———— that.
4. Do not be angry ———— me.
5. The members agreed ———— the committee.
6. Divide the tickets ———— the girls in the club.
7. I beg to differ ———— you on that point.
8. The boys took the ring ———— Jean.
9. Put the checkers ———— the box.
10. Jim is quite different ———— George.

Conjunctions

Discuss what the conjunction *and* joins in the following sentences:

1. Snow and ice formed weird patterns on the windows.
2. The wind roared and raged all night.
3. He and I could not wait until morning.
4. A cold and waning moon peeked through a cloud bank.
5. We moved off quietly and quickly.
6. Across the clearing and into the bush we made our way.
7. The journey was long and we had no time to lose.

A conjunction that joins two words, two phrases, or two clauses, which are used the same way in a sentence is a *co-ordinate conjunction.*

Two thoughts which are related and of equal value may be joined by a co-ordinate conjunction to form a compound sentence. Examine the following compound sentences:

8. Man has not conquered outer space *and* this is a challenge to many scientists.
9. Man has not conquered outer space *but* the time for this achievement may be fast approaching.
10. Man has not conquered outer space *or* a trip to the moon would be a possibility.
11. Man has not conquered outer space *yet* this may soon become a reality.

The conjunction *and* is used to add one idea to another. *But* or *yet* are used to show a contrast between two ideas. *Or* expresses an alternative idea or choice of ideas. Two ideas which are related and of equal value may be combined effectively in a compound sentence if the proper co-ordinate conjunction is used.

EXERCISE 1: Combine each of the following pairs of sentences into a compound sentence by using the proper conjunction.

1. Water always flows down hill. Eventually it will reach the ocean.
2. Water freezes at thirty-two degrees. The salt in ocean water prevents this from happening.
3. Moisture from the winter snow may be retained. It may be allowed to run off in spring floods.
4. A heavy flow of water may be held back by a dam. This overflow may be used to generate electricity.
5. Canada has many great power developments. The increasing demands of Canadian industry will require more of them.

Conjunctions:

Examine the words in the following sentences which introduce the subordinate clauses:

1. I knew *that* the koala bear is found in Australia.
2. Metal expands *when* it is heated.
3. *Because* light travels faster than sound, a flash of lightning can be seen *before* we hear the thunder.

A word which introduces a subordinate clause and joins it to some other word in the sentence is a *subordinate conjunction.*

Two thoughts which are related and equal in importance may be joined together in a compound sentence. When one thought is less important than the other, the two thoughts may be combined into a complex sentence by making the less important thought a subordinate clause. In this case a knowledge of subordinate conjunctions will enable the writer to construct strong effective complex sentences.

4. The water in the bottle froze into ice. The expansion of the ice cracked the bottle.

These two thoughts can be combined into a strong complex sentence as follows:

5. Because water expands on freezing, the formation of ice in the bottle cracked it.

EXERCISE 2: Making use of the subordinate conjunctions found on page 233, combine each of the following pairs of sentences into a more effective complex sentence.

1. The planet Saturn may be viewed through a telescope. Then the rings of Saturn may be seen.
2. The most familiar planet to us is the earth. We live on it.
3. The smallest planet, Mercury, is difficult to see. It is near the sun.
4. Mercury comes between the earth and the sun. Then it looks like a black dot against the sun.
5. Pluto is very far away. We know very little about it.
6. You would need an oxygen tank to breathe properly on Mars. The atmosphere on this planet does not contain enough oxygen.
7. Uranus and Neptune are about the same size. Neptune is farther from the sun.
8. The earth revolves about the sun. Other sky bodies also revolve about the sun.
9. We can watch the sky on a starry, moonless night in summer. Then we can see shooting stars most easily.
10. Some meteors enter the earth's atmosphere. The heat created by the speed of their travel causes them to glow.

Conjunctions:

1. *Like* is a preposition and should never be used as a conjunction. *As* or *as if* should be used instead.

Right: Mary looks *like* her mother.
Wrong: You must do it like Bill does.
Right: You must do it *as* Bill does.
Right: It looks *as if* it might storm.

2. *Except* is a preposition and should not be used in place of the conjunction *unless*.

Right: Everyone could go except me.
Wrong: Except the garden is weeded I cannot go.
Right: Unless the garden is weeded I cannot go.

3. Some conjunctions are used in pairs. They are called *correlative conjunctions.*

Either you *or* I may go.
Both Jean *and* Joan were there.

The most common correlative conjunctions are:

neither——nor	either——or
not only——but	both——and
whether——or	nor——nor

Correlative conjunctions must always be placed directly before the words or groups of words which they connect.

Wrong: She neither brought an umbrella nor rubbers.
Right: She brought neither an umbrella nor rubbers.

4. The use of too many *and's* or *but's* should be avoided. Two thoughts which have been joined in this manner may be more effective by using a semi-colon. Note the following:

Daylight was breaking through the leaves; we had not a moment to lose.

5. Another method of eliminating *and* or *but* is to use a semi-colon followed by one of these words:

besides, furthermore, hence, however, nevertheless, accordingly, so, therefore, then, still, yet, otherwise

I was there; however, I did not see it.
She was absent on Monday; nevertheless, the work must be completed.

6. Note the incorrect use of *and* in the following expression:
Wrong: Try and do it.
Right: Try to do it.

Interjections

Sometimes certain words are used to express some sudden or strong feeling.

> *Hurrah!* We won.
> *Oh!* What have I done with it?
> *Ah!* There it is.

Words such as *Hurrah, Oh,* and *Ah* are called *interjections.* An interjection is usually followed by an exclamation mark, but occasionally a comma may be used. In this latter case, the sentence frequently closes with an exclamation mark.

> Alas! I could not be chosen. Alas, I could not be chosen!

PARTS OF SPEECH

The way in which a word is used in a sentence determines its part of speech. The parts of speech are used in the following ways:

1. Noun
   (a) bare subject of a verb   (c) subjective completion of a verb
   (b) object of a verb   (d) object of a preposition
                (e) indirect object of a verb

2. Pronoun may have same relations as *noun* above.

3. Verb
   (a) bare predicate of its subject

4. Adjective
   (a) modifies a noun or pronoun   (b) subjective completion of a verb

5. Adverb
   (a) modifies a verb   (b) modifies an adjective
             (c) modifies another adverb

6. Preposition
   (a) introduces an adjective or an adverb phrase and shows the relation between the noun or pronoun in the phrase to the word which the phrase modifies.

7. Conjunction
   (a) A co-ordinate conjunction joins two words, two phrases, or two clauses used the same way in a sentence.
   (b) A subordinate conjunction introduces a subordinate clause and joins the clause to the word it modifies.

8. Interjection
   Has no relation.

Parsing

Parsing means to give the grammatical relationship of a word and to tell its part of speech.   Note that it is the use of a word in a sentence that determines its part of speech.

1. Iron is an important mineral.

    Iron—bare subject of the verb "is"—noun

    is—bare predicate of its subject "Iron"—verb

    an—indefinite article

    important—modifies the noun "mineral"—adjective

    mineral—subjective completion of the verb "is"—noun

2. Many mothers iron on Tuesday.

    Many—modifies the noun "mothers"—adjective

    mothers—bare subject of the verb "iron"—noun

    iron—bare predicate of its subject "mothers"—verb

    on—introduces the adverb phrase "on Tuesday" and shows the relation between the noun "Tuesday" and the verb "irons"—preposition

    Tuesday—object of the preposition "on"—noun

3. The steel industry requires iron ore.

    The—indefinite article

    steel—modifies the noun "industry"—adjective

    industry—bare subject of the verb "requires"—noun

    requires—bare predicate of its subject "industry"—verb

    iron—modifies the noun "ore"—adjective

    ore—object of the verb "requires"—noun

4. You and I iron very quickly.

    You—bare subject of the verb "iron"—pronoun

    and—joins the pronouns "You" and "I"—conjunction

    I—bare subject of the verb "iron"—pronoun

    iron—bare predicate of its subject "You and I"—verb

    very—modifies the adverb "quickly"—adverb

    quickly—modifies the verb "iron"—adverb

Parsing:

EXERCISE 1: Parse each of the italicized words in the following sentences by giving its relationship and by naming its part of speech. Study the examples on the previous page.

1. A *light* wind blew from the ocean.
2. From the shore we could see a faint *light*.
3. *Light* our fire now.
4. Heavy winds *break* dead branches from our elm tree.
5. The repair crew had soon mended the *break* in the line.
6. The stream runs *fast*.
7. Those people *fast* one day in every seven.
8. *Running* is good exercise.
9. A *running* horse is difficult to photograph.
10. The story was *excrutiatingly* funny.

EXERCISE 2: Compose sentences using each of the following words as the part of speech indicated.

1. jingle—noun
2. garden—verb
3. paint—adjective
4. quite—adverb
5. like—verb
6. like—preposition
7. quiet—noun
8. spring—adjective
9. than—conjunction
10. that—pronoun

EXERCISE 3: Parse each word in each of the following sentences.

1. Aluminum is a light metal.
2. At Arvida in Quebec is a large aluminum factory.
3. Iron and coal are used in the manufacture of steel.
4. A very large steel plant operates in Hamilton.
5. Forsythia is a colourful shrub in the spring.
6. That garden was full of colour.
7. That is a new variety of petunia.
8. Portuguese sailors explored the west coast of Africa.
9. Hand me a map of the ocean routes.
10. In the fading light the view is quite picturesque.

Review V

EXERCISE 1: (a) Draw a chart similar to the one below and analyse the following sentences by putting the parts of the sentence in the proper spaces:

1. Water is our most useful and abundant liquid.
2. In homes, on farms, in factories, water has many important uses.
3. An adequate supply of clean pure water is one of our basic needs.
4. Without water you could live for only a few days.

	1.	2.	3.	4.
Bare Subject				
Mod. of B.S.				
Bare Predicate				
Mod. of B.P.				
Object				
Mod. of O.				
Subjective Completion				
Mod. of S.C.				

(b) Now analyse graphically the following sentences:

5. The soil in the forest is one of nature's reservoirs.

6. Forests assist the maintenance of a steady flow of clean water.

7. Most surface water contains several kinds of impurities.

8. To kill disease bacteria chlorine is added to water in small, scientifically controlled amounts.

9. Epidemics of typhoid fever have almost disappeared since the introduction of modern water purification methods.

10. You should drink four or five glasses of water every day.

286

Review:

EXERCISE 2: (a) State whether each of the following sentences is simple, compound, or complex.

(b) Select the principal clauses.

(c) Select the subordinate clauses and tell their kind and relation.

1. Some of the trees in our forests were towering giants when Columbus discovered America.

2. If Canadians learn to use the forests wisely, they will benefit in many ways.

3. A policy which provides for the selective cutting of trees maintains a continuous yield.

4. Conservation is essential to the welfare of all Canadians and it is the responsibility of every citizen.

5. We have learned that the forest industries rank among our most important.

6. Vast quantities of the lumber that is required for building purposes are produced each year.

7. Because newspapers require such large amounts of newsprint, the manufacture of pulp and paper ranks among our most important industries.

8. The chief enemies of our forests are forest fires, insect and plant diseases, and careless lumbering practices.

9. Many people have stated that our future prosperity is linked with the wise use of our forests.

10. We should all dedicate ourselves to the support of those measures which are aimed at the conservation of our forests.

EXERCISE 3:

1. Write each of these common nouns and beside it write a proper noun which corresponds with it.

| island | girl | ocean | month | poet |
| province | strait | planet | day | sea |

2. Write the plural form of each of the following:

| tomato | roof | ox | piano | 7 |
| loaf | child | larva | sheep | dwarf |

Review:

EXERCISE 4: Write the following sentences and insert the proper punctuation marks.

1. Mary please lend me your atlas
2. Our hemisphere the western hemisphere is shown on the first page
3. The boys maps of this hemisphere are on the bulletin board
4. What is the worlds largest continent
5. North America ranks third in size South America ranks fourth
6. The childrens library has a reference section about these continents.
7. The Womens Association is sponsoring a map contest
8. Ive suggested that youll enter your best effort
9. The fathers committee will do the judging
10. Which map of yours will you enter

EXERCISE 5: Write the following sentences correcting any pronoun which has been used improperly.

1. Who did you see on your trip?
2. Please lend the road map to Gerald and I.
3. We brought the postcards back with me.
4. It was her that took the pictures.
5. We visited Jean which we hadn't seen for two years.
6. She is older than I.
7. Was it they who used to live in Winnipeg?
8. Us girls keep a steady correspondence.
9. It was Jean and me who have those stamp collections.
10. I and she have been friends for many years.

EXERCISE 6:

1. Use the adjective form of each of the following words in a sentence:

Europe   twinkle   agree   friend   mischief

2. Use the comparative form of each of the following adjectives in a sentence:

cool   important   many   cautious   heavy

3. Use the superlative form of each of the following adjectives in a sentence:

happy   good   much   exciting   large

Review:

1. Use the adverb form of each of the following words in a sentence:

speed   careful   true   noise   skill

2. Write the comparative form of each of the following adverbs in a sentence:

quickly   cheerfully   soon   well   early

3. Correct any errors in the following sentences and give a reason for any change you made.

    (a) She spoke harsh to me.
    (b) The board feels roughly.
    (c) He wasn't hardly tall enough.
    (d) Frozen food only can be kept in the freezing compartment.
    (e) We never went nowhere.

EXERCISE 8: Select the adjective phrases and the adverb phrases from the following sentences and state what each modifies.

1. Tin is one of our useful metals.
2. Men have used tin since ancient times.
3. The early Phoenicians made voyages to Britain for this precious metal.
4. After them the Romans voyaged to the Tin Isles.
5. In modern times tin is still one of our useful metals.
6. Cans of perishables are coated with tin before food is put into them.
7. Most cans are made from steel with a coating of tin.
8. Tin can be rolled into extremely thin sheets called tinfoil.
9. Tinfoil is used for wrapping by many food companies.
10. Most of the world's supply of tin comes from the Far East.

EXERCISE 9: Write each of the following phrases in two different sentences, using the phrase as:

    (a) an adjective phrase
    (b) an adverb phrase

        1. in the cellar
        2. from Montreal
        3. beside the river
        4. over the mountain
        5. to the cottage

Review:

EXERCISE 10: Select the verbs and verb phrases from the following sentences and tell whether they are transitive, intransitive, or copula.

1. Rice is one of the most important food crops.
2. Many people of the Far East use rice as their main food.
3. It requires a great deal of water for growth.
4. Rice is first planted in small seed beds.
5. Then the plants are moved to the fields for planting.
6. Each field has a bank of earth around it.
7. Then the field is flooded.
8. The farmers set out the young plants in the mud.
9. The rice is ripe towards the end of September.
10. Then the water is drained off the fields.

EXERCISE 11: A verb must agree with its subject in person and number.
Write the following sentences making the proper change in any verb which could not be considered correct and give your reason for the change.

1. Neither Jane nor Margaret were here.
2. The day go by very quickly.
3. Jim, with his sisters, were waiting for us.
4. Each of the girls has an equal chance.
5. The team was late in arriving.
6. Everybody are going to the lake.
7. There goes your friends.
8. Five dollars is the cost of the glove.
9. The duck and the goose is in separate cages.
10. The committee have planned the program.

EXERCISE 12:

1. State the tense of each verb or verb phrase.
   (a) We shall visit Halifax next summer.
   (b) I have seen a picture of the Citadel.
   (c) My uncle lives across the harbour in Dartmouth.
   (d) He lived in Vancouver several years ago.
   (e) We shall have visited both coasts by next summer.

2. Write the following sentence changing the verb to (a) past tense, (b) future tense, (c) present perfect tense, (d) past perfect tense, (e) future perfect tense.
   We go to the library every Saturday.

Review:

EXERCISE 13: Write each of the following sentences, selecting the proper
preposition. Be prepared to give the reason for your
choice.

1. She was angry (with, at) me.
2. Divide the candies (between, among) Pat and me.
3. I differ (with, from) his opinion about the animal.
4. My jacket is different (with, from) yours.
5. We ran from the orchard (in, into) the house.
6. Divide the cards (between, among) Bill, Tom, and Charlie.
7. They took the knife (from, off, off of) Terry.
8. The class agreed (with, to) the plan for the excursion.
9. Norah is quite different (from, than) Janice.
10. She put the books (in, into) the carton.

EXERCISE 14:

1. A co-ordinate conjunction joins two words, two phrases, or two clauses
which are used the same way in a sentence. Select the co-ordinate conjunctions
from each of the following sentences and tell what kind of words, phrases, or
clauses each joins.

(a) Quietly but quickly we set off down the path.
(b) John and I were certain of the direction.
(c) The stars blinked and twinkled through the leaves.
(d) From the clearing or near the lake we heard a noise.
(e) We crept silently towards it and there in the dim light was a fox.

2. A subordinate conjunction introduces a subordinate clause and joins
the clause to the word it modifies. Select the subordinate conjunctions from
each of the following sentences.

(a) Because quinine is used in the treatment of malaria it is a valuable
drug.
(b) Malaria may be contracted when you are travelling in tropical
countries.
(c) Quinine is extracted from the bark of the cinchona tree after it has
been ground into a fine brown powder.
(d) Although the tree is not fully grown until it is eight or nine years
old the bark can be taken from it when it is three years old.

EXERCISE 15: From the sentences of the first question of Exercise 14
select the following:

1. a proper noun
2. a first person, plural pronoun
3. a predicate adjective
4. a definite article
5. a pronoun object of a preposition

291

Review:

EXERCISE 16: Tell how each of the italicized words is used in the sentence and then state what part of speech it is.

1. Brazil is the largest *country* in South America.
2. *It* is larger than the United States.
3. The Amazon *with* its tributaries is the world's greatest river system.
4. Along it *stretches* vast tropical forests.
5. Huge alligators, boa constrictors, *and* rattlesnakes infest the area.
6. The chief *source* of wealth is in the coffee plantations.
7. Next to coffee, cotton is *now* the leading export of the country.
8. In *iron* ore Brazil is one of the richest countries in the world.
9. Cacao, like sugar cane, is an old crop of *this* tropical land.
10. Today rubber from the Amazon Lowland is of little *importance*.

EXERCISE 17: Use each of the following parts of speech in a sentence according to the directions given.

1. the pronoun "her" as an object of a preposition
2. the conjunction "but" joining two adverbs
3. the adjective "silent" as subjective completion of a verb
4. the adverb "too" modifying another adverb
5. the adverb "very" modifying an adjective
6. the plural possessive form of the noun "man"
7. the conjunction "and" joining two adverb phrases
8. the subordinate conjunction "if" introducing a subordinate adverb clause
9. the pronoun "that" used as a relative pronoun
10. the past perfect tense of the verb "see"

EXERCISE 18: Select the correct word from each pair in brackets and be prepared to give a reason for your choice.

1. Everyone must do (his, their) best.
2. I (shall, will) be thirteen years old next week.
3. Tell the dog to (lie, lay) down.
4. Try (and, to) do the printing carefully.
5. I saw (their, there) new car.
6. It was (she, her) that did it.
7. Have they (gone, went) home yet?
8. He (don't, doesn't) like it.
9. (Is, Are) either of the answers correct?
10. This is the (cooler, coolest) side of the street.

APPENDIX

Material for Handy Reference

OPENING EXERCISES

Perhaps your classroom is one in which a group of pupils conducts the opening exercises each day. If so, you have an opportunity to practise your reading and speaking skills in a real audience situation. If you attend a large school, you may have additional practice of this kind when the weekly or bi-weekly assembly is held for the classes of your division in the auditorium.

If the pupils of your class are already participating in the opening exercises, the following suggestions may be of help in improving everyone's contribution. On the other hand, if your class has not adopted a procedure somewhat similar to that outlined below, this information may be of even more use to you. It will help you and your teacher in organizing a programme for the opening exercises which will enable you to practise using your language skills in interesting and purposeful activities.

Read this section OPENING EXERCISES carefully. Prepare to answer the questions that are found on page 298.

Opening Exercises:

OPENING EXERCISES in the classroom might include the following:

1. O, Canada or The Maple Leaf
2. The Bible Reading
3. The Lord's Prayer
4. The Morning Hymn
5. Reports on Current Events
6. A Poem, Short Story, or Song
7. The Salute to the Flag
8. God Save the Queen

For an assembly programme item 6 above usually becomes a FEATURE which may be either a dramatic or a musical presentation. It is prepared by a group of pupils from the class in charge on that particular day. This FEATURE is usually followed by the principal's announcements.

SOME HELPFUL HINTS:

1. THE CHAIRMAN: With the teacher's help the chairman has three main tasks: (a) to plan the programme for the day, and to obtain the co-operation of the pupils who are to be responsible for presenting the various items; (b) to make the arrangements whereby the classroom or auditorium is prepared for the exercises or assembly; (c) to conduct the programme by announcing the items, and by introducing the participants.

The chairman should speak distinctly at all times. Between items on the programme he should wait for all noise to subside before making the next announcement. When a participant has done well he may comment on that pupil's contribution: Thank you, John, for that report. Your use of the map helps us to remember the legend of the lost continent of Atlantis.

Note: When the chairman is a girl she is always addressed as *Madam Chairman*, NOT as Madam Chairlady.

2. THE BIBLE READING: Select the passage the day before it is to be used. Write on the chalkboard the book, the chapter, and the number of the first and last verse. *Example:* St. Luke 2: 41-52.

All who participate should practise reading the selection silently and orally. Pupils should be familiar with the pronunciation key which appears in most Bibles near the title page. They should use this key to determine the pronunciation of all the proper nouns before the devotional period of the opening exercises begins.

To determine how well the members of the class have remembered the content of the passage, the leader might prepare three or four questions which will be asked as soon as the reading is completed.

Opening Exercises:

3. THE PRAYER: The prayer is usually conducted by the pupil who leads the Bible reading. This pupil should speak so as to be heard, and in a manner which will result in the prayer being said slowly and meaningfully.

4. REPORTING CURRENT EVENTS: (a) One pupil may be selected to report on the news for each of the following headings: (i) World News; (ii) National News; (iii) Provincial News; (iv) Local or Community News; (v) Sports News.

In some classrooms only one kind of news is reported on each morning from Monday to Thursday. On Friday one pupil reviews the most important items and another presents a digest of the sporting news of the week.

The news items should *not* be read from the clippings that are brought to class. Each item should be reported on orally in a few well-composed sentences.

Pupils reporting news items should be able to explain the meaning of any word used in their reports. Unfamiliar names of people and places should be written on the chalkboard. The location of all places mentioned in the report should be pointed out on a map of suitable size.

Clippings brought to class should be mounted on a bulletin board. Coloured strings, fastened with thumb tacks, which run from the clippings to the appropriate spots on a world map, help to provide an interesting display. If the bulletin board is really used for *current* events it must be changed frequently to be kept up to date.

The items selected for these reports to the class must be of real interest to pupils of Grade VIII. News reports of crimes should *not* be chosen. Only a few reports of accidents can be classified as being sufficiently important to be called current events. It is far better to have a few items reported that are significant than to have many items none of which are of any importance.

(b) To encourage all pupils to skim read at least the front page of the daily paper, some teachers write four or five questions on the chalkboard before the class comes into the room in the morning. After the pupils' reports on current events have been given these questions are uncovered. Sometimes points are given to the rows or teams that are able to answer best orally.

Opening Exercises:

REMEMBER: 1. *Select the news items carefully.*

2. *Talk about the items. Do not read them.*

3. *Be brief by giving only the important facts.*

4. *Use a map or globe to show the location of the place where the event occurred.*

5. *Know the pronunciation of all the words used in your report.*

6. *Present new or unusual words on the chalkboard.*

5. THE FEATURE: Dramatic presentations may be of several types: (i) a play found in the reader or in another book; (ii) a play composed by members of the class which is based on a story in the reader, or on some incident known to the class; (iii) a radio play or a puppet show in which it is possible for all the lines to be read.

Choral presentations may be either the musical variety, or that in which poems are spoken in unison by a voice choir. In both types there are often parts for solo voices.

A theme for the feature presentation can often be selected by referring to the ALMANAC section of this book.

6. THE EVALUATION: Before the opening exercises are concluded a class evaluation or criticism of all the participants may be held. This should *not* be done every day, but if carried out about once a week it can be an interesting and valuable activity. Remember that a complete criticism will present comments on the good points as well as draw attention to those that need to be strengthened.

The chairman should call upon the members of the class to appraise the work of those who participated. Of course the pupils should also comment upon the manner in which the members of the audience took part.

For the leaders these characteristics should be considered:

1. Preparation: —evidence of careful preparation
   —news items selected for importance and for interest
   —ability to summarize
   —use of oral reading skills

2. Manner and Poise: —posture; standing erect
   —no distracting movements of face or arms
   —looking at the audience
   —enthusiasm or interest
   —confidence

Opening Exercises:

3. Speech: —speed and volume suitable for easy listening
  —conversational tone
  —accurate pronunciation and clear enunciation
  —absence of "ah's" and "um's" and repetitions
  —well-composed sentences used throughout
  —no errors in grammar

4. Method of Presentation: —news, told or read
  —use of maps, chalkboard sketches, suitable pictures to illustrate items
  —use of chalkboard to present new or unusual words
  —reaction of the audience

In evaluating class participation these points should be considered:

1. Did all pupils co-operate to provide an attentive audience?
2. Did all pupils participate when called upon?
3. Did pupils sit or stand properly at all times?

In closing the evaluation period the chairman might ask if any pupils wished to make suggestions whereby the general procedure of the opening exercises might be improved.

EXERCISE 1: After reading carefully the previous four pages prepare to answer the following questions orally.

1. In a pupil-conducted opening exercises period what are the chairman's three duties?

2. In what two ways may maps be used in conjunction with the classroom study of current events?

3. When a girl is chairman how is she addressed?

4. What may be done by the leader of the Bible reading to encourage the members of the class to read attentively?

5. Recite the six points to remember when selecting, preparing, and presenting current events reports.

6. Why is it preferable for a pupil to report orally on each news item rather than to read from a clipping?

A CRITIC SHEET: On the next page is a sample of a critic sheet that has been used successfully by Grade VIII classes. The material in italics has been taken from the reports made by the pupils.

Sheets of this type are duplicated and a copy is distributed to each pupil at the close of the exercises. After sufficient time for them to be completed has been given, they are collected. The pupils who participated are given an opportunity to read them. The teacher, after reading them, may present a summary of their contents to the class.

CRITIC SHEET

In commenting on each participant keep these points in mind:

1. POSTURE and POISE: Distractions? Eyed the audience?
2. SPEECH: Volume? Speed? Tone? Grammar?
3. PRESENTATION: Reading or talking? Illustrations?
4. PREPARATION: Evidence of time spent? Choice of material?
   Use of reading or speaking skills?
5. AUDIENCE: Co-operation? Attentiveness? Posture?

CHAIRMAN:	*David might have spoken more loudly. His posture was excellent. He conducted the exercises well, and thanked, in a different way, each person who took part.*
BIBLE READER:	*Frank rocked back and forth when reading although he showed that he had practised and that he knew what he was reading. He hurried too much at the beginning and started before we were ready.*
SPORTS NEWS:	*George gave interesting sports news but had his fingers in his pockets while telling it. He looked solemn.*
LOCAL NEWS:	*Mary's news was well chosen. She should have studied it more and have been able to talk to us about it clearly. The use of the map would have helped. Her pronunciation and enunciation were good.*
CANADIAN NEWS:	*Donna's presentation was well done except for some of the words. She should make sure of them all.*
WORLD NEWS:	*John's news was of real interest. He could be heard very well. His posture and manner were excellent.*
CLASS: OR AUDIENCE	*Some pupils were fidgeting at times. Everyone should refrain from laughing when a person at the front mispronounces a word.*
SUGGESTIONS:	*There should be some form of punishment for those who do not bring their news. Everyone should prepare his news before giving it and not have to refer to the clipping. Each morning somebody should be asked to give a poem. I should like to hear some humorous poems.*

Current Events

To develop the ability to make wise judgements, to practise picking out the main facts in a news item, and to develop the ability to make an oral report effectively and with confidence, follow these suggestions:

Thirteen-Year-Old Publishes History Book

AUCKLAND, N.Z. (CP)—The historian of the town of Waiuku, near Auckland, has completed a long task. Six years of research and preparation went into a history of the district which he has just published. He is now aged 13.

Starting at the ripe old age of seven, Brian Muir began to keep a scrap book in which he recorded all he heard about the early history of his town and district.

Snatches of information, sketches of early life, clippings from newspapers all went into the scrap books until several were filled.

So Brian determined to collect the story of the district in a printed book.

He drew on early newspapers, souvenir pamphlets published at the time of local celebrations, other printed records and historical references to the town and its surroundings.

Not content with that he called on old-timers in the neighborhood and asked them to tell their stories of pioneering days.

The result is a 120-page book "Waiuku and District," which has just been published.

1. Select a news item that is of interest to people of your age.

2. After the family is finished with the paper, cut the item out.

3. Read the clipping several times silently. Underline or tick the important details. Use a dictionary to find the meanings of new words. Locate the places mentioned on a map.

4. Practise giving a brief oral summary of the news item in well-composed sentences.

5. Take the clipping to school. Read it silently before making your report. Prepare the illustrations and the map you wish to use.

6. Without referring to the clipping, give your oral report. Point out the places on the map. Use the chalkboard to present new words and sketches to illustrate your presentation.

7. Be prepared to read orally any portion of the clipping which might answer any question which your classmates might ask about your report.

Your report on the news item reproduced on this page might be as follows:

What is perhaps the world's newest history book has just been published by its thirteen-year-old author. Brian Muir, who lives near Auckland, New Zealand (Point to the map.) started when he was seven to write the history of his town and district. He read all he could about it. He asked questions. He listened to the older people talk. Now after six years of research and writing his 120 page book called Waiuku and District has been printed. Perhaps Brian's success will encourage those of us who have difficulty in writing a story of more than one paragraph.

300

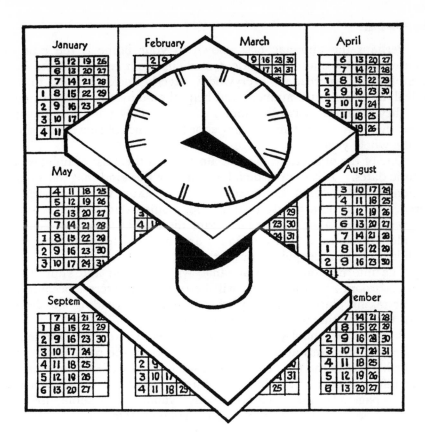

THE ALMANAC

Almanacs, or annual calendars with seasonal information of interest to farmers, sailors, and others were prepared by the ancient Greeks and Egyptians long before the birth of Christ. After printing was invented in the fifteenth century it was possible to distribute almanacs more widely. The Farmer's Almanac, which has been published annually in the United States since 1792 is, perhaps, the oldest periodical of its kind in America. Years ago the popularity of the almanac was such that a copy of it was found hanging on a nail in almost every kitchen. At that time it was probably read more frequently than any other book except the Bible.

Some modern almanacs are published for specific purposes. The *Nautical Almanac*, first issued in 1914, presents information of particular interest to mariners. The *Air Almanac*, introduced in 1937, has been adapted to meet the requirements of air navigation.

The Almanac:

Perhaps the almanac best known in your home is the type distributed free by one of the patent medicine companies. These books often boast that readers everywhere eagerly look forward to their arrival, and find entertainment and helpful guidance in the information that they contain. Like the almanacs of old, they tell about the stars, about the phases of the moon, and about the times of sunset and sunrise for the whole year.

One of the attractions of most almanacs is their list of holidays and historic dates. It is to provide information of this kind that the almanac section of DEVELOPING LANGUAGE SKILLS—GRADE VIII has been prepared. It will be a handy reference for finding dates which mark the anniversaries of some of the important discoveries and inventions. It includes the dates of many religious and national festivals, and of the birthdays of some people whose work has benefited all mankind.

The information in this almanac will help you and your teacher plan classroom activities which will be of greater interest because they will be taking place on the day when you will be reading and hearing about the same theme or topic outside of school.

Because the school year runs from September to June, the months will be arranged in that order. For each month the number of entries will be limited to the ten or twelve considered to be of most interest. If more information of this kind is required consult the books which are listed on page 327 and which are usually available in a public library.

After noting the importance of a particular date one or more of the following activities may be carried out:

1. Consult reference books and prepare an oral or written report on the discovery, invention, or historical event. Use maps or illustrations, which you may have to make, in the presentation of your report.

2. Find poems or stories suitable for the occasion. Practise reading these silently and orally before reading them to the class.

3. Arrange a display of models, drawings, and pictures to be accompanied by oral or written explanations, or plan a programme, to mark certain anniversaries.

4. At the end of a month write puzzle-pen-portraits of the famous men and women in the almanac for that period. (See page 29.)

The activities suggested above are only a few that might be used. You, your classmates, and your teacher will be able to plan many more. Although you will not find facts about the sun, the moon, the stars, and the tides in this almanac, the information that is presented here should be interesting and useful during your year in Grade VIII.

"Let us now praise famous men, and the fathers that begat us."

Ecclesiasticus xliv: 1

The Almanac:

SEPTEMBER

Before the calendar was revised by Julius Caesar in 46 B.C. September was the seventh month of the year. Its name comes from the Latin word *septem* meaning *seven*. Its flower is the morning glory. Its birthstone is either the sapphire or the beryl.

1—The provinces of Alberta and Saskatchewan were founded in 1905.
2—World War II began, 1939.
6—First Canadian television station officially opened in Montreal, 1952.
8—First air mail from Montreal to Vancouver, 1928.
10—The Soo Canal opened, 1895.
13—Battle of the Plains of Abraham, 1759.
15—Russia was proclaimed a republic, 1917.
20—The franchise in Canadian federal elections was extended to women, 1917.
21—The autumn equinox occurs on or about this date each year.
26—R.M.S. *Queen Mary* launched at Glasgow, Scotland, 1934.

OCTOBER

The name for this month is derived from the Latin word for *eight*. The flower is the cosmos. The birthstone is the opal.

4—Feast of St. Francis of Assisi.
—First air mail service in Canada, 1927.
—Miles Coverdale published the first English Bible, 1535.
5—R.C.M.P. vessel *St. Roch*, an eighty-ton schooner, completed an eastward journey through the North West Passage, 1942. The voyage began June 9, 1940. (See Oct. 16.)
8—Edmonton, now Canada's "Oil City"; was incorporated, 1904.
9—The Great Chicago Fire, 1871. Each year the Governor-General of Canada usually decrees that the week in which the ninth falls will be observed as Fire Prevention Week.
11—Y.M.C.A. Founder's Day, Sir George Williams, 1821-1905.
12—Columbus Day in honour of his arrival in the New World in 1492.
16—R.C.M.P. vessel *St. Roch* completed its westward voyage through the North West Passage from Dartmouth, N.S. to Vancouver, B.C., 1944. The voyage began on July 22, 1944. (See Oct. 5.)
18—Alaska Day—Alaska transferred to the United States of America, 1867.
23—Fredericton was made the capital of New Brunswick, 1896.
24—United Nations Day—The UN was founded in 1945.
25—The Battle of Balaklava, 1854. (Read Tennyson's poem *The Charge of the Light Brigade*.)
31—Hallowe'en: The eve of All-Hallomas or All Saints' Day is an autumn festival inherited from pagan times. It corresponds to the spring festival of reawakening.

303

NOVEMBER

The name for this month is derived from the Latin word meaning *nine*. The chrysanthemum is the flower of the month. The topaz is the birthstone.

1—All Saints' Day.

3—Penny Postage introduced in Canada, 1890. (See January 9.)

6—First session of the Canadian Parliament at Ottawa, 1867.

7—Donald Smith drove the famous last spike at Craigellachie, B.C., to complete the first Canadian transcontinental railway, 1885.

11—Remembrance Day.

14—Toronto made the capital of Ontario, 1849.

19—President Abraham Lincoln delivered the Gettysburg Address, 1863.

24—Discovery of Tasmania, 1642.

27—The first vessels passed through the first Welland Canal, 1829.

30—Birthday of Sir Winston Churchill, statesman, 1874.

—St. Andrew's Day, which everyone of Scottish ancestry celebrates.

(*Note:* Young Canada's Book Week, sponsored by the Canadian Library Association is held during November.)

DECEMBER

The name for this month comes from the Latin word *decem* meaning *ten*. The birthstone is the turquoise. The flower is the holly.

6—The Halifax Explosion, 1917.

7—First successful heavier-than-air flight made by the Wright Brothers at Kitty Hawk, North Carolina, 1903.

8—Timothy Eaton opened a dry goods store in Toronto, 1869.

12—The first trans-Atlantic wireless signal received by Marconi at St. John's, Newfoundland, 1901.

—The Statute of Westminster became effective, 1931.

13—"Bad Luck Day" for turkeys. Why?

—New Zealand discovered, 1751.

21—The winter solstice occurs on or about this date each year. Winter begins.

24—The Treaty of Ghent, 1814: The people of Canada and the United States have been at peace with one another since that date.

25—Christmas: Read the Scriptures, Matthew 2: 1-12 and Luke 2: 1-20.

30—Birthday of Rudyard Kipling, 1865-1936.

(*Note:* Watch the daily papers during this month for an account of the close of the shipping season at the port of Montreal.)

The Almanac:

January

This month is named after the Roman two-headed god, Janus, because it looks backward to the past year and forward to the new. Its birthstone is the garnet and its flower is the carnation.

1—The National Holiday of Scotland.
2—The Royal Mint opened in Ottawa, 1908.
4—Birthday of Isaac Newton, English scientist, 1642-1727.
6—Epiphany, the twelfth day after Christmas. (See St. Matthew 2: 1-2.)
7—Birthday of Sir Stanford Fleming (1827-1915), the Scottish-Canadian who devised Standard Time adopted in 1883.
9—Penny postage established in Britain, 1840. (See November 3.)
11—Birthday of Sir John A. MacDonald, Canadian statesman, 1815-1891.
14—Birthday of Albert Schweitzer, 1875.
20—The first English Parliament met, 1262.
25—The birthday of Robert Burns, Scottish poet, 1759-1796.
—St. Paul's Day.
26—Australia Day, the anniversary of the arrival of the first colonists from England, 1788.
—Thomas A. Edison patented the incandescent electric lamp. (See Feb. 11.)
29—Queen Victoria instituted the Victoria Cross for valour, 1856.

February

The name for this month is derived from the Latin word *februa* meaning *the feast of purification*. It was the month of purification amongst the ancient Romans. The primrose is the flower of the month. The amethyst is the birthstone.

2—Candlemas.
—Groundhog Day.
6—Death of King George VI and accession of Elizabeth II, 1952.
9—France ceded Canada to Britain, 1763.
11—Birthday of Thomas A. Edison, inventor, 1847-1931.
12—Birthday of Abraham Lincoln, 1809-1865.
14—Valentine's Day.
15—Birthday of Galileo, Italian astronomer, 1564-1642.
19—Birthday of Copernicus, Polish astronomer, 1473-1543.
22—Birthday of George Washington, 1732-1799.
23—Birthday of George Frederick Handel, 1685-1759.
27—Birthday of H. W. Longfellow, poet, 1807-1862.
28—Right Honourable Vincent Massey was sworn in as the first Canadian-born Governor-General, 1952.

The Almanac:

MARCH

In the old calendar this was the first month of the year. It was called *Martius* after *Mars*, the Roman god of war. The bloodstone is the stone and the jonquil is the flower for the month.

1—St. David's Day, dedicated to the patron saint of Wales, on which all loyal Welshmen wear a leek or a daffodil and gather to sing the songs that praise their homeland.

—TCA airmail service inaugurated, 1939.

3—"The Star Spangled Banner" became the national anthem of the United States of America, 1931.

6—Birthday of Michelangelo, 1475-1564, a man of many talents.

11—Bank of Canada commenced operation, 1935.

12—Birthday of William Lyon Mackenzie, 1795-1861, Canadian political leader.

13—"Standard Time," a system devised by a Canadian, Sir Stanford Fleming, was adopted in 1884.

17—St. Patrick's Day.

21—The spring equinox occurs about this date. Winter ends. Easter is on the first Sunday after the first full moon following the spring equinox.

26—Birthday of Cecil Rhodes, 1853-1902, British statesman.

28—Gunpowder first used in Europe.

31—Newfoundland was admitted to the Canadian federation as the tenth province, 1949.

APRIL

The name of this month comes from a Latin word meaning "to open." The daisy is the flower and the diamond the stone for April.

1—April Fool's Day.

2—Birthday of Washington Irving, 1783-1859, American writer.

6—Robert E. Peary, 1856-1920, American explorer, discovered the North Pole in 1909.

10—Birthday of Jack Miner, 1864-1944, Canadian naturalist. National Wild Life Week is held annually during the week in which April 10 falls.

18—Ontario's first newspaper, the Upper Canada Gazette, founded at Newark (Niagara-on-the-Lake), 1793.

21—Birthday of Queen Elizabeth II, 1926.

23—St. George's Day, in honour of the patron saint of England.

—The birthday and the date of the death of William Shakespeare, 1564-1616.

25—Birthday of Oliver Cromwell, 1599-1658, English general and statesman.

—Birthday of Guglielmo Marconi, 1874-1937, Italian inventor. (See Dec. 12.)

27—Birthday of Samuel Morse, 1791-1872, inventor.

The Almanac:

MAY

The name is derived from *Maia*, one of the seven daughters of Atlas, who held the weight of the world on his shoulders. The hawthorn and the emerald are the flower and the stone for this, the fifth month of the year.

1—May Day: On this date the ancients celebrated the return of spring with the lighting of bonfires or with a flower festival. Nowadays many people honour the day by crowning a May queen, by dancing around a Maypole, or by distributing May baskets.

4—Birthday of John James Audubon, 1785-1851.

5—Napoleon Bonaparte, 1769-1821, died on the Island of St. Helena.

12—National Hospital Day, honouring the birthday of Florence Nightingale, 1820-1910, "The Lady with the Lamp."

18—Landing of the United Empire Loyalists at Saint John, New Brunswick, 1783.

23—Captain William Kidd, 1645-1701, known as "Captain Kidd," British privateer and pirate, hanged for piracy in London.

24—Birthday of Queen Victoria, 1819-1899.

27—The English Parliament enacted the Habeas Corpus Act, 1679.

29—Mount Everest scaled for the first time by Hillary and Tensing, 1953

30—Joan of Arc, 1412-1431, French heroine, was burned at the stake.

—Memorial Day (U.S.A.).

(*Note:* The Monday before May 25th is celebrated as the Queen's Birthday.)

JUNE

This month was named after Juno, who was the wife of Jupiter, the king of the Roman gods. The honeysuckle is the floral emblem. The pearl is the gem of the month.

1—Coronation of Queen Elizabeth II, 1953.

2—Birthday of Leonardo da Vinci, 1452-1519, a man of many talents.

6—D Day, 1944, when the greatest armada in history crossed the English Channel to land in France.

10—Establishment of the United Church of Canada, 1925.

11—Hawaii became a territory of the U.S.A., 1900.

15—King John signed the Magna Carta at Runnymede, 1215.

19—The first Jesuits arrived in Canada, 1625.

21—The summer solstice when the northern hemisphere has the longest day of the year.

22—Sir Wilfrid Laurier, 1841-1919, became Prime Minister of Canada, 1896.

24—St. Jean de Baptiste Day.

27—Birthday of Helen Keller, 1880-   , whose work on behalf of the blind and the deaf has made her world famous.

(*Note:* The second Sunday in June is observed as Children's Day, Flower Sunday, or Rose Day in many parts of Canada.)

For July and August only a few items are presented in this almanac as schools are usually closed during these months for the summer vacation. There is one date, however, which should be celebrated at school before the holidays begin. To mark this occasion a programme should be planned and presented, perhaps outdoors, on one of the last days. Parents might be sent written invitations to attend. It would be a celebration to mark

CANADA'S BIRTHDAY
JULY 1, 1867

Canadians have heard a great deal about early American frontiersmen such as Davy Crockett, Daniel Boone, Paul Revere, and General Custer. Two Canadian historians were asked to name ten swashbuckling Canadians whose derring-do matched that of the Americans. These professors named explorers Henry Kelsey, Anthony Henday, Etienne Brulé, Sieur de la Salle, Alexander Mackenzie, David Thompson, Pierre Radisson, Médard Groseilliers, the Indian chief Tecumseh, and Adam Dollard who died in the siege of an Ottawa River outpost and thus saved Montreal in its early days. For good measure these learned gentlemen added the names of Pierre La Vérendrye and Indian warrior Joseph Brant.

Another Canadian scholar lists D'Arcy McGee, William Lyon Mackenzie, and Louis Joseph Papineau as colourful historical figures whose deeds should be well known to every Canadian boy and girl.

Canada also has her heroines. The names of Madeleine de Verchères, Jeanne Mance, Madame de la Tour, Laura Secord, Susanna Moodie, and Catherine Parr Traill remind us that women, too, played their part in pioneer days.

There are, of course, many historical characters in addition to those named above who, because of what they did for the development of our country, should also be regarded as heroes or heroines.

A programme in celebration of Canada's birthday provides an opportunity to honour our national heroes, the men and women of our colourful history.

July

The Anglo-Saxons called it "Maed-monath" because the meadows were in bloom. Before the present name was given in honour of Julius Caesar it was known as Quintilis, meaning the fifth month. Until about 1800 July was pronounced to rhyme with *newly* and *truly*. The flower of the month is the water lily. The stone is the ruby.

1—The British North America Act created the Dominion of Canada, 1867.

—Prince Edward Island entered Confederation, 1873.

(*Note:* See the book list on page 328.)

3—Birthday of Samuel de Champlain, 1567-1635.

9—Upper Canada passed a law forbidding the importation of slaves, 1793.

12—The Battle of the Boyne, 1690.

15—Manitoba entered Confederation, 1870.

20—British Columbia entered Confederation, 1871.

22—An inscription on a Pacific Coast sea-side rock was carved. It reads: "Alexander Mackenzie, from Canada by land, 22nd July, 1793."

31—Canada acquired the North West Territories, 1870.

August

When this was the sixth month in the calendar it was known as *Sextilis*. The present name was given in honour of Augustus Caesar, emperor of Rome from 27 B.C. to A.D. 14 Its stone is the sardonyx and its flower is the poppy.

4—Canada entered World War I, 1914.

5—The first atomic bomb to be used in warfare was dropped on the city of Hiroshima, Japan, in 1945 during World War II.

6—Official opening of the new Welland Canal, 1932.

10—The Feast of St. Lawrence.

—Jacques Cartier entered the Gulf of St. Lawrence, 1536.

—The first sod was turned for the St. Lawrence Seaway and Power Project, 1954.

15—The Panama Canal opened, 1914.

26—The first television broadcast, 1936.

THE SENTENCE AND ITS PARTS

I. THE SENTENCE

1. A sentence is a group of related words expressing a complete thought.

2. Kinds of sentences according to function:
   - (a) I read an exciting book. —Assertive
   - (b) Have you read this exciting book?—Interrogative
   - (c) Read this exciting book. —Imperative
   - (d) What an exciting book this is! —Exclamatory

3. Order in the sentence:
   - (a) Natural order (the subject at the beginning)
     The bats flew out of the cave.
   - (b) Inverted order (the subject at the end)
     Out of the cave flew the bats.
   - (c) Split order (the subject in the middle of the predicate)
     Out of the cave the bats flew.

4. Kinds of sentences according to construction:
   - (a) Victoria is the capital of British Columbia. —Simple
   - (b) Victoria is the capital of British Columbia and —Compound
     it is situated on Vancouver Island.
   - (c) Victoria, which is the capital of British Columbia,—Complex
     is situated on Vancouver Island.
   - (d) Victoria, which is the capital of British Columbia,—Compound-
     is situated on Vancouver Island and it is visited   complex
     by many tourists each year.

5. Variety in the sentence:
   - (a) Use different kinds of sentences.
   - (b) Use inverted and split order in sentences.
   - (c) Combine ideas into simple, compound, and complex sentences.

A knowledge of the ways to obtain variety in the sentence can be used to improve both spoken and written English.

II. THE PARTS OF THE SENTENCE

Note: Before a sentence is analysed, it should always be expressed in natural order.

1. Subject—the part of the sentence that tells what you are talking about.
   One of the oldest cities | is Quebec.

2. Predicate—the part of the sentence that says something about its subject.
   Quebec | *is one of our oldest cities.*

A knowledge of subject and predicate is needed to be able to rearrange the order in sentences to obtain variety. It should also be useful in detecting and avoiding the use of sentence fragments.

The Sentence and Its Parts:

3. Bare subject—
    (a) Buttercups | bloom in the summer.
    (b) The yellow flowers | brighten the fields.

4. Bare predicate—
    (a) Buttercups | bloom in the summer.
    (b) Some girls | are gathering bouquets.

5. Modifiers of the bare subject—
    (a) (Four) (little) girls (in red dresses) | ran across the lawn.
    (b) (Some) (winter) apples (from Ontario) | are sent to England.

6. Modifiers of the bare predicate—
    (a) John | runs [quickly].
    (b) Birds | fly [south] [in the autumn].

7. Object—the completing part of the sentence that
              (i) completes the bare predicate
              (ii) receives the action of the bare predicate.
    (a) The first settlers built log cabins.
    (b) Bell invented the telephone.

8. Subjective completion—the completing part of the sentence that
              (i) completes the bare predicate
              (ii) describes or means the same as the subject.
    (a) Alice seems angry.
    (b) Father is a doctor.

9. Indirect object—the completing part that tells **to whom** or **for whom** the action of the bare predicate was performed.
    (a) Tom gave me the apple.
    (b) His mother bought the girls some grapes.

A knowledge of object and subjective completion is useful in determining whether the subject or object form of the pronoun is required in a sentence.

Complete graphic analysis of the sentence:
    (a) Mackenzie | discovered (a) (famous) river.
    (b) He | was (a) (fur) trader.
    (c) (This) (famous) (Canadian) explorer | has given (his) name [to a great river].

The relationship of the words in a sentence is shown by analysis. This relationship determines the name given to each part of the sentence.

311

THE PARTS OF SPEECH

1. NOUN—a word which names a person, a place, a thing, or an unseen thing or quality.

    (a) Kind: (i) common—boy   city   musician
                (ii) proper— Tom   Ottawa   Mozart

    (b) Number: (i) singular—man   city   sheep
                (ii) plural— men   cities   sheep

    (c) Possessive forms:
        (i) the *boy's* books   (a singular noun)
        (ii) the *boys'* books   (a plural noun ending in s)
        (iii) the *men's* coats   (a plural noun *not* ending in s)

    (d) Use:
        (i) bare subject—*Coffee* grows in Brazil.
        (ii) object   —Brazil grows *coffee.*
        (iii) subjective completion—This drink is *coffee.*
        (iv) object of a preposition—Coffee grows in *Brazil.*
        (v) indirect object—She gave the *men* coffee.

2. PRONOUN—a word that takes the place of a noun.
    (a) Kind: (i) personal—*I* brought *them* with *me.*
             (ii) interrogative—*Who* was there?
             (iii) demonstrative—*That* is the new store.
             (iv) indefinite—*Some* of the boys shouted.

    A pronoun which introduces a subordinate clause and also acts as a conjunction is known as a *relative* pronoun.
    A state *which* borders Canada is Maine.

    (b) Number: (i) singular—I, you,   he,   her,   this
                (ii) plural —we, you,   they,   them,   these

    (c) Case: (i) nominative (subject form)
                is used in the sentence as
                    subject of the verb   —*I* was there.
                    subjective completion—It was *I.*

            (ii) objective (object form)
                is used in the sentence as
                    object of the verb—   Tom raced *me* to the tree.
                    object of the preposition— Give it to Tom and *me.*
                    indirect object of the verb—Give *me* the book.

The Parts of Speech:

3. VERB—the bare predicate of a sentence.

(a) Single word verb: Tom *runs* fast.

(b) Verb phrase:

Auxiliary Verb	Principal Verb
is	running
has	been
has been	playing

(i) Tom *is running*.
(ii) He *has been* here.
(iii) Mary *has been playing* the piano.

(c) Kind: (i) transitive (requires an object to complete it)
(ii) intransitive (requires no completing part)
(iii) copula (requires a subjective completion)

(d) A verb must agree with its subject in number and person.

(i) A singular verb is used
—with a subject singular in number.
—with singular subjects joined by *or* or *nor*.
—with subjects containing the words, *each, every, either, neither, any, one, none,* which refer to persons or objects considered singular.
—with a subject naming a sum of money.

(ii) A plural verb is used
—with a subject plural in number.
—with subjects joined by *and.*

(iii) The form of the verb usually changes with a subject which is third person singular when used in the present tense.

I go.	We go.
You go.	You go
He goes.	They go.

(e) Tense:
(i) The verb is said to be in the *present tense* when it indicates that an action is taking place or that something exists at the present time.

Our team *plays* hockey now.

(ii) The verb is said to be in the *past tense* when it indicates that an action has taken place or that something existed at some time in the past.

Our team *played* hockey yesterday.

(iii) The verb is said to be in the *future tense* when it indicates that an action will take place or that something will exist at some time in the future.

Our team *will play* hockey tomorrow.

When *shall* and *will* are used as auxiliary verbs for the simple future tense, use *shall* with *I* and *we*, and *will* with all other subjects.

(iv) The verb is said to be in the *present perfect tense* when it indicates that an action is finished or is complete at the present time.

The train *has arrived*.
I *have given* my answer.

(v) The verb is said to be in the *past perfect tense* when it indicates that an action was completed at some time in the past.

The train *had arrived* before we left home.

(vi) The verb is said to be in the *future perfect tense* when it indicates that an action will be completed at some time in the future. The rule for the use of *shall* and *will* is the same as for the simple future tense.

The train *will have arrived*.

(vii) The future of promise or determination is used to emphasize the promise or to express determination. The rule for this is just the opposite to that for writing the simple future tense.

When writing a paragraph it is important to avoid shifting from one tense to another.

(f) Principal Parts:

Present Tense	Past Tense	Perfect Participle
see	saw	seen
come	came	come
do	did	done
go	went	gone
lay (transitive)	laid	laid
lie (intransitive)	lay	lain

The Parts of Speech:

4. ADJECTIVE—a word that describes or modifies a noun.
   (a) Kinds:
   - (i) proper   *Canadian* winters are cold.
   - (ii) pronominal   This is *my* pen.
   - (iii) descriptive   He wore a *pointed* hat.
   - (iv) predicate   The sky is **cloudy**.

   (b) Articles:
   - (i) the indefinite article—a, an
   - (ii) the definite article—the

   (c) Comparison of adjectives:

Kind	Positive Degree (describing one noun)	Comparative Degree (comparing two nouns)	Superlative Degree (comparing three or more nouns)
(i) regular	tall	taller	tallest
(ii) phrasal	valuable	more valuable	most valuable
(iii) irregular	good	better	best

   (d) Use:
   - (i) modifies a noun   —This is an *exciting* book.
   - (ii) subjective completion—This book is *exciting*.

   (e) Adjective phrase: a group of words made up of a preposition **and a** noun or pronoun—

   in the tree   to Toronto   with him

   (f) An adjective phrase usually follows the word which it modifies.
   - (i) The birds *in the tree* sing sweetly.
   - (ii) The trip *to Toronto* was interesting.
   - (iii) The one *with him* was his cousin.

5. ADVERB—a word that modifies a verb, and adjective, or another adverb.
   (a) Comparison of adverbs: The degrees of comparison of adverbs are similar to those of adjectives.
   - (i) positive   —John runs *quickly*.
   - (ii) comparative—John runs *more quickly* than Tom.
   - (iii) superlative   —In the first race John ran **most quickly**.

The Parts of Speech:

(b) Use: An adverb can modify

    (i) a verb   John runs *quickly.*

    (ii) an adjective   John is *very* quick.

    (iii) another adverb   John runs *very* quickly.

(c) Adverb phrase: a group of words made up of a preposition and a noun or pronoun.

    (i) The rabbit jumped *through the hedge.*

    (ii) The dog ran *after it.*

Note: The position of a phrase in a sentence often determines whether it is an adjective phrase or an adverb phrase.

—The boy *on the bicycle* is the paper boy.   (adjective phrase)

—The boy sits *on the bicycle.*   (adverb phrase)

6. PREPOSITION—a word that introduces a phrase and shows the relationship between its object and the word which the phrase modifies.

The book *on* the desk is mine.

Note: A preposition always requires the object form of the pronoun.

—Give the book *to me.*

—Give the book *to* Mary and *me.*

7. CONJUNCTION—a joining word.

(a) The *co-ordinate conjunction* joins words, phrases, or clauses used the same way in a sentence.

    (i) The puppy runs *and* jumps.

    (ii) We raced down the hill *and* across the bridge.

    (iii) The rain had stopped *but* the lake was rough.

(b) The *subordinate conjunction* introduces a subordinate clause and joins the clause to the word it modifies.

    (i) I hurried *because* I was late.

    (ii) Rover came *when* I whistled.

(c) *Correlative conjunctions* are used in pairs.

    (i) *Either* you *or* I may go.

    (ii) *Both* Jean *and* Joan were there.

8. INTERJECTION—a word used to express some sudden or strong feeling.

Hurrah!   We won.

Well!   What do you think of that?

GRAPHIC ANALYSIS USING SYMBOLS WITH SIGNIFICANCE

To make the best use of the time spent in analysis, pupils may show the relationship of the parts of the sentence by drawing these symbols beneath or around the particular parts.

These symbols have been designed to help the pupils *think* carefully about the relationship of each word or phrase that is marked by them.

1. ～～～～～～～ A *single wavy line* is drawn under the *bare subject.*

2. _____ A *single straight line* is drawn under the *bare predicate.*

3. ══════════ *Two straight lines* mark the *object* to indicate that this word has what may be called for the sake of emphasis, a double relationship to the verb:

    (a) It completes the incomplete verb.

    (b) It represents the receiver of the action expressed by the verb.

4. ════════ *One straight line and one wavy line* mark the *subjective completion.* The straight line indicates that this word completes the incomplete verb. The wavy line indicates that this word modifies, or refers to, the subject.

5. (   ) *Round brackets* are used to indicate *all* modifiers that have the value of an *adjective.*

6. [   ] *Square brackets* are used to mark all modifiers of adverb value. As the modifier of the verb is always an adverb, the symbol is designed from the straight line used to indicate the verb.

7. ⬭ An *oval* is drawn around a *co-ordinate conjunction* to indicate its linking or joining function.

8. ════════ *Three straight lines* mark the *indirect object.* Two lines show its relationship to the verb, and the third represents the omitted preposition.

Note: Arrows, drawn above the line of writing, from the modifier to the word it modifies, may prove to be valuable, especially in the early stages of detailed analysis.

PUNCTUATION

1. THE PERIOD is used:
    (a) After abbreviations. Ont. Wed. Nov.

    (b) At the end of assertive and imperative sentences.
        Winnipeg is the capital of Manitoba.
        Find it on the map.

2. The QUESTION MARK is used after an interrogative sentence.
    In what province is the Fraser River?

3. THE EXCLAMATION MARK is used:
    (a) After interjections.   (b) After exclamatory sentences.
        Oh! Hurrah! No!   How exciting it is!

4. The COMMA is used:
    (a) To set off the name of a person spoken to.
        Mary, please lend me your dictionary.

    (b) To separate words or phrases in a series.
        It was a warm, bright, moonlit evening.
        From the east, from the west, from the north, and from the
        south the raiders swept down upon the camp.

    (c) To set off the words *yes,* or *no.*   Yes, you may come.

    (d) To set off words of explanation.
        Mr. Smith, the principal, addressed the assembly.

    (e) To set off expressions such as *however, for example, indeed, to be sure,*
        nevertheless, too.
        You will note, however, that the top is missing.

    (f) To set off the date of the month from the year.   July 1, 1867.

    (g) To set off the parts of an address.
        Mr. John Smith,
            123 Pine St.,
            London, Ont.

    (h) After the salutation and complimentary closing of a friendly letter.
        Dear George,   Yours truly,

    (i) To separate a quotation from the explaining words.
        "I found the book," he replied, "where I left it."

    (j) After long introductory adverbial modifiers.
        When the game was almost finished, the goalie collapsed.

    (k) Between long principal clauses.
        We spent many hours writing our story, but the other group
        produced a better one.

Punctuation:

5. QUOTATION MARKS are used:

   (a) To enclose the exact words of the speaker.

   > Mary said, "I have a new book."
   > "What is the name of it?" inquired Sue.
   > "What a striking cover design!" added Lois.
   > "This book," continued Mary, "was written by a Canadian."

   (b) To enclose the title of a story, book, or poem.

   > I have read "David Copperfield" this year.

6. The COLON is used:

   (a) When listing a number of items.

   > Each person will bring the following:
   > > bathing suit
   > > towel
   > > sun glasses

   (b) After the salutation of a business letter.

   > Dear Sir:

   (c) Between the hour and minute figure of a time.

   > School dismisses at 11:45 a.m.

7. The SEMI-COLON is used sometimes in place of a co-ordinate conjunction.

   > The sun was setting; we had not a moment to lose.

8. The APOSTROPHE is used:

   (a) In forming possessives.

   > This is Joan's pen.

   (b) In forming the plurals of letters, figures, and words.

   > Write two lines of a's, 7's, and but's.

   (c) To show that a letter has been omitted in a contraction.

   > I haven't any money.

9. The HYPHEN is used:

   (a) To join parts of compound words.

   > good-bye   sugar-cane   old-fashioned

   (b) To divide a word at the end of a line. The division must be made between two syllables.

   > govern- ment   station- ary   agree- ably

USING QUOTATION MARKS TO RECORD CONVERSATION

The examples on this page illustrate the use of quotation marks to record conversation. Notice that the exact words used by the speaker, which might be called THE QUOTATION, are inside the quotation marks. The words that indicate who spoke, and which tell something about the speaker and the manner in which the words were spoken, might be called THE EXPLAINING WORDS. The explaining words are not included within the quotation marks.

Sentences in groups (a) and (b) illustrate the use of quotation marks in unbroken quotations of one sentence. Those in group (c) illustrate their use in broken quotations of one sentence. The sentences in group (d) illustrate the use of quotation marks in a quotation of more than one sentence.

(a) 1. "We shall go on Saturday," said father.   (Assertive)

2. "What time shall we leave?" asked Mary.   (Interrogative)

3. "Let me decide that later," replied father.   (Imperative)

4. "What a time we'll have!" shouted Bill.   (Exclamatory)

(b) 1. Father inquired, "Is all your homework done?"

2. Slowly Bill replied, "Some arithmetic is unfinished."

3. Father said sternly, "Get at it."

4. After looking disgustedly at Bill, Mary exclaimed, "How silly boys are!"

(c) 1. "While at the museum," the teacher explained, "keep your pads and pencils handy."   (Imperative)

2. "Is it necessary," asked the fellow who always seemed to be full of questions, "to write down something about everything we see?"   (Interrogative)

3. "That is a question," sighed the teacher, "which only you, Bill, could ask."   (Assertive)

(d) 1. "Each of these three early civilizations," the guide slowly and clearly explained, "depended for their food on the harvest of one main crop. In Central America corn or maize was the basic food. In the time of the pharaohs wheat was the staff of life for the Egyptians. For these people who lived in this part of Asia, rice was the most important item in their diet. Look carefully in each of these display cases. Which group constructed the most elaborate buildings?"

HOW TO APPRAISE WRITTEN COMPOSITION

Purpose: (i) to discover the weaknesses in need of corrective treatment and to praise where praise is due; NOT merely to list the pupil's errors;

(ii) to *appraise* by considering thought *and* structure *and* the mechanics of writing in terms of the capabilities of the individual pupil of that grade level; NOT according to standards based on adult accomplishment.

Method: Use a marking schedule. (See Schonell: BACKWARDNESS IN THE BASIC SUBJECTS—page 484.) Assign three separate marks and a percentage score.

A. THOUGHT AND VOCABULARY: (Maximum marks—12)

What effect has the writer on the reader?

(i) Clearness of expression; (ii) originality of ideas; (iii) interest of material; (iv) word choice: lack of monotonous repetition, absence of hackneyed phrases and slang, apt selections.

B. STRUCTURE: (Maximum marks—7)

How well is the paragraph put together? Are the sentences well constructed?

(i) Effective topic and summary sentences; (ii) sentences in order with a good degree of coherence; (iii) sentences are varied to suit the thought and purpose according to: (a) function, (b) construction, (c) order of the parts; (iv) absence of (a) sentence fragments, (b) infantile sentences, (c) run-on sentences, (d) dangling modifiers; (v) accuracy of paragraphing in multi-paragraph stories; (vi) tense consistency or absence of tense shift.

C. MECHANICAL ACCURACY: (Maximum marks—6)

How accurately is the work written?

(i) Spelling; (ii) punctuation; (iii) grammar; (iv) omissions and repetitions of syllables and words.

General Comment: In marking the pupil's written work two vertical lines, which divide the width of the page in three equal parts, may be drawn on a clear space either at the top or bottom of the sheet. As the teacher reads the composition, the comments and marks with respect to THOUGHT AND VOCABULARY are recorded in the left hand column; those for STRUCTURE in the centre column; and those for MECHANICAL ACCURACY in the right hand column. The three marks when totalled and multiplied by four provide a percentage score.

The merit of this marking scheme arises from the fact that the pupil, on receiving his paper after the teacher's appraisal, can be shown in which phase of writing he happens to be weakest. When he writes next he should concentrate on improving this greatest weakness, and strive to equal or better his score in the other two columns.

USING CAPITAL LETTERS

1. The first word in a sentence has a capital letter.

2. In written conversation the first word of each sentence used by the speaker has a capital letter.

> (a) The teacher said, "The first word needs a capital. Study the next example carefully."

> (b) "Here you see," the teacher explained, "that the completing part in a broken sentence needs no capital."

3. In poetry each line begins with a capital letter, unless the poet wrote it otherwise.

4. Proper nouns and their abbreviations require capitals:
Buildings: the Parliament Buildings; the City Hall
Churches: the United Church; the Roman Catholic Church
Days, months, holidays: Saturday, January, Hallowe'en
Historical events and documents: the Magna Carta; the British North America Act; the Battle of Queenston Heights
Organizations: the Home and School Association; the Parent-Teacher Association; the Boy Scouts
People: Sir John A. Macdonald; Sir Wilfrid Laurier; Mr. Robt. Cooke
Places: Vancouver, New South Wales, South Porcupine
Political parties, languages and races: Liberal, Conservative, Cooperative Commonwealth Federation, Social Credit; Chinese; Negro
Religious words: Bible, God, Jesus, the Saviour, the Virgin Mary, the Old Testament

5. Proper adjectives which are made from proper nouns:
Britain—British exports; France—the French government

6. In TITLES the first word and all other important words require a capital letter. The articles and prepositions have small letters, except a long preposition.

> "From Dawn to Dusk"   "The Brave Warrior"
> "Listening Within the Gates"   "A Journey to the Moon"

7. Nouns that show OCCUPATION have a capital when part of the name.

> Is that Professor Smith?   —Mr. Smith is a professor.
> Send for Doctor Brown.   —We do not need a doctor.

Using Capital Letters:

8. Nouns that show RELATIONSHIP have a capital when used as part of a person's name or as a word of address.

> This came from Uncle Fred. —When did you write to your uncle?
>
> Will you give this to your mother? —Yes, Father, I shall do that.

9. Words such as river, street, avenue, road, mountain, school, company, require capitals when they form part of a name.

> the Saskatchewan River;   Main Street;   Blantyre Road;
>
> Welland Avenue;   Snow Mountain;   St. Dennis School;
>
> Eastwood Junior High School;   the Ajax Thimble Company

10. Here are THREE TROUBLE MAKERS:

(a) The names of the seasons do *NOT* have capitals unless one of the above rules applies.

> In the spring boys collect marbles and in the fall they gather chestnuts.

(b) The names of the points of the compass do *NOT* have capitals when they indicate direction.

> News comes to us from the north, the east, the west, and the south.

> When the names of the points of the compass are used to refer to a part of the country or the world, they *DO* require capitals.

> Canada's biggest oil fields are in the West.

> We listened to a lecture by a reporter who had visited the Middle East.

(c) Names of school subjects do *NOT* require capitals unless the above rules apply *OR* unless they are names of languages.

> Do you like grammar, composition and literature?

> I like English but I prefer social studies, science, and arithmetic.

> Next year I am going to take French, Latin and Spanish.

ABBREVIATIONS

This list contains many of the abbreviations which are seen quite frequently. A complete list will be found in the dictionaries named on page 326.

A.D.	Anno Domini (in the year of our Lord)	D.D.	Doctor of Divinity
		D.D.S.	Doctor of Dental Surgery
Alta.	Alberta	Dec.	December
A.M. or	ante meridiem	Dr.	Doctor
a.m.	(before noon)	D.S.T.	Daylight Saving Time
Apr.	April	D. Th.	Doctor of Theology
A.R.C.T.	Associate of the Royal Conservatory, Toronto	D.V.M.	Doctor of Veterinary Medicine
A.S.	Anglo-Saxon	E.S.T.	Eastern Standard Time
A.S.T.	Atlantic Standard Time	Feb.	February
Aug.	August	Fri.	Friday
Ave.	Avenue	Geo.	George
B.A.	Bachelor of Arts	G.M.T.	Greenwich Mean Time
B.B.C.	British Broadcasting Corporation	Hon.	Honourable
		H.P.	horse power
B.C.	British Columbia, Before Christ	IHS	This is really a symbol derived from the Greek word for Jesus, and standing for His name.
B.D.	Bachelor of Divinity		
B. Ed.	Bachelor of Education		
B. Paed.	Bachelor of Pedagogy	I.N.R.I.	Jesus of Nazareth, King of the Jews (from Latin).
B.E.M.	British Empire Medal		
B. L.S.	Bachelor of Library Science	Jan.	January
Blvd.	Boulevard	Jas.	James
Bros.	Brothers	Jos.	Joseph
B. Sc.	Bachelor of Science	K. of C.	Knights of Columbus
C.A.	Chartered Accountant	Lab.	Labrador
Capt.	Captain	LL. B.	Bachelor of Laws
C.B.C.	Canadian Broadcasting Corporation	M.A.	Master of Arts
		Man.	Manitoba
C.C.F.	Co-operative Commonwealth Federation	Mar.	March
		M.C.	Master of Ceremonies, Military Cross
Chas.	Charles		
C.I.O.	Congress of Industrial Organization	M.D.	Doctor of Medicine
		Messrs.	Messieurs (plural of Mr.)
C.O.D.	Cash On Delivery	M.L.A.	Member of the Legislative Assembly
Col.	Colonel		
C.P.R.	Canadian Pacific Railway	Mlle.	Mademoiselle (Miss)
C.S.T.	Central Standard Time	Mme.	Madame (Mrs.)
C.Y.O.	Catholic Youth Organization	M.O.H.	Medical Officer of Health
		Mon.	Monday
D.V.A.	Department of Veterans' Affairs	M.P.	Member of Parliament, Military Police

Abbreviations:

M.P.P.	Member of Provincial Parliament	Rt. Hon.	Right Honourable
m.p.h.	miles per hour	Sask.	Saskatchewan
Mus. Bac.	Bachelor of Music	Sat.	Saturday
N. B.	New Brunswick	Sept.	September
N.B.	note well (L. nota bene)	S. J.	Society of Jesus
Nfld.	Newfoundland	St.	Saint (male) or street
Nov.	November	Ste.	Sainte (female)
N.S.	Nova Scotia	Sun.	Sunday
O.B.E.	Order of the British Empire	Supt.	Superintendent
Oct.	October	T.B.	Tuberculosis
Ont.	Ontario	T.C.A.	Trans-Canada Airlines
P.C.	Privy Councillor	Thos.	Thomas
P.E.I.	Prince Edward Island	Thurs.	Thursday
Phm. B.	Bachelor of Pharmacy	T.K.O.	technical knock out
Ph. D.	Doctor of Philosophy		(a term used in pugilism)
P.M. or	post meridiem—after noon	treas.	treasurer
P.S.	postscript	Tues.	Tuesday
P.S.T.	Pacific Standard Time	U.K.	United Kingdom (of Great Britain and Northern Ireland)
P.T.A.	Parent Teacher Association		
P.Q.	Province of Quebec		
Q.C.	Queen's Counsel	U.N.	United Nations
Que.	Quebec	U.S.A.	The United States of America
R.F.D.	Rural Federal Delivery (U.S.A.)		
		vol.	volume
Rev.	Reverend	Wed.	Wednesday
R.I.P.	May he rest in peace (L. Requiescat in pace.)	Wm.	William
		Y.M.C.A.	Young Men's Christian Association
R.M.C.	Royal Military College		
R.N.	Registered Nurse	Y.M.H.A.	Young Men's Hebrew Association
Robt.	Robert		
R.R.	Rural Route	Y.W.C.A.	Young Women's Christian Association
R.S.V.P.	Reply if you please (Fr. Répondez s'il vous plaît)		
		Y.W.H.A.	Young Women's Hebrew Association

Abbreviations for titles (Col.) and degrees (M.D.) and honours (Q.C.) are generally used when writing names on an envelope. If in doubt whether the use of an abbreviation is permissible always write the word or words in full.

BOOK LISTS

The authors of DEVELOPING LANGUAGE SKILLS—GRADE VIII—have found the books listed below to be worthy of recommendation for the purposes indicated.

REFERENCE BOOKS FOR PUPILS' USE:

1. BRITANNICA JUNIOR. (15 volumes) Encyclopaedia Britannica.
2. COMPTON'S PICTURED ENCYCLOPEDIA. (15 volumes) F. E. Compton and Co.
3. WORLD BOOK ENCYCLOPEDIA. (18 volumes) The Quarrie Corporation.

DICTIONARIES FOR PUPILS' USE:

1. THE CANADIAN TEACHING DICTIONARY. Clarke, Irwin.
2. A DICTIONARY FOR BOYS AND GIRLS, WEBSTER'S ELEMENTARY DICTIONARY. Allen.
3. WORDS AND THEIR MEANINGS. Copp Clark.
4. THE WINSTON DICTIONARY FOR CANADIAN SCHOOLS. Holt, Rinehart & Winston.

DICTIONARIES FOR SCHOOL OR CLASSROOM LIBRARY:

1. FOWLER, H. W.: A DICTIONARY OF MODERN ENGLISH USAGE. Oxford.
2. THE CONCISE OXFORD DICTIONARY. Oxford.
3. LARGE-TYPE CONCISE DICTIONARY (Annandale). Ryerson.
4. WEBSTER'S STUDENTS' DICTIONARY.

PROFESSIONAL BOOKS FOR THE TEACHER:

1. Corbin and Perrin: GUIDE TO MODERN ENGLISH. Scott, Foresman, 1955 (Gage).
2. Gurrey, P.: THE TEACHING OF WRITTEN ENGLISH. Longmans, Green, 1954.
3. McKee, P.: LANGUAGE IN THE ELEMENTARY SCHOOL. Thos. Nelson & Sons, 1937.
4. Ministry of Education Pamphlet No. 26: LANGUAGE—SOME SUGGESTIONS FOR TEACHERS OF ENGLISH AND OTHERS. Her Majesty's Stationery Office, 1954. (U.K. Information Office, Ottawa).
5. Schonell, Fred J.: BACKWARDNESS IN THE BASIC SUBJECTS. Clarke, Irwin, 1948.
6. Watts, A. F.: THE LANGUAGE AND MENTAL DEVELOPMENT OF CHILDREN. D. C. Heath, 1944.

GUIDE TO MODERN ENGLISH provides the teacher with an alphabetically arranged list of grammatical items. This 200-page section is particularly useful.

BACKWARDNESS IN THE BASIC SUBJECTS contains the marking scheme referred to in the foreword and described on page 321.

Book Lists:

The following books will be found useful in obtaining information regarding some of the THEMES FOR CREATIVE WRITING described in Chapter V.

These books may be found on the BIOGRAPHY or FAMOUS PEOPLE shelf of a school or public library.

Nisenson & Dewitt: ILLUSTRATED MINUTE BIOGRAPHIES. Grosset and Dunlap, 1953.

Pringle, Patrick: WHEN THEY WERE GIRLS. Harrap & Co., 1956.
(This book contains twelve stories of famous women.)

Pringle, Patrick: WHEN THEY WERE BOYS. Harrap & Co., 1954.
(This book contains sixteen stories of famous men.)

Stevens, W. O.: FAMOUS MEN OF SCIENCE. Dodd Mead, 1952.

Stevens, W. O.: FAMOUS HUMANITARIANS. Dodd Mead, 1953.

Milne, L. J. & M. J.: FAMOUS NATURALISTS. Dodd Mead, 1952.

Carlson & Hixon: SCIENCE MILESTONES. Windsor Press, 1954.
(This book presents the dramatic stories of over sixty trailblazers of science, people who made scientific history.)

Wallace, W. S.: BY STAR AND COMPASS. Ryerson, 1953.
(This book contains stories of Canadian explorers.)

Unstead, R. J.: GREAT PEOPLE OF MODERN TIMES. A. & C. Black, 1956.

Bolton, S. K.: LIVES OF GIRLS WHO BECAME FAMOUS. Crowell Co., 1952.

Crowther, J. G.: SIX GREAT SCIENTISTS. Hamish Hamilton, 1955.
(This book is one of a series of ten books of biographies: Englishmen, English women, Explorers, Inventors, Novelists, Missionaries, Aviators, Railwaymen, Poets, Sailors.)

Macmillan N.: GREAT AIRMEN. Bell & Sons, 1955.
(In this book will be found the stories of all the famous aviators from the Wright Brothers to those of the rocket age.)

Adams & Kimball: HEROINES OF THE SKY. Doubleday Doran, 1942.

Bakeless: STORY LIVES OF GREAT COMPOSERS. Lippincott, 1953.

Boynick, D. K.: CHAMPIONS BY SETBACK. Crowell Co., 1954.
(The stories of ten men who conquered great physical handicaps to make their mark in the world of sport are presented in this book.)

Block, Irvin: THE REAL BOOK ABOUT EXPLORERS. Garden City, 1952.

Pratt, Viola: FAMOUS DOCTORS. Clarke Irwin, 1957.
(This book is the first of a series called CANADIAN PORTRAITS which will tell the stories of outstanding Canadians.)

Book Lists:

DeWitt, Wm. A.: ILLUSTRATED MINUTE BIOGRAPHIES, Grosset and Dunlap, 1953.

Davis, Mac: 100 GREATEST SPORTS HEROES, (Illustrated), Grosset and Dunlap, 1954.

Buehr, Walter: SHIPS AND LIFE AFLOAT, Chas. Scribner's Sons, 1953.

(This book is an illustrated history of the development of ships and navigation. It describes the life, the craftsmanship, the discipline, the food, and the costumes of mariners, in both peace and war.

The following books will supply information on the Almanac items:

1. FAMOUS FIRST FACTS by J. N. Kane (H. W. Wilson & Co., New York, 1950).

2. EVERY DAY'S A HOLIDAY by Hutchison and Adams (Harper, New York, 1951).

3. ANNIVERSARIES AND HOLIDAYS by M. E. Hazeltine (American Library Association, Chicago, 1944).

4. THE AMERICAN BOOK OF DAYS by George W. Douglas (H. W. Wilson & Co., New York, 1948).

5. HIGH DAYS AND HOLIDAYS—A. H. Foster, Ryerson, 1956.

The following Books are recommended for use in preparing the programme in honour of Canada's birthday.

Brown, Harman, and Jeanneret, THE STORY OF CANADA, Copp Clark, 1950, and THE TEACHER'S MANUAL.

Creighton, Louella, CANADA: THE STRUGGLE FOR EMPIRE, Dent, 1962.

Tait, George E., FAIR DOMAIN, Ryerson, 1960.

Tait, George E., ONE DOMINION, Ryerson, 1962.

INDEX

330

331